TEACH YOURSELF BOOKS

APPROACHING LITERATURE

NTC *NTC Publishing Group*

TEACH YOURSELF BOOKS

APPROACHING LITERATURE

Sue Collins

NTC *NTC Publishing Group*

Long-renowned as *the* authoritative source for self-guided
learning – with more than 30 million copies sold worldwide –
the *Teach Yourself* series includes over 200 titles in the fields
of languages, crafts, hobbies, sports, and other leisure activities.

This edition was first published in 1993 by NTC Publishing Group,
4255 West Touhy Avenue, Lincolnwood (Chicago), Illinois 60646 –
1975 U.S.A. Originally published by Hodder and Stoughton Ltd.

Library of Congress Catalog Card Number: 93-83169

Printed in England by Cox & Wyman Ltd, Reading, Berks

CONTENTS

PREFACE

A work of literature is something which belongs to all of us. When we read it, we give it life; when it lives for us, it changes the way we think and feel: the writing and the reading of a novel or a poem become the two halves of a shared experience. Without a reader, a book is nothing. With every new reader, it takes on uncharted possibilities.

The enormous interest in the theory of what we call *literary criticism* is in part an attempt to define this elusive relationship. Can the study of literature ever be an objective, scientific discipline – as the heirs of the Russian Formalists would claim it can? Or is criticism itself a kind of *creative writing*, on a par with the text it seeks to illuminate – as the thematic critics would have us believe? If I approach literature armed with my favourite ideology – Marxist, Feminist or psychoanalytical – shall I have a clearer picture of what literature *really* is? If I try to analyse the patterns of parallels and contrasts in a text in the same way an anthropologist analyses different versions of a myth, will my analysis bring me closer to the text's 'true' message?

In the last 50 years, literary criticism has become an arena for intense theoretical debate, and the results of that debate are still with us. They have been far-reaching. Certain works of literature which we thought were familiar to us will never look the same again.

The debate goes on, and meanwhile the literary texts are still there, waiting for us to read them. We approach them with all our inevitable prejudices – literary, social, political and personal – and whether we are literary theorists or not, we can try to make sense of them and discuss them in a way which will be intelligible to others who may or may not share our own convictions.

My own approach owes more to the classroom than it does to academic journals: trying to teach literature objectively can be a one-sided and sterile business. What students readily talk about is, to use Emily Dickinson's phrase, what 'takes the top of our heads off'. What we need to do is not to forbid ourselves to talk about the tops of our own heads, but to give ourselves a language to do it in, a language which will help us pinpoint the source of our emotional response and communicate it to others. We can all react to literature, with gasps of admiration or shudders of distaste. But those gasps and shudders are not always easy to understand, let alone put into words. If we want others to gasp or shudder as we did, we need to look again more closely, and find reasons to explain why we felt as we did. Without a cool analysis of the text, there is no criticism. Without a warm response to it, any criticism there is is pointless.

In writing this book, I have become aware that readers are just as important to literature as the texts under discussion. In my opinion – and it is an opinion shared by a number of eminent critics – literature is not something fixed, static, perfected, but something which is dynamic and cumulative, which relies every day on new readers to become what it is in the process of becoming. Far from dismissing first reactions, I have encouraged readers to explore them, in the conviction that daring to respond – even 'inappropriately' – is the first step in understanding the structural organisation which directly or indirectly stimulated that initial response.

Some very valuable criticism has been written from overtly Marxist or Feminist viewpoints. My own preferences are for an unsystematic initial approach, for few hypotheses. In my view, 'What have we here?' is always an appropriate question for the literary critic to ask. If we cannot categorise a work of literature because we lack the concepts or the vocabulary, so much the better. We shall have to make something up in order to explain it to ourselves.

This book is really a book of questions. I have probably answered some, but I have almost certainly raised more than I have answered. If there are answers to them, they are in the minds and experiences of individual readers. To study literature is to become aware of a heady mixture of delights and problems, and to become capable of living with it. For if we can learn to be good readers of literature, that is only the beginning. The best kind of education doesn't try to protect us from life, but to give us the tools to deal with it. My hope is that by the time they reach the end of this book, my readers will be more than able to look after themselves!

INTRODUCTION: ──── WHAT IS ──── LITERATURE?

──────── Art and writing ────────

If we study literature, there is almost invariably a kind of ghost hovering over us, demanding, 'What makes you think this is literature anyway?' If we want to go on reading literature seriously, re-reading it to understand it better, we have to deal with the ghost. We have to silence it effectively or find a way of ignoring it. We have to decide that, even if we cannot define it precisely, for our own purposes at least, we do know what literature is.

Part of literature's problem is its medium. If we want to create a sonata or a picture, a statue, a building or a patchwork quilt, we have first to learn to handle the medium. We have to learn about musical notation or technical drawing, pigments and perspective, the properties of different fabrics. But the medium of literature is language, something we have all used since we were toddlers with what is – if we only stop for a moment to analyse what we are saying – an astonishing degree of sophistication. At two we were competent users of the medium of oral literature; at five or six we were writers. I can sit down now and write a note to someone, almost without thinking about it. What is it that stops my letter from being a work of literature? What is it that stops the four-year-old's sweet, funny, illuminating chance remarks from being an orally transmitted poem?

These questions seem simple. In practice, we should scarcely hesitate. Yet in theoretical terms they are very difficult indeed to answer.

Dictionaries rarely define literature more precisely than as an art which has to do with writing and books. There is even a tendency to define the terms *literature* and *literary* in a way which is distinctly circular. Literature is a collective term for what is literary; what is literary pertains to literature. Small wonder that the debate about what literature really is has inspired theoretical treatises.

For our purposes, it is surely enough to recognise that the debate is there and that the ambiguities exist. Literature is a written art which is not readily definable, which we as readers must struggle again to define each time we read a piece of writing which moves, delights or changes us in a special way.

In practice, the difficulties tend to fade when we come to grips with a real piece of writing. Our initial responses are often more reliable than we give them credit for: often we 'just know' a piece of writing is literature, even though on first reading we are hard put to say why. If we distrust our subjective reactions, we can at least learn what other readers before us have designated as literature by reading the acknowledged classics. Perhaps there is a recognisable quality in them which will act as a yardstick for the judgement of all the potential literature we might read in the future?

What we are really learning as we question ourselves about our own responses, or read and re-read the classics, is an art of reading. For whatever else it may be, literature is a kind of writing which carries more than one meaning, and which as such deserves to be read thoughtfully and with attention. There are kinds of language which are functional in a very obvious, single way – such as the telephone message from the dentist's receptionist, the news bulletin, the shopping list – and there are kinds of language which, by not communicating a single, straightforward message, are making us wonder, and question, and dream.

Exercise 1

Read the following pieces of writing as carefully as you think you need to in order to understand them. Then answer the questions which follow.

Mr Ashdown, buoyed by a rise in the opinion polls, was ostensibly in Boulogne to underline his commitment to European unity. But the visit allowed a glimpse of the Liberal Democrat leader on one of the few forms of transport as yet untried in the course of this hectic election tour. It was a catamaran with a capacity to bring on queasiness even among those travelling the length and breadth of Britain by Dan Air.

Old Seadog Ashdown, the former Royal Marine, was more than a match, refusing his sea-sickness pill and then contradicting his minders about the likely sailing time needed with a 'stern wind'.

The Independent 30/3/92

Don't miss out – reply today!

Claim your super free gift that's already waiting for you, grab your chance to win something **really** special in our Great £25,000 Prize Draw – and look forward to spending your £10 Discount Voucher on **anything** you please from [our] latest catalogue. YOU JUST CAN'T LOSE!

Send your Free Gift Claim Form back to us **right away**. Just pop it in the envelope provided – you don't even need a stamp.

We look forward to hearing from you soon.

(*Advertising letter*)

The Sacred Spine

It will always be invisible, it will
have hair on it, but that will be false,
and skin, but that will be stretched over
the branches like a sweater dipped in alum.
It will hang from the mouth
like a piece of paper or a large caterpillar.
It will twist over doubly
like a ravenous birch.
It will lie rigid.
It will scream out,
trying to find a position.
It will turn in pain,

trying to escape, trying to release
itself, trying to live again
without fear and exhaustion,
trying to float once more, trying to rest, trying to rise
in the fine dust and the feathers,
in the wet leaves and the grass and the flowers,
on the bleached wood and the pillows and the warm air
and the weeds and the water.

Gerald Stern

Questions

(a) How long do you think it took you to read each of these pieces of writing? Estimate the times and write them down.

(b) Are there any conclusions you can draw from this?

(c) Which of these pieces of writing was the most persuasive?

(d) In which was the meaning clearest?

(e) Can you pick out any 'literary' features in either of the first two passages?

(f) Which of these three pieces of writing do you think is likely to linger in your memory the longest?

——— Literature and history ———

In some ways it is hard to dissociate literature from history: each work of literature is produced by an individual or a group of individuals living at a particular time and in a particular place. Whether or not a writer intends to reflect his or her age and its ideological and cultural values, those values are embedded in every decision – conscious or unconscious – that he or she makes. Not only the world we live in, but also the way in which we see it, and the language in which we describe it, are all in a sense historical. The forms we have inherited from our ancestors were not available to the writers of a hundred or more years ago; some of the forms which were available to them are no longer available to us. A writer today is not free to write in the language of Chaucer without making a particular *extra* statement full of ironies. Whether we are aware of them or not, the cultural and linguistic values of our own century have filtered through to us, to colour everything we write or read today.

The reader also brings his or her *baggage* of history: we cannot 'forget about' the rise of Nazism to read Nietzsche more purely; we cannot decide not to know about recent developments in Eastern Europe as we read Karl Marx. We can't even 'unlearn' our everyday language of slang, journalese, cliché and bad grammar to study Donne or Shakespeare. However hard we try, we cannot possibly put ourselves inside the skin and consciousness of readers or audiences of another century. Yet, if we try, we may discover meanings in a work of literature that we never suspected – and be forced to abandon some of the meanings we found in it as readers of our own time.

Literature can, of course, be studied – and has been studied – as a historical document. If we look at a novel by Dickens for what it can tell us about life in the Victorian period, we shall not be short of answers. They may be oblique answers. We may suspect them of being unreliable, or at the very least exaggerated. And we may also find ourselves thinking that *Hard Times* or *Little Dorrit* is after all a more limited book than we had first thought.

The fact is that, though literature can in one sense be accounted for historically, what is special to literature – i.e. the ability to delight us in unforeseen ways, to greet us intimately even across the all but insurmountable barriers of changing values and social behaviour and speech-habits – is not linked to what we usually think of as history in any very direct or obvious way. As René Wellek argues convincingly in Wellek and Warren's *Theory of Literature* (published for the first time in 1949), even what we usually call literary history or the history of literature is very rarely what it claims to be. Library shelves are still full of books which group and discuss writers in a historical time-sequence. But the book which truly links history with aesthetic values is still a rarity.

Exercise 2

Read the following descriptive passage from a 19th century realist novel carefully, trying to absorb its tone and literary qualities as well as the more immediate information it carries.

The paper-mills of Angoulême are well-famed: during the last three centuries they had of necessity established themselves along the Charente and its tributaries, where waterfalls were available. At Ruelle the State had set up its most important foundry for naval cannons. Haulage, post-houses, inns, wheelwrights' workshops, public transport services, all the industries which depend on roads and waterways clustered round the base of Angoulême in order to avoid the difficulties presented by access to the town itself. Naturally tanneries, laundries and all water-side trades remained within reach of the Charente, which was also lined with brandy warehouses, depots for all kinds of goods in transit. And so the suburb of L'Houmeau became a busy and prosperous town, a second Angoulême, arousing resentment in the upper town where the administration, the Bishop's palace, the course of justice and the aristocracy remained. For this reason L'Houmeau, despite its increasing activity and importance, was a mere appendage of Angoulême. The nobility and the political authority held sway on high, commerce and finance down below: two social zones, everywhere and constantly hostile to each other; as a consequence, it is difficult to guess which of the two towns more cordially hates its rival.

(Balzac, *Lost Illusions*)

Draw a line down the centre of a large piece of paper, dividing it into two columns. Now read the passage again, making notes as you go. In one column, list everything which tells you something about the historical period in which the novel was written (in this case that period coincides loosely with the period in which the novel is set). In the second column list anything you can say about the passage and its 'contents' which is *not* immediately and obviously related to a study of its period.

When you have finished, compare your two lists. What light do they cast on the passage? What light to they cast on your own values? Were the two 'categories' easy or difficult to separate? Was our implied definition of history too narrow here? What does history mean when we study the text of a work of literature?

Exercise 3

Read the following short passage from George Orwell's *Nineteen Eighty-four* and answer the questions which follow.

The voice from the telescreen paused. A trumpet call, clear and beautiful, floated into the stagnant air. The voice continued raspingly:

"Attention! Your attention, please! A newsflash has this moment arrived from the Malabar front. Our forces in South India have won a glorious victory. I am authorized to say that the action we are now reporting may well bring the war within measurable distance of its end. Here is the newsflash –"

Bad news coming, thought Winston. And sure enough, following on a gory description of the annihilation of a Eurasian army, with stupendous figures of killed and prisoners, came the announcement that, as from next week, the chocolate ration would be reduced from thirty grammes to twenty.

Winston belched again. The gin was wearing off, leaving a deflated feeling. The telescreen – perhaps to celebrate the victory, perhaps to drown the memory of the lost chocolate – crashed into "Oceania, 'tis for thee". You were supposed to stand to attention. However, in his present position he was invisible.

"Oceania, 'tis for thee" gave way to lighter music. Winston walked over to the window, keeping his back to the telescreen. The day was still cold and clear. Somewhere far away a rocket bomb exploded with a dull, reverberating roar. About twenty or thirty of them a week were falling on London at present.

Questions

(a) Imagine you are reading this passage when it was first published in 1949, and then again in the present. What in your relationship with it has changed?

(b) What has remained the same?

(c) Would one of your two readings be a *better* reading, or would they both be equally valuable?

(d) Try to write down your reasons for answering this last question in the way you have.

───── Biography and insight ─────

It would take, at the very least, a gifted psychiatrist to be able to trace the complex links between a mind and the works of art it produces. The fact that the medium of literature is language, so that we all to some extent understand what it seems to be saying, should make us doubly cautious. There is no reason why a work of literature should reflect the life of its creator and his or her personal characteristics any more directly than a painting or a piece of music. Literature is always in some sense fictional. As soon as I regard what I am creating as *literary*, my voice is no longer entirely my 'real' voice. Even when I say 'I', or 'you', I am putting a kind of distance between the 'I' and my everyday factual self, between the 'you' and the person I know. If we resort to biographies of its author in order to explain a novel or a poem, we are confusing two different kinds of truth. Literature can tell us the truth about its author and ourselves, on condition that it is allowed to lie.

Biography as a tool of interpretation is far from reliable. We can read 20 books about the Brontës and still not be at all clear about how this wealth of biographical information fits the fictional landscape of *Wuthering Heights*. Is Emily Brontë Cathy? Is she Heathcliff? Or is she the young Catherine? Is the 'real' Emily Brontë in the leaping firelight of Wuthering Heights, or is she swinging in the trees of the Thrushcross Grange garden? Is she haunting the moors or is she buried under them? Or is she all and none of these things?

When we approach a piece of writing through the life of its author we may feel it brings us closer. Information about a writer's life and personal habits may make it easier for us to empathise with the 'I' of the book itself; they may sensitise us to underlying themes or patterns of metaphor. But the themes and metaphors were in the book before we read about the writer's life. We may be distorting their importance. We may be trying to reduce all the possible meanings of this novel or poem to the one set of meanings which the facts of the writer's life have brought to the surface. If what we really want is a friend, why don't we make friends rather than read works of literature?

The trouble is that literature *does* offer psychological insight, *does* offer possibilities of intimacy probably greater than any we ever achieve in our real lives. But it is the work itself – its tone and stance, its whole organisation, as much as its subject – which does this best. As such, the biography of a writer is no more interesting than our own. Certain writers, admittedly, have their own dramatic *stories*: what we touch of life by studying the life of Hans Andersen is, certainly, poignant and thought-provoking. But what we learn of life by studying his stories is something different: the grief and hopelessness, claustrophobia and exhilaration, belong to anyone who can respond to them; they will have significance for new readers when the facts of his own childhood and adolescence are long forgotten.

Exercise 4

The following short extract is in fact not from a biography or autobiography, but from a novel which is generally thought to use a considerable amount of real autobiographical material. Read it and compare it with the lines of poetry which follow.

> I don't know how long I sat there, watching the woman in purple and wondering if her pursed, pink lips would open, and if they did open, what they would say.
>
> Finally, without speaking or looking at me, Miss Norris swung her feet in their high, black, buttoned boots over the other side of the bed and walked out of the room. I thought she might be trying to get rid of me in a subtle way. Quietly, at a little distance, I followed her down the hall.
>
> Miss Norris reached the door of the dining-room and paused. All the way to the dining-room she had walked precisely, placing her feet in the very centre of the cabbage roses that twined through the pattern of the carpet. She waited a moment and then, one by one, lifted her feet over the door-sill and into the dining-room as though stepping over an invisible shin-high stile.

> > (Sylvia Plath, *The Bell Jar*)

> No novice
> In those elaborate rituals
> Which allay the malice
> Of knotted table and crooked chair,
> The new woman in the ward
> Wears purple, steps carefully

Among her secret combinations of eggshells
And breakable humming birds,
Footing sallow as a mouse
Between the cabbage-roses
Which are slowly opening their furred petals
To devour and drag her down
Into the carpet's design.

(Sylvia Plath, from *Miss Drake Proceeds to Supper*)

How much more are we given in the poem than in the more straight-forward prose version? If we have read the whole of *The Bell Jar*, we will know that this scene takes place in a psychiatric ward in which the narrator of the story is herself a patient. How far does this information explain the poem? How far does it not explain the poem?

—————— Waiting for the train ——————

There is no doubt that our response to literature is affected by our expectations. If we are told a piece of writing is a poem and we find ourselves forced to read it as if it were 'a piece of chopped-up prose', we shall judge it more harshly than we should if we had approached it as prose in the first place. If we know in advance that a book is generally thought of as a great work of literature, we may well find ourselves overruling our own authentic responses in favour of what we know we *ought* to be seeing and feeling in it. Rather than put ourselves in the risky situation of a real critic and coming to grips with what puzzles or repels us, we often prefer simply to label ourselves insensitive, uncultured or stupid.

But one of the worst things we can do as readers of literature is to overrule our own first reactions. Accepting them provisionally, using our initial spontaneous response as a basis for questions and answers which may later alter that response and make us read the poem or story differently, is something we can all bring to our own understanding of literature.

We are not 'wrong' to have certain expectations of what we read – to want or need a book to be truthful or passionate or witty, compelling or difficult, full of killing or full of human relationships. Without its passengers, the train will be empty – what is a poem that no one has ever read? Yet a work of literature is not designed *for* its readers as individuals, any more than the train is designed to suit the personal tastes of any one of its passengers. I may hate the blue upholstery. Blue may be the colour of the dressing-gown my father died in. But I get into the train, I lean back against the blue, and I may begin to experience it differently. And the way I recoiled at first may be a part of something far more complex which is just beginning.

We as readers are individuals, as surely as the writers themselves are. Our personal experience and attitudes, even to some extent our prejudices, are necessary. Literature defines itself against them. No writer can realistically hope to affect his or her readers uniformly. The best a writer can hope is that the individual responses of readers should add up to something, that in our various ways we might react to a book as if it were a necessary answer to an individual question in each of our own lives.

Genre is a French word meaning 'kind'. Literary genres are kinds or classes of literature. These days we tend to think of the three major genres as poetry, drama and the novel, while being aware of others, such as biography, autobiography, the short story, the essay and even literary correspondence. But the idea of literary genre is wider and deeper than this simple classification implies. It is related to the whole question of reader-expectation. We may not find it easy to define a novel or a poem, or even a play, but, directly or indirectly, we have been exposed to them since childhood. Even if we have never been to the theatre, we have a mental picture of what a play is. We know what a novel does. We know how we feel about someone we see reading a book of poetry. *Genres* or literary kinds are far from being abstract concepts. When Aristotle in the *Poetics* formally differentiated between epic and lyric, tragedy and comedy, he was in a sense less of a theorist than a recorder. Genre is a bridge of expectation and understanding between the act of writing and the act of reading. Writers can use that bridge, or attempt to blow it up, but the reader will be waiting on the opposite bank.

Exercise 5

Read the following published extract from a writer's personal diary attentively and answer the questions.

Underlying all my anxiety there is a great bargaining going on, a kind of bartering which weighs up undisclosed values and half-hidden treasures; and this dispute is slowly rising up and forcing its way into the daylight. Time presses. The whole truth, which I could not tell to Max, I owe to myself. It is not a beautiful truth, and it is still a bit feeble and scared, and slightly perfidious. So far all it can do is to whisper to me in short sighs: 'I don't want . . . I mustn't . . . I'm afraid.'

Afraid of getting old, of being betrayed, of suffering. A subtle choice guided my partial sincerity while I was writing that to Max. That particular fear is the hair-shirt which clings to the skin of nascent Love and contracts there as he grows. I have worn that hair-shirt; one does not die of it. I would wear it again . . . *if I could not do otherwise.*

'If I could not do otherwise . . . ' This time the formula is clear. I saw it written in my mind and I see it there still, printed like a judgement in small, bold capitals. Now at last I have taken the true measure of my paltry love and brought my real hope into the open: the hope of escape.

Questions

(a)   How far do you relate to this writer and her concerns?

(b)   How far does this diary extract resemble any other diary you have ever read?

(c)   How sincere is this writer being?

Exercise 6

Read the following three prose passages. How would you describe each of them? Do they fall into a convenient literary genre or category? Can you try to define each in terms of the expectation it sets up in you personally as a reader? How do you judge each in terms of those expectations?

The blast of cold was followed by days of high wind and sun, a dazzling air as light dappled through leaves, all in motion. Now we have Scotch mist, and it looks like rain, badly needed. Yesterday I managed to sow all the annuals, and more pansies, fighting blackflies that swarmed around my face the whole time. It was a relief to get it done, the worst spring job. Now for a while I can enjoy the garden as the great spring sequence proceeds. The daffodils are nearly over, but tulips and bleeding heart have opened.

It is a catastrophe to have five baby woodchucks under the barn, though they are adorable, like small toy bears. Of course, they have eaten down the hollyhocks. But I take these disasters more philosophically than I used to. I am learning not to take it all too personally, I guess, and not to mind failure. The garden is growth and change and that means loss as well as constant new treasures to make up for a few disasters. The blue pansies are wonderful this year. Blue is the most exciting color in the garden, I think. And these blues are everywhere now: Virginia bluebells, grape hyacinths, blue primroses, and wood anemones. Soon there will be bluebells in the little wood and wild phlox here and there.

All these matters drew my thoughts to the subject of idolatry, which was severely censured at the missionary meeting. I cross-examined my Father very closely as to the nature of this sin, and pinned him down to the categorical statement that idolatry consisted in praying to any one or anything but God himself. Wood and stone, in the words of the hymn, were peculiarly liable to be bowed down to by the heathen in their blindness. I pressed my Father further on this subject, and he assured me that God would be very angry, and would signify His anger, if anyone in a Christian country, bowed down to wood and stone. I cannot recall why I was so pertinacious on this subject, but I remember that my Father became a little restive under my cross-examination. I determined, however, to test the matter for myself, and one morning, when both my parents were safely out of the house, I prepared for the great act of heresy. I was in the morning-room on the ground-floor, where, with much labour, I hoisted a small chair on to the table close to the window. My heart was now beating as if it would leap out of my side, but I pursued my experiment. I knelt down on the carpet in front of the table and looking up I said my daily prayer in a loud voice, only substituting the address 'O Chair!' for the habitual one.

No Getting Down

Now the film has been exposed to the Californian light I have to wind it back to New York in the cramped camera of this bus. I feel the sadness of having turned my back on the Pacific, of being headed east again, of having seen America. I'm dreading it, but I have a reading to do in Boston. If you want you can skip all the disomfort and go straight back to New York and Vicky. After all, what are books for, I'd join you, but . . .

I see the one attractive girl in the bus is already paired with a late-arriving young hunter in single shoulder patch and binoculars. He lets her look through them and they see the same thing. A pity.

I have Cliff and his sister Tania, teenagers whose breaking up parents have packed them off with sandwiches to live with an aunt in Salt Lake City. He handsome, protective, precocious, asking me questions about my background and saying 'Majestic!' to every-thing, she tired and old and weepy at fourteen, looking up to him who's going to be a statesman and a foreign correspondent some day.

Yucca Flats. Trees like madmen.

'Looks like they don't believe in getting too close to one another,' says Cliff.

It is characteristic of some of the very best literature to be difficult to define. In retrospect, we may have a category to fit even the most formally inventive writers, but in their time the greatest experimenters are particularly problematic in critical terms because they seem to be exploding the forms they are using and transforming them into some-thing which no longer fits our ready definitions. *Ulysses, The Waves*, Robbe-Grillet's *In the Labyrinth* or John Barth's *Floating Opera* are novels to us now. When we try to appreciate them, we bring to them all our knowledge of novels past and present, including the revolutions in vision that they themselves have made possible. When they first ap-peared, *the novel* could hardly accommodate them. Literary genre is not a matter of categories which are reliable, a convenient tape-measure for anything a writer can produce. They are something organic, something which is constantly shifting and changing. They are not absolutes; they are as fluid as the corporate identity of a school run entirely by its pupils.

———— Meeting the train ————

While we cannot ignore the weight of literary tradition which makes us expect certain qualities of a play, a novel, an autobiography, a collection of poetry, we should be aware that what first signals *novel* to us is one signal among many. What we expect of a work of literature has a lot to do with what we have so far absorbed about literature. But it also has a lot to do with factors which seem to have very little to do with literature at all.

We come to each new work of literature as we come to anything new in our lives. When the train comes, we know it *ought* to be the train to London, but it might not be. Even though it displays the usual head-code, it might stop short at York, or be diverted to Oxford.

We stand on the platform with our luggage round our feet, but we are never quite sure whether we might have to leave some of it behind or wait for the next train. The best writers will find space for us and all our luggage – but we may well not recognise our own cases when we come to get off.

———— Commentary ————

Exercise 1

(a)   Reading speeds are fairly individual, but I would guess that most of us would read the first passage fairly steadily and would skim the second in less time than it takes to think about an answer. The poem, while there is nothing obviously obscure or difficult about its language, probably took longer. I suspect most of us will have read it more than once.

(b)   Any conclusions you can draw surely have little to do with the actual language in which these examples are written. Nothing about the sentence-structure or the vocabulary is incomprehensible. Our reading-speed and the attention we are willing to give to a piece of writing probably have a lot to do with our past experiences of writing apparently of the same kind. Most of us will have scanned many advertising letters very similar to the second extract and feel confident we know in advance what they are going to contain.

If the poem took us longer, the reason is surely to do with the central question it contains. We have clear words and startlingly vivid pictures, but they are all organised round a central 'it' which is never identified. What *is* this 'Scared Spine'? What does 'sacred' mean? What does 'spine' mean? (It means at least three things.) Where is it? What is happening to it? And where are we?

(c) The first passage is subtly persuasive. The word 'ostensibly', with its implied question, already puts us on our guard. 'Hectic' carries not just a single meaning, but a host of connotations. But the real tool of persuasion here is humour, which grows, from the dead-pan 'length and breadth of Britain by Dan Air' with all its implications of smallness and parochialism, to the more overt 'Old Seadog Ashdown' and 'stern wind'.

The persuasive tactics of the second extract are very transparent. Capital letters, emboldening, repetition of sums of money, all are used as so many heavy, blunt instruments. The most interesting word here in my opinion is the little word *pop* in 'just pop it in the envelope provided'. An inoffensive enough word, apparently, yet think of the kind of context in which this expression is normally used, and you will see that it establishes a kind of familiarity between writer and reader which is highly suspect.

The poem is not persuasive in the normal sense. It is highly suggestive – of what, we are not quite sure. Are we in a personal context? Or a sexual context, or a religious one? The pictures we see are of a natural world tormented, and they are powerful and troubling partly *because* we cannot attach them definitively to anything. This is as potent as persuasion, but it is its opposite. The reader is being *opened up* to something without being *persuaded to* anything.

(d) The meaning is probably clearest in the first passage. If the meaning of the second passage is clear, it may well be because we have long experience of this kind of language and how it can be used for just such a purpose.

(e) Nothing strikes me as literary in the first passage, though a different context could make it literary by giving it additional (ironic?) meanings. (Imagine it as a passage 'quoted' in a serious novel about the destructiveness of nationalism or party politics.) It would surely be almost impossible for anything to be at all literary in the context of the second passage, but the handling of the word 'pop' is potentially intelligent and resonant and funny enough to be worthy of a poet.

(f)   Surely most readers will answer in favour of the poem? Whether you react to it with pleasure or with anxiety or even anger, the unexplained images will surely remain in your mind, even if only as an irritant. For me, this is a particularly haunting poem because it *will not* allow itself to be explained. There is nothing elitist or mystifying about what it is *saying* and yet it remains mysterious. It sensitises us to its images' mixture of pain and natural beauty by trapping us in its unstated question and not letting us out.

Exercise 2

Your left-hand column will probably fill up very quickly with all the information we have here about the 19th-century development of river-side industry and its social implications. In your right-hand column you may have almost nothing, or you may have a sequence of questions – about the relevance of paper-mills to the subject of the novel, about the river and its possibilities as a symbol, about the social divisions as the framework of the novel's plot.

Whatever your own response to these categories, the exercise should be useful as a way of becoming aware of your receptiveness to different kinds of information at different levels of a literary text.

Exercise 3

(a)   This mixture of sinister, manipulative 'Newsflash' and inescapable humiliations would have seemed both more and less of a reality in 1949. Now we live with it, but its guises are more insidious and less dramatic that they were in Orwell's imagination. The detail of the chocolate is interesting. It would have a whole string of emotive connotations to 1949 readers and would have lent a kind of felt immediacy to the other ingredients of Winston's day-to-day existence. Now, for most of us, rationing is hearsay, or at least only a very dim memory. Standing to attention for a National Anthem has also become a rare occurrence in most people's lives. Only a small minority of readers would now be able to relate Orwell's rocket-bombs to personal memories of bombs falling on London.

(b)   The effects of gin have not changed, nor the element of sympathetic voyeurism in the reader's relationship with Winston. The odd conjunc-tions – of music, propaganda, sweets and bombs – are as disturbing now as they were just after the Second World War (when sweets were dropped with aerial propaganda). Perhaps they are even more disturbing now that they are no longer part of our everyday experience.

(c) and (d)   This is a subject critics, scholars and individual readers can argue about at great length. Your answers to these two questions will help you to pinpoint your own position inside the debate. In my opinion, there is something important in literature which survives to trigger a subtly different set of responses in each generation. To privilege the initial, contemporary set of responses over our later ones is to deny literature's very real capacity for survival.

Exercise 4

Much of the information is similar: the woman is in purple and walks with exaggerated care across the carpet's cabbage-rose design. But in the poem the very first line gives the reader a special relationship with her. This painstaking ritual is part of a view of the world. There is a consciousness here which is at risk and at the same time 'no novice'. There is no 'I' in the poem, and this brings us closer to the 'she', who is seen at the same time from the outside (the mouse image) and from within. The eggshell, humming bird and devouring imagery replace the stile. The observed exaggerations and deliberateness of the woman in the prose passage become something much more suggestive – secret, intimate (the furred petals remind us of furred tongues), fragile and intensely vulnerable.

If we know the story of *The Bell Jar* we can visualise this scene clearly in context. Esther is observing a new patient in her ward. What follows clarifies Esther's attitude to this new acquaintance. The two patients sit down for supper and wait an hour together 'in a close, sisterly silence' until it is time for the meal to be served. In the second stanza of the poem, the bird images become even more frequent, finally fusing together in a central metaphor in which Miss Drake is herself transformed. To follow the images is to follow the madwoman's own deluded consciousness. To follow the implied 'I' of the poem through the images is to follow her own changing conception of herself. The biographical information we glean from *The Bell Jar* may help us to visualise the scene and explain something of the poem's genesis, but the meaning of the poem goes far beyond Esther's interpretation of the same incident.

Exercise 5

In fact, this extract was not taken from a personal diary but from an autobiographical novel, Colette's *The Vagabond*, based closely on her own experiences, both in a relationship and in her other life as a professional dancer. Your answers to the questions will obviously in a sense have been falsified by the trick I have allowed myself to play on you in this exercise. Reread your answers and try to work out how far they were conditioned by the false information I gave. Would you now answer them differently? Are my questions in fact appropriate to the discussion of a novel?

What were your reactions to this exercise? Do you feel cheated or irritated? Does a writer owe it to his or her readers to signpost clearly what genre he or she is writing in, allowing us to *tune in* to the appropriate set of responses and criteria?

Exercise 6

These passages are all chosen because, while they obviously display certain literary characteristics, and are written by writers of recognised seriousness, they are in themselves difficult to define. The second passage is perhaps the easiest, being written in formal language, with a coherent narrative development and a poignantly funny dramatic climax. The first passage could be a hard one to classify. Trying to come to grips with it stylistically, we might well describe it as *unpretentious*. It is an odd mixture of rather self-consciously *written* description ('a dazzling air as light dappled through leaves') and colloquial elements ('of course', 'I guess'). In fact we have a movement from the 'literary' to the ordinary: most of us could come up with a gardening diary not very different from parts of the second paragraph.

The second extract is in fact taken from Edmund Gosse's auto-biographical *Father and Son*. The first extract is from May Sarton's *Diary of a Solitude*, and its unassuming, thought-provoking mixture becomes moving and comprehensible when we read it in the knowledge that this is a writer's personal diary, written honestly, yet with a view to publication. The third extract is from Hugo Williams' unclassifiable 'travel book' (is it really a travel book?), *No Particular Place To Go*. Part of the charm of this book is that it defies categorisation.

How far were these functional identities in fact perceptible in the passages themselves? Look at them again. Look at your answers to the last two questions in this exercise and reassess them in the light of this new information. Do these writers have us where they want us from the first word, or is expectation something more global, less easy to analyse?

I

THE NOVEL

———

1

— STORY, PLOT, TIME —

—————— Fiction and story ——————

No one, as far as I know, has ever managed to define exactly what a novel is. We can take an 18th-century novel like Richardson's *Pamela* and put it side by side with a recent novel like Margaret Atwood's *Cat's Eye*, and at first the two will seem to have nothing in common. One is visibly 'old-fashioned', its language now dated and awkward, written in the form of letters exchanged by imaginary characters. The other at first reads more like a kind of diary, starting in the present and 'wandering' back to tell of the past events that have made that present a point of crisis. Yet we have no difficulty, as we read on, in recognising that both these two works are novels. We feel the weight of them in our hands; we turn the pages; and as we turn the pages a story begins to take shape, a story which not only intrigues us in itself but which prompts us to ask questions about the characters, their motivation and their values, and provokes us to re-examine our own. Almost by instinct, we come back to the only definition of the novel that seems possible, the famous definition the novelist E M Forster put forward in 1927 and which has never been superseded: 'Well – I don't know [. . .] a novel's a novel [. . .] I suppose it kind of tells a story [. . .].' If we have read enough novels to begin to realise how many *other* things novels can do, we might even echo with Forster himself the regretful 'Yes – oh dear yes.'

Even in its beginnings, the novel has always told stories. Our English word 'novel' has the same origins as the German word *Novelle* and the French word *nouvelle* which both describe a short fictional narrative, somewhere between a regular novel and what we think of as a short story. All these words were derived from the Latin word for 'new'. In several other European languages the word for novel is something like *roman* or *Roman*, reflecting the fact that in the course of the Middle Ages a whole body of stories grew up across Europe, many of them around the legend of King Arthur and his knights. These stories were part of a new growth in writing, not in Latin, but in the old European languages known as *Romance*. They became known as *Romances*. They had – oh dear, yes – stories. They also used fiction and fantasy as a way of conveying deeply held values and serious thoughts about various aspects of the author's own life and society. This is what we tend nowadays to expect of our serious fiction. But this social focus, more or less latent in the novel's early ancestors, was not to be exploited fully until the writers associated with a 19th-century development called Realism were to change the expectations of readers of fiction in Europe and North America for ever.

Story and plot

Most, if not all, novels are built around a plot of some kind. Even ones that at first glance seem plotless generally prove on examination to have some sort of unifying sequence of events hidden beneath the surface. Sometimes the events will be presented to us in the wrong order. Sometimes we almost have to reconstruct the events for ourselves if we are to make sense of what is happening *here and now*. But there is invariably a story of some kind, and if the novel is a novel and not just a kind of fairy-tale, the story has to be of a sort which will make us ask the appropriate questions. Most of us are very accustomed, from our childhoods, to the sort of story that makes us ask *and what happens next*? The plot of a novel may well make us ask, *What next?* but it almost always also prompts us to ask how and why and whether. It is above all the reasons *why* a character is moved to commit a given action that link him or her to other characters and their desires or ambitions. 'The plot thickens,' we say. A *thick* plot, with all its implications for character and motivation, will ultimately hold a reader's interest better than a *thin* story. Small wonder that some of the greatest of novelists like Dickens or Dostoyevsky sometimes wove plots of astonishing complexity.

Exercise 1

Each of the following is a brief summary of a short work of fiction (tale or short novel). Take time to read and digest them as well as you can. Think about the interest that each would hold for you as a reader of serious fiction and the kind of questions the story might raise as it unfolded. Then work through the more specific points, trying to formulate in each case an answer that *you yourself* find satisfactory. (Remember that a literary criticism question rarely has a 'right' answer, though it may sometimes have 'wrong' or inadequate ones. Any answer that you can justify is worthy of serious attention.)

> As a mother sits at the bedside of her sick child, Death comes and snatches him from her. The woman follows, desperately questioning the Night, a rosebush and a lake and winning answers to her questions by sacrificing her songs, her blood and her eyes. She crosses to the other side where Death has a greenhouse of human souls, and searches among the plants for her own child. When Death returns to interrogate her, she, in a frenzy, threatens to uproot two plants at her feet. Then Death gives her back her eyes and shows her a vision of two futures, one of them happy and one tragic, telling her that one of them is her child's own. She, frightened at the tragic possibilities, begs Death to save her child by taking him away from her.
>
> (Hans Andersen, *The Story of a Mother*)

> A middle-aged writer, tired and overwrought after intense concentration on his work, goes out for a walk, meets an ambiguous stranger and conceives a sudden desire for a change of scene. He makes the journey to Venice, cutting an ineffectual figure in an altercation with the gondolier on his arrival. Shortly afterwards in his hotel he notices a Polish family also staying there, and in particular the very beautiful fifteen-year-old son, Tadzio. He

watches the boy closely, analysing and savouring his own reactions. Feeling the city to be unhealthy, he makes plans to leave, but there is a mix-up about his luggage and he finds himself staying on in Venice, watching Tadzio, more and more deeply under his spell, until rumours of cholera begin to circulate and the Polish family is on the point of leaving. The writer, by now half mad and uncharacteristically vulgar both in his tastes and his personal appearance, watches the boy in a fight on the beach, seems to communicate with him momentarily as Tadzio stands on the shoreline; then collapses and is taken to his room. Later that night he dies.

(Thomas Mann, *Death in Venice*)

The old man is now fishing alone after a spell of bad luck that has forced his boy companion to leave him regretfully for a luckier boat. He rows out into the morning darkness, knowing he will find fish. He baits his lines and waits. Eventually, from a particular kind of pulling far out on one line, he senses 'his' fish. He prepares; talks aloud to the fish; waits. At noon he hooks him.

Then there is a long slow struggle: the old man must wait, far from land and help, for the fish to tire. The sun goes down and he sits out the night, eating some of his catch and trying to rest, until the fish wakes him by jumping. He is exhausted, but at last the great fish is beaten and lashed alongside the boat. Soon after the old man turns the boat for home, sharks come after the dead fish's blood. The old man defends his catch with all the strength he has left, but by the second night, when he returns to harbour, the great fish is only a skeleton and the old man himself near death. The boy tells him that, luck or no luck, from now on they will fish together.

(Ernest Hemingway, *The Old Man and the Sea*)

Questions

(a) How complicated are these stories? Which seems to be the most complex, and which the simplest?

(b) Which involves the largest number of characters?

(c) Which would hold, for you, the greatest element of suspense?

(d) Does there seem to be any connection between 'suspense' and complication?

(e) Does any of these outlines seem to cry out to be longer or larger than a story or short novel can allow?

Try not to rush your answers to these questions: they are designed to help you become more aware of how plot functions in a work of fiction. When you have thought about them as fully as you can, you can turn to the **Commentary** at the end of the chapter where suggestions of possible ways to work through them are given. These suggestions are by no means exhaustive. You may well have had other ideas of your own which are equally valuable.

How important is plot?

Plot is not the easiest feature of a novel to analyse, because the best kind of plot is invisible, so deeply embedded in a pattern of cross-motivation among characters that events seem to happen almost of themselves, with a kind of *rightness* that makes us think, 'This is what life is like,' yet not obviously enough to be predictable. In the best novels, plot and character are almost impossible to separate: one character pushes another to provoke a third, who then acts in such a way as to have repercussions for the first. The best novels have no use for magic, or divine intervention, or Tay Bridge disasters. The characters meet, in given circumstances, and that is enough – Anna Karenina meets Vronsky, Jane Eyre is shut into the red room by Mrs Reed, Middlemarch just *is*.

All the same, we, as readers of fiction, are conditioned to have certain expectations of a thread or story-line which will seize and hold our interest and make us keep reading even if characters or setting or ideas are not immediately appealing. On the first page of a novel, the writer usually makes some concession to these expectations of ours. The emphasis he or she chooses in the opening paragraphs conditions our reactions to what follows. Is this going to be a novel with a story? Is the story going to be compelling? Or is our thirst for 'stories' being held in abeyance while we absorb other 'more serious' considerations of time, place, atmosphere or psychology?

Exercise 2

Each of the following extracts is the opening of a novel or a story. Read them all carefully and imagine how you would react to each as a 'taster' of imaginary events to come.

I did not kill my father, but I sometimes felt I had helped him on his way. And but for the fact that it coincided with a landmark in my own physical growth, his death seemed insignificant compared with what followed. My sisters and I talked about him the week after he died, and Sue certainly cried when the ambulance men tucked him up in a bright-red blanket and carried him away. He was a frail, irascible, obsessive man with yellowish hands and face. I am only including the little story of his death to explain how my sisters and I came to have such a large quantity of cement at our disposal.

(Ian McEwan, *The Cement Garden*)

Ursula and Gudrun Brangwen sat one morning in the window-bay of their father's house in Beldover, working and talking. Ursula was stitching a piece of brightly coloured embroidery, and Gudrun was drawing upon a board which she held on her knee. They were mostly silent, talking as their thoughts strayed through their minds.

'Ursula,' said Gudrun, 'don't you *really want* to get married?' Ursula laid her embroidery in her lap and looked up. Her face was calm and considerate.

'I don't know,' she replied. 'It depends how you mean.'

(D H Lawrence, *Women in Love*)

Once upon a time there dwelt near a large wood a poor wood-cutter, with his wife and two children by his former marriage – a little boy called Hansel, and a girl named Grethel. He had little enough to break or bite; and once, when there was a great famine in the land, he could not procure even his daily bread; and as he lay thinking in his bed one evening, restless and sorely troubled, he sighed, and said to his wife, 'What will become of us? How can we feed our children when we have no more than we can eat ourselves?'

(The Brothers Grimm, *Hansel and Grethel*)

Once upon a time there lived in Berlin, Germany, a man called Albinus. He was rich, respectable, happy; one day he abandoned his wife for the sake of a youthful mistress; he loved; was not loved; and his life ended in disaster.

(Vladimir Nabokov, *Laughter in the Dark*)

Questions

(a)   What questions does each extract provoke you to ask? Are they 'what then?' questions? Or are they questions that begin with 'how' or 'why'?

(b)   Do the first three openings use suspense to make us read on? Is suspense used in the same way in each of them?

(c)   Is it still possible to talk about 'suspense' where the last extract is concerned? What kind of suspense would it be?

(d)   The last extract is a famous beginning. The author has chosen, for some reason, to give away the story of his book in advance in his first two sentences. Is this likely to ruin the reader's relationship with the book, or make it more interesting?

——— Towards 'plotlessness' ———

More than any of the preceding extracts or remarks, this last short passage from Nabokov's *Laughter in the Dark* should have made you question your own attitude to the charm of story-telling in fiction. You may have felt intrigued about a writer who would dare to break the rules in this way; or you may have felt exasperated, telling yourself that the work was not worthy of your attention; or again you may have felt vaguely worried, wondering what was the 'proper' way to respond to a device that was so obviously literary. Whatever your initial reaction, try not to lose sight of it as you go on to look more closely: it is a barometer of how our expectations of a certain kind of literature have been formed through the ages. The most innovative of writers cannot entirely ignore the tradition of which he or she is a part. He or she is always, at some very deep level, digesting it or reacting against it.

Nabokov is not alone in questioning the place of *plot* in the novel. In England we seem to take less readily to experiments of this kind, but in other European countries and in North America writers have been more adventurous. The French novelist and film-maker Alain Robbe-Grillet has produced novels which at first sight seem almost plotless. If we are looking for an easy story, the almost endlessly repetitive scenes seem very boring. Only the occasional small jarring detail tells us that there *is*, after all, a human consciousness and a human story here: then the whole novel, like a shattered windscreen in reverse, fits itself fleetingly into an intricate pattern of cracks and little pieces.

Even in England, several important novelists of the last 50 years have come to interpret plot differently. What *has* become current, even in popular fiction, is the notion that *plot* is not necessarily based on a story which develops through time in a straightforward way, not necessarily *linear*. Frequently, it is more a matter of going *backwards*, revealing past events and deeper levels of character and motive to us as we read on. Great novelists have, of course, always done this. We are only just beginning to come to grips with Dostoyevsky's *Idiot* by the time the novel ends. We understand Hardy's Tess fully only at the end of the book when she appears against the timeless landscape of Stonehenge. But some novelists have changed the emphasis of story-telling more self-consciously and systematically and produced a recognisably different kind of novel.

Lawrence Durrell was one of those who saw the underlying structure of the novel as progressive revelation rather than as a linear *story*. There *is* a story, of course. But the four novels that make up *The Alexandria Quartet* and the more recent *Monsieur* and its sequels treat the reader as if he or she were something of a detective, unpeeling the 'truth' layer by layer like an onion, rather than planting it like a bulb and watching it grow. Most readers still find this approach to plot difficult and off-putting. But if we think of the more innovative fictions that we are accustomed to watching on film and television, it may be easier to see how our expectations of what a plot is or is not are subtly changing.

Exercise 3

Keep a diary of any *fictions* you come across over a period of time – say, two or three weeks. This could include not only any novels or short stories you read (from *any* source), but also films, theatre, radio and television, and even any stories you hear told by people you meet. Think about how each story developed. Did it progress more or less in a straight line, with one event or action giving rise to another? Or did it sometimes work visibly backwards or *inwards*, uncovering actions or motives perhaps already half-suggested? At the end of your diary, go back and think about your own reactions to the form taken by *plot* in each case. How frequently did variations from the conventional pattern occur? Would you have noticed them if you hadn't been asked to? Did they change the way you felt about the characters and their fictional lives?

Exercise 4

William Faulkner's *The Sound and the Fury* is one of the most remarkable examples of a plot that is based on gradual revelation. To achieve it, Faulkner uses an unusual time-sequence and a very special character, Benjy, who makes no comforting distinctions between past and present. Read the following short passages from the early part of the novel very carefully. It reads oddly, but for a good reason. Try not to be put off by its strangeness, and just *listen* to the words as if you were listening to a child speaking, or perhaps to a poem.

> [. . .] There was a flower in the bottle. I put the other flower in it.
> 'Ain't you a grown man, now.' Luster said. 'Playing with two weeds in a bottle. You know what they going to do with you when Miss Cahline die. They going to send you to Jackson, where you belong. Mr Jason say so. Where you can hold the bars all day long with the rest of the looneys and slobber. How you like that.'
> Luster knocked the flowers over with his hand. 'That's what they'll do to you at Jackson when you starts bellering.'
> I tried to pick up the flowers. Luster picked them up, and they went away. I began to cry.
> 'Beller.' Luster said. 'Beller. You want something to beller about. All right, then. Caddy.' He whispered. 'Caddy. Beller now. Caddy.'
> 'Luster.' Dilsey said from the kitchen.
> The flowers came back.

Now look at this passage, taken from much later in the book, and answer the questions that follow.

[. . .] 'Is you gwine hush, er ain't you?' Luster said. He got up and followed and came upon Ben squatting before a small mound of earth. At either end of it an empty bottle of blue glass that once contained poison was fixed in the ground. In one was a withered stalk of jimson weed. Ben squatted before it, moaning, a slow, inarticulate sound. Still moaning he sought vaguely about and found a twig and put it in the other bottle. 'Whyn't you hush?' Luster said, 'You want me to give you somethin' to sho nough moan about? Sposin I does dis.' He knelt and swept the bottle suddenly up and behind him. Ben ceased moaning. He squatted, looking at the small depression where the bottle had sat, then as he drew his lungs full Luster brought the bottle back into view. 'Hush!' he hissed. 'Don't you dast to beller! Don't you. Dar hit is. See? Here.[. . .]'

Questions

(a) What is happening in these two passages?

(b) Are the events clearer in the first extract or the second?

(c) What additional information does Faulkner give us in the second extract?

(d) Is some kind of a story beginning to emerge?

—— Time ——

More and more contemporary writers and critics seem to agree that the most fundamental problem that faces the novelist is the problem of time. How is he or she to compress the duration of a life-span or even longer into the limited few hours taken by the actual process of reading?

As we have seen, the way in which the novelist chooses to solve this problem is closely linked to his or her conception of what the novel can or cannot do, and to the relative emphasis he or she chooses to place on traditional elements of plot and character.

It is almost always rewarding to look closely at how time is handled in a novel. We may at first feel that we are being manipulated by such devices as flashbacks. Sometimes, when the past intrudes without warning in a character's unspoken thoughts (as it does in writers as different as James

Joyce and Rosamond Lehmann) we may feel vaguely angry because the illusion of a *whole* fictional world is broken. It is chastening to catch ourselves thinking as we go about our daily lives and see what part past and future play in a real present. In our everyday thoughts and conversations we jump backwards and forwards between then and now all the time. It is only in fiction that we seem to find the mixture difficult to handle.

But juggling with time is one of the most economical ways in which a novelist can create an illusion of depth. The young David Copperfield, the 'I' who 'is born' in the first chapter, is already seen through the defeats and survivals of the mature man, and means more to us than if he were not. The clean slate of his beginning is already covered with half-erased handwriting, and is all the more interesting for that. The simple past comes to us with a voice-over that says, 'This is how I have become what I am now.' We lose part of the *suspense*, but we gain something better, something perhaps not very different from what Nabokov offered us more provocatively in the first two sentences of *Laughter in the Dark*.

Exercise 5

The time-structure of L P Hartley's novel, *The Go-Between*, is in some ways similar to that of *David Copperfield*. Although Hartley's novel is much shorter and less complex than Dickens', both consist almost entirely of an extended 'flashback', reconsidered and interpreted to varying degrees by a maturer consciousness. In a sense the book's story suffers: even at the beginning we know something of what became of the hero; we know at least that his mature voice is sane and fairly ordinary, and that he is going to survive whatever happens to him. (Unless the writer is very sloppy or very eccentric, the 'I' viewpoint already, of course, tells us this.) But Hartley is already, even in his first sentence, making us curious about other things. He uses a list of small physical objects to put us into a frame of mind that is firmly retrospective. It is as if we were in his attic, or our own, sorting through a box of old momentoes, their significance half forgotten. What could be more natural than to wonder about them and the past they represent? What more natural than to open the diary, read a few pages and then sit back on our haunches, musing, filling in the gaps? The whole novel is built on this interplay between past and present, memory and its lapses, certainty and uncertainty. The device of the diary – and it is, after all, only a device, and a transparent one at that – helps the reader to accept in fiction what he or she would have no trouble accepting in his or her own life.

Here is the opening of the Prologue. Read it closely twice, and then answer the questions:

> The past is a foreign country: they do things differently there.
>
> When I came upon the diary it was lying at the bottom of a rather battered red cardboard collar-box, in which as a small boy I kept my Eton collars. Someone, probably my mother, had filled it with treasures dating from those days. There were two dry, empty sea-urchins; two rusty magnets, a large one and a small one, which had almost lost their magnetism; some negatives rolled up in a tight coil; some stumps of sealing-wax; a small combination lock with three rows of letters; a twist of very fine whipcord, and one or two ambiguous objects, pieces of things, of which the use was not at once apparent: I could not even tell what they had belonged to. The relics were not exactly dirty nor were they quite clean, they had the patina of age; and as I handled them, for the first time for over fifty years, a recollection of what each had meant to me came back, faint as the magnet's power to draw, but as perceptible. Something came and went between us; the intimate pleasure of recognition, the almost mystical thrill of early ownership – feelings of which, at sixty-odd, I felt ashamed.

Questions

(a)   Who are 'they' in the first sentence?

(b)   Why does the narrator say '*the* diary'?

(c)   Imagine you were going through the things of someone who had died, and these were the objects you found. What might they suggest about a life?

(d)   Look carefully at the last sentence of the second paragraph. Who or what is the *Go-Between* here?

Exercise 6

Look at the following two extracts from Iris Murdoch's novel, *A Word Child*.

It was Friday morning and I was just leaving for the office. Darkness had not yet really given way to day. There might have been some sort of yellow murk outside, but I did not pull back the curtains to look at it. I had swallowed two cups of tea and was my usual hateful early morning self. I emerged from the flat onto the bright electrically lit landing and closed the door behind me. The curious smell was still there. Then I stopped dead.

On the opposite side of the landing, not far from the lift, a girl was standing. I saw at once that she was, wholly or partly, Indian. She had a thin light-brown transparent spiritual face, a long thin fastidious mouth, an aquiline nose: surely the most beautiful race in the world, blending delicate frailty and power into human animal grace. She was not wearing a sari, but an indefinably oriental get-up consisting of a high-necked many-buttoned padded cotton jacket over multi-coloured cotton trousers. She was not tall, but in her gracefulness did not look short. Her black hair in a very long very thick plait was drawn forward over one shoulder. She stood perfectly still, her thin hands hanging down, and her large almost black eyes regarding me intently.

I felt shock, pleasure, surprise, alarm. Then I recalled Christopher's words, completely forgotten since, about a coloured girl looking for me. Fear. For *me* surely no one could search with an amiable motive. I was about to speak to her when the fact of the silence having lasted, as it seemed, so long made speech impossible. How after all could this girl, such a girl, concern me?

In the morning (Friday) I had breakfast in Paddington main line station, at the buffet on platform one, eating toast and marmalade at a table out on the platform, near to the most moving war memorial in London which represents a soldier of the first war, dressed in his trench warfare kit with his greatcoat over his shoulders, standing in a calm attitude and reading a letter from home. I sat there on the platform for some time and watched the departure of the seven-thirty for Exeter St David's, Plymouth and Penzance, the seven-forty for Bath, Bristol Temple Meads and Weston-Super-Mare, the eight o'clock for Cheltenham Spa, Swansea and Fishguard Harbour, and the eight-five for Reading, Oxford and Worcester Shrub Hill. I felt now much less exalted and much more frightened: not frightened really of anything that could happen in the world, but frightened of my own mind, of sudden vistas of new kinds of pain. How could I so *love* someone whom I could never see or know, the person indeed who was of all the farthest from me, the most ineluctably separated? What awful suffering, not yet felt, not yet revealed, would this involve? Was this the punishment, the expiation, the end, the dark hole into which I would finally disappear? Yet even then I knew that from myself I would not disappear. I would go on indestructibly, day after day, week after week, year after year, and I would not break down and no one would ever hear me scream. That was the worst of it. And with this worst was interwoven the fact and miracle of love with all its gentleness and its vision and its pure joy.

As you read these two passages for the second time, ask yourself whether the Friday morning of the second extract is the same Friday morning or a different one. What might make the reader think they are the same? What might suggest they are not?

Why might a novelist want to create an illusion of time's standing still?

Resolution

The conventional fairy-tale has a happy ending. Hans Andersen's fairy-tales often have an ambivalent ending. Very many of the most powerful 19th-century novels (*Jude the Obscure, Anna Karenina, Germinal*) end disastrously, and most readers find this no less satisfying. What seems to be so fundamental to the fictional tradition as to be almost a physiological need, is that a story should end *somehow*.

Increasingly, in our own times, serious novelists have tried to break away from a traditionally emphatic ending: life itself does not *end* in satisfying ways. Married couples do not live happily ever after, nor does everything stop in the tragedy of a bereavement. Whole civilisations may perish, but in real life the grass soon pushes up between the paving-stones. Surely the way in which a work of fiction ends should reflect this?

The central character in an influential French novel of the 1920s claimed that a novel should end as if with the words: 'could be continued', and readers of fiction since the turn of the century have had to become more used to ambiguous or open endings. At the end of D H Lawrence's novel, *Sons and Lovers*, the hero, Paul Morel, takes his first step down into the valley. What that step means is for the reader to work out.

Usually, there *are* clues. If we go back and re-read what has gone before, even the most ambiguous of endings usually holds some kind of resolution. Sometimes an open ending, by making us vaguely uncomfortable, even helps us to see tensions that we have not really been aware of earlier.

Here, too, the novelist's handling of time is important. The predominantly retrospective novel like *David Copperfield*, or *Great Expectations*, or *The Go-Between* works towards a fictional present, ending when the teller reaches the point at which he is telling the story. Implicit in that present is an open and undetermined future. When Dickens responded to a friend's disappointment at the original ending of *Great Expectations* by changing it to a 'happy' one, he was changing not just the fictional destinies of Pip and Estella, but the meaning of the whole book.

Exercise 7

John Fowles' novel, *The French Lieutenant's Woman* is probably unique in its blend of modern techniques and period atmosphere. At the end of the book, the author presents us with two alternative outcomes.

At a crucially dramatic moment in the final scene, the heroine, Sarah, steps in to explain her own behaviour and resolve tensions that have been building throughout the novel:

> [. . .] he ground his jaws shut, turned on his heel and marched towards the door.
>
> Gathering her skirt in one hand, she ran after him. He span round at the sound, she stood lost a moment. But before he could move on she had stepped swiftly past him to the door. He found his exit blocked.
>
> 'I cannot let you go believing that.'

Seven pages later, the sequence is repeated and resolved in a different way:

> [. . .] he ground his jaws shut, turned on his heel and marched towards the door.
>   'Mr Smithson!'
>   He took a step or two more; stopped, threw her a look back over his shoulder; and then with the violence of a determined unforgivingness, stared at the foot of the door in front of him. He heard the light rustle of her clothes. She stood just behind him.
>   'Is this not proof of what I said just now? That we had better never to have set eyes on each other again?'

Read these two short extracts again carefully, looking particularly at the point at which the two diverge, and try to answer the following questions:

(a) Do you gain the same impression of Sarah's character from both?

(b) Does the author use the same kind of language in both?

(c) Which do you find the more satisfying?

(d) Do you wish your preferred ending were the only ending?

————————— **Commentary** —————————

Exercise 1

(a) Complex as they seem, these stories are in fact very simple as examples of *plot* in fiction. Merely to list the characters and their interrelationships in a novel by Dickens, George Eliot, or Tolstoy, would be a gigantic undertaking. As they stand, I would say that the second plot is the simplest of the three and the first is arguably the most complex. (The exercise of summarising cannot be entirely objective, and decisions about which ramifications of plot to include or exclude are ultimately personal. If you go back to the original stories, you may summarise them differently and come up with very different answers.)

(b)   Almost any answer is acceptable here, provided you have thought through what you mean by a character in this context. If a character is a fictional entity which works on another to generate feelings and actions, then the child in the first plot is certainly a character. So is the sea in the third or the big fish, or the sharks. The other members of the Polish family in the second summary, however, do not seem to enter the equation in any serious way.

(c)   This, again, is a personal matter. If you are a mother yourself, you may find suspense even in the obviously symbolic world of the first summary. I suspect most readers would be most involved in the third summary.

(d)   On the face of it, no. But Hemingway's plot is a very simple struggle framed in a more complex one. While the old man is battling with the fish, the novel seems emptied of all else. At that central point of conflict – which fills up the largest and most memorable part of the book – no irrelevant consideration is allowed to intrude.

(e)   It is difficult to see how either the first or the third plot could be the plot of a longer work of fiction. The second plot, however, with its suspicious stranger, its gondolier, its hotel full of guests, has the makings of a far larger cast waiting in the wings. Thomas Mann has chosen to focus on one man's struggle with perfection, just as Hemingway has. But here society seems to lie in wait under a thin crust of artistic decision-making.

Exercise 2

(a)   The third extract, as you would expect of a fairy-tale, seems to me to elicit primarily 'what then?' questions. In the second extract, while there are underlying 'what then?' questions here (*Will* Ursula get married? Will Gudrun?), the most important questions already have to do with character and motivation (What can Ursula mean? What kind of person is she to be thinking of marriage already in these terms?). The first extract has something in common with the fourth extract, in that it is already anticipating, telling the reader the outcome of an important part of the story. We are not permitted to ask what is going to happen to the narrator's father. We know already that he is to die. So instead we find ourselves asking *how* and *why* he died and what kind of a relationship the son had with the father. The question implicit in the last sentence, however, dwarfs all the others. Victims of McEwan's shock tactics, we find ourselves asking simply, *'Cement????'* The one word holds a wealth of questions, of all descriptions. The fourth extract is in some ways similar. We are not *allowed* to ask 'what?', so our curiosity is immediately focused on the 'how' and the 'why?'. We may also become suddenly conscious of ourselves as readers of a novel and of the novelist as a potential manipulator, as we ask ourselves such questions as 'Now what does Nabokov mean by telling us all that in advance?'

(b)   Yes: it is possible for characters and their relationships to generate, if not suspense, exactly, at least a kind of excitement. But we are intrigued rather than on tenterhooks. I would guess that for most readers it was the sheer surprise of Ian McEwan's cement that generated the most impatience to read on.

(c)   Yes, I think it is, but it has to do with *how* and *when* events will take place rather than with the nature of the events themselves. In fact, suspense implies that we suspect that something is about to happen. Logically if we *know* it will happen (as we surely know the shark will attack in *Jaws*), the suspense is all the greater.

(d)   This is a question which you can only answer for yourself. Personally, I enjoy the enforced change of focus. All the same, there are obviously contexts (e. g. detective or science fiction novels) in which this kind of beginning would be destructive. Jokes, however, often begin with 'Have you heard the one about the man who . . . ?'

Exercise 4

(a)   In both cases Luster is teasing Benjy by hiding the flowers Benjy loves behind his back, then producing them again.

(b)   Although the actual words and sentence-structure are simpler in the first passage, it is surely easier to understand what is happening from the second.

(c)   What Luster says and the way he speaks are similar in the two extracts. The only obvious difference is in the way Faulkner has punctuated them. What changes is the point of view. In the second passage the two characters are seen from the outside. Ben is named. The scene is set briefly. We see what the 'flowers' consist of, and how and why they vanish and reappear.

(d)   As we begin to understand in retrospect what was missing in the vision of the character (Ben) who was telling the story in the first extract, we see that his odd way of looking at the world is itself a part of the story. Perhaps the second paragraph also begins to make sense. The whole novel is built on this principle of gradual revelation.

Exercise 5

(a)   We are not told who 'they' are. 'They' must be someone the narrator knows and someone we as yet are unfamiliar with. 'They' are also 'other people', a vaguely hostile, alien class of beings with whom the narrator once had a relationship, but to whom he no longer belongs.

(b)   'The' seems to imply that a diary has already been mentioned, its importance already demonstrated. It establishes a kind of intimacy between us and the narrator: it is as if he has already confided a secret to us, and his past has become something that must concern us too.

(c)   Most of these objects suggest in their various ways that something which once was potent, painful, binding, has now lost its power. They also suggest a collector, a preserver of memories, perhaps someone secretive and slightly insecure, who liked things that came in pairs. By their uncared-for appearance they suggest sadness and neglect: a human being has been lost or changed beyond recognition.

(d)   The 'Go-Between' in this sentence is the emotion that seems to pass back and forth between these childhood objects and the 60-year-old who is rediscovering them. Perhaps the book's title refers to this, as well as to the more obvious rôle the child Leo is to take as messenger between the lovers later in the story.

Exercise 6

The two Friday mornings are, in commonsense terms, obviously not the same: the narrator is in two different places; there is no obvious connection between the Indian girl of the first extract and the 'love' of the second extract. Not only the setting but the narrator's emotions seem to tell us that this is a later Friday: we have progressed from fear and panic at the recognition that something unknown is beginning, to the certainty that, whatever drama life throws at him, he will survive. We have also moved from a place where extraordinary things may begin to happen to a place in which *the miracle of love* competes for our attention with very ordinary trains to comically banal destinations. Yet the central 'I' who questions himself remains the same. 'Can this be happening to me?' he seems to be saying, and in his dramatic, flowery way, 'Can I cope?' The fact that all this is still happening on a Friday seems to emphasise both that time is passing and that the character himself is standing still. It is as if *every* Friday, regular as clockwork, he meets his emotional Waterloo.

There are, of course, many reasons why a novelist might want to create this effect. In this particular book, the way time is handled contributes to our view of the hero as a kind of Peter Pan figure, unable or unwilling to face up to the banality of a truly adult relationship. It also invites us to draw parallels between one part of the plot and another, and manipulates our reactions subtly by creating a pattern of expectation: as we read on in the book, we come almost to cling to certain fixtures of the calendar in the way the hero, Hilary Burde, does. It is against this backdrop that the real drama can begin.

Exercise 7

(a)   No. The Sarah who runs to the door, hesitates, cries out in the first extract is not the same as the Sarah who follows Charles to the door in the next extract and addresses him formally, as if on cue.

(b)   No. The language Sarah uses is more considered and more self-consciously *period* in the second extract. The language used in the body of the narrative also seems slightly more melodramatic in this passage ('the violence of a determined unforgivingness').

(c)   The answer to this must be subjective. You will no doubt choose the ending which fits best with your own experience of man-woman relationships. Readers of the whole book will no doubt choose the ending which best fits their conception of Sarah. But we should not forget that what has implications for Sarah has implications for Charles too, and for his capacity for self-deception. While both endings are possible, John Fowles is undoubtedly implying that one is more real than the other.

(d)   I should think every *normal* reader would prefer a single ending. As we have seen, endings are built into our expectations of the novel. In a period novel, they are surely built in even more. The success or otherwise of John Fowles' device depends on our reacting in the expected way, with confusion, frustration, even anger.

2

—— CHARACTERS ——

—— What is character? ——

In a novel by L M Montgomery, written for older children, the fictional heroine writes in her diary:

> November 11, 19-
>
> 'Last night Aunt Ruth found me reading *David Copperfield* and crying over Davy's alienation from his mother, with a black rage against Mr Murdstone in my heart. She must know *why* I was crying, and wouldn't believe me when I told her.
>
> '"Crying over people who never existed," said my aunt Ruth incredulously.
>
> '"Oh, but they *do* exist," I said. "Why, they are as real as *you* are, Aunt Ruth. Do you mean to say that Miss Betsy Trotwood is a delusion?"'

(Emily Climbs)

Most of us, and especially those of us who have enjoyed reading novels from childhood, are surely familiar with this phenomenon – the fictional character who absorbs and dominates our imagination to such an extent that he or she evokes in us a real emotional response. It is fortunately still not unusual for a reader to cry over a character, or to think of a fictional character with something very close to affection, or anger, or dislike. Discussing the fiction we have read, we are very often tempted into realms of conjecture beyond the scope of the narrative, fleshing out a character's past ('But perhaps there was more unhappiness in her childhood than the author tells us?'), a character's future ('Well, she's obviously going to lead him a merry dance!') or even alternative plot-lines in explicit contradiction to what we are actually told in the novel itself ('If he hadn't led such a hand-to-mouth existence and thought so much about philosophy . . . ').

In criticism, as in our spontaneous human reactions, it is often very easy to forget, at least momentarily, that a fictional character is after all only a collection of words printed on paper – no more and no less. Even the least *functional* of characters has his or her function. If we have an impression of human characteristics, it is because specific words are used to give us this impression. If we carry in our heads an impression that seems to go beyond the words, it is because the author is using words, and the interaction of words, to put it there.

In a sense, Miss Betsy Trotwood is indeed a delusion. So is Aunt Ruth. In a more sophisticated, more modern, context, the L M Montgomery passage quoted above could be full of ironies.

There are, of course, different degrees of emotion to be felt. Intense feeling is not always appropriate. If Jane Austen were to give us real sympathy for Emma's father, Mr Woodhouse, we should all end up feeling threatened and disparaging any part of *Emma* that did not take place under his roof at Hartfield. Traditionally, a novel gives us an illusion of life. But we are used to seeing life from a single viewpoint, and even the most enlightened viewpoint is at times melodramatic and reductive. A novel which practised real equality for its characters is difficult even to imagine. Perhaps it was this impossibility that Virginia Woolf had in mind when she wrote *The Waves*.

Most, if not all novels, are based on a hierarchy of characters. In general, we accept that the principal characters are to create an illusion of life, that they are to be *three dimensional*, that we cannot talk about their function without examining the entire structure of the book to which they belong. If they are provocative or mysterious, so much the better. We smile at Emma's little vanities, but we are waiting for her serious-ness. Her meddlings govern the first half of the story, and the growth of her understanding puts every character, including her blundering self, into perspective in the second. Mrs Bates, on the other hand, is *two-dimensional*, *flat* – summed up completely by her function as Jane Fairfax's loved, infirm, elderly relative.

Jane Fairfax herself might seem to be a minor character. For much of the book she is only a name other characters admire and gossip about, an irritatingly *perfect* standard Emma is forced to measure her own qualities and accomplishments by. In Emma's relationships with other characters in the book, Jane Fairfax has a definite and limited function to perform. Yet she still manages to be mysterious. In the end, how we feel about Mr Knightley and Emma, the novel's hero and heroine, depends on how we feel about Jane.

Some of the most memorable characters in fiction do seem somehow to *escape* their functional requirements, without being mysterious or even emotive in the usual sense. They are the caricatures, the *larger than life* figures we find so often in Dickens to amuse or half-frighten us, the minor characters of more modern comic novels, or the Poirots and the Lord Peter Wimseys. Why a caricature is appropriate obviously varies from circumstance to circumstance. In 19th-century novels associated with Realism, caricature often seems to be a way of producing the illusion of a world crawling with eccentricities and conflicting ambitions. In a comic context, this kind of character is often the butt of social criticism. In any context, this is a kind of character that we are used to. For a 19th-century reader, Mr Micawber or the Veneerings would have been a source of delight. To us, in the 20th century, they may well still bring delight, but they also flatter us with something like reassurance. We are comfortable in this somewhat grotesque company. We are entertained in a way we understand. No real effort is being asked of us.

In fiction, even more than in poetry or drama where the demands of the medium are more clear-cut, effort is an important concept. How much work should the reader be expected to do? Is the novel to unfold in front of us effortlessly, as if we were ensconced in some imaginary armchair? Is it to transport us magically to some other mental place? May we relax, suspend our critical faculties, and expect the novelist to do all the work for us? Or should we take it that we are at least to 'put two and two together', to foresee events and build character from fragments of behaviour and dialogue, to induce a character's 'identity' from the clues a writer gives us?

We do this all the time in our day-to-day existence. We know only what we see and hear. We never know the people around us totally. Yet we often find ourselves called on to interact with them as if we did. Why is it then that in novels we expect things to be clearer?

It could be that constructing reasoned hypotheses about characters' motivation not only forces us to think but also reminds us that we are thinking. As we become aware of ourselves, the novel's own world becomes less complete, less compelling. We can no longer see it quite so clearly. Someone has come into our private cinema and turned on the lights. The disbelief we had suspended is hovering somewhere uncomfortably just above our heads.

In practice, we tend to co-operate with the author more than we realise. When Percy Lubbock in his work on the novel, *The Craft of Fiction*, first published in 1921, made the important distinction between *telling* and *showing*, he saw *showing* as one of the greatest resources a creator of fictional characters had at his or her disposal. Once we get used to it, surely it is more exciting, more immediate, somehow more 'real' to work out for ourselves that a character is self-satisfied, or ambitious, or in love, than it is to be handed those qualities explicitly on a plate? What is likely to be disturbing is not so much the fact that our cinema is lit or in darkness, but any *variation* in that lighting. We can get used to the light if it stays on – if an author is asking us consistently to participate in the creative process. It is when an intrusive narrator pops in and out of a narrative that we become uncomfortable: if the lights flicker or dim and then come on again unexpectedly, we might get caught with the tears still running down our faces.

To describe or not to describe?

Every fictional character we meet in literature is first met through words. In novels and stories which make little claim to be formally inventive, those words may take the form of a description. Sometimes dialogue, or behaviour or reputation precede them. Sometimes we see events through a character's own eyes and description of that character would then be intrusive. Yet even where it is patently artificial, personal description has impressed itself so deeply on our expectations of how a character should be portrayed that many novelists – some of them minor and others by no means minor – have found it almost impossible to dispense with. We have only to think of the number of fictional characters who look at themselves in mirrors. The characters of novelists as diverse as George Orwell and Colette have fallen back on mirrors to gloss over the artifice.

When characters are described indirectly, the description is more logically accounted for in the narrative, and so, theoretically at least, less obtrusive. We have already mentioned the device of the mirror. A fictional diary, letter, notes, or even a page of dialogue, can contain information about one character in the voice of another. These *mediated* portraits are doubly interesting because we have to interpret them. They may be a pack of lies. We know they tell us something about the describer as well as about the character who is being described. We may have to hold back, stop ourselves from concluding too quickly: it could be pages, or even hundreds of pages, before we know just how flattering or jaundiced or unwittingly revealing a likeness this is.

Exercise 1

For a few days, keep a diary noting the people you meet for the first time, together with those you come into contact with yet know only slightly. Ask yourself what impressions you have retained about their personal characteristics, and then, more importantly, try to pin those impressions down to actual information that has passed between you. Where are your impressions coming from? Is it from how those people look, or what they are wearing? Is it from the way they speak, or what they have said or done? How strong an impression do you retain of the character of someone you have only spoken to on the telephone or heard on the radio?

Exercise 2

Write down the names of three of the most memorable characters in the fiction you have read. Do you have a mental picture of what they look like? Does that picture come from the author's own description or from somewhere else? Go back and look at the novels in question to see how comprehensively, and at what point, your characters were described.

Think about the fictional characters you meet in films or on television. Is your conception of character altered by being embodied in the face and physique, voice and clothes of an actor? Can you think of any television characters who are referred to by the others but who never make a personal appearance? Do they *exist* for you through their reported behaviour in the same way as the characters you see?

Think of television or film dramatisations of novels you had previously read. How often was your impression of the characters deepened by the physical representation? How often were you disappointed?

Exercise 3

Another way of portraying character indirectly is through his or her relationship with an object. In our lives, we surely feel that the things which surround us and which we use every day begin to look a bit as we do ourselves. Our homes, whether by design or default, tend to reflect our personalities. In fact we frequently decorate and furnish them with this aim in view. Our clothes take on the shape and smell of our bodies, and perhaps more than our bodies. In a novel by Elizabeth Bowen, the characters decide to leave a kind of 'personality capsule' of themselves in an underground hiding-place, a box of personal 'clues':

> 'Clues to reconstruct *us* from. Expressive objects. What really expresses people? The things, I'm sure, that they have obsessions about: keep on wearing or using, or fuss when they lose, or can't go to sleep without. You know, a person's only a *person* when they have some really raging peculiarity – don't you notice that, Mrs Coral, with all your friends?'

In this particular novel, *The Little Girls*, the legacies of character and time are important themes. But almost all fiction links character and objects implicitly to some extent.

The links may be elusive. Sometimes even a vestige of association is enough. But if an object is openly cherished, so much the better. The wonderful old heroine of Flaubert's story, *A Simple Heart*, is characterised by the things she loves – a shell box, a little girl's plush hat, a moth-eaten stuffed parrot, a painting of the Holy Ghost. Félicité *is* all of these things – breakable and velvety, mangy and exotic, sentimental and visionary. Few techniques could have dramatised the paradoxes so effectively.

Read the following extracts carefully, and try to answer the questions which follow:

'[. . .] Is this where you live?' he asked, nodding towards the projecting wing off the far side of the garage.

'Yes,' Vic said, pulling the corners of his mouth into a smile. He went back to his snail cleaning. It was an unattractive aspect of snail raising, cleaning the mess off the glass sides of the tank with a razorblade, and he loathed it when Mr Cameron strolled over to watch him, still whistling. To Vic's surprise, he was whistling part of a Mozart concerto.

'Where'd you get all those?' he asked.

'Oh – most of them were born here. Hatched.'

'How do they breed? In the water?'

'No, they lay eggs. In the ground.' Vic was washing the inside of a tank with a rag and soap and water. Delicately he detached a young snail that had crawled up on the part of the glass he was washing, and set it down on the earth inside the tank.

'Look like they'd be good to eat,' Mr Cameron remarked.

'Oh, they are. Delicious.'

'Reminds me of New Orleans. Ever been to New Orleans?'

'Yes,' Vic said, with finality. He began on another tank, first detaching with his hands or the razorblade the snails of all sizes that were sleeping on the sides of the glass. He looked over at Mr Cameron and said, 'I wish you wouldn't take the screen off, if you don't mind. They crawl out very easily.'

(Patricia Highsmith, *Deep Water*)

The new boy had perhaps not noticed our procedure, or if he had he felt too scared to attempt it himself, for he was still holding his cap on his knees when prayers were over. His was one of those composite pieces of headgear in which you may trace features of bearskin, lancer-cap and bowler, night-cap and otterskin: one of those pathetic objects that are deeply expressive in their dumb ugliness, like an idiot's face. An oval splayed out with whale-bone, it started off with three pompons; these were followed by lozenges of velvet and rabbit's fur alternately, separated by a red band, and after that came a kind of bag ending in a polygon of cardboard with intricate braiding on it; and from this there hung down like a tassel, at the end of a long, too slender cord, a little sheaf of gold threads. It was a new cap, with a shiny peak.

(Gustave Flaubert, *Madame Bovary*)

Mr and Mrs Veneering were bran-new people in a bran-new house in a bran-new quarter of London. Everything about the Veneerings was spick and span new. All their furniture was new, all their servants were new, their plate was new, their carriage was new, their harness was new, their horses were new, their pictures were new, they themselves were new, they were as newly married as was lawfully compatible with their having a bran-new baby, and if they had set up a great-grandfather, he would have come home in matting from the Pantechnicon, without a scratch upon him, French polished to the crown of his head.

For, in the Veneering establishment, from the hall-chairs with the new coat of arms, to the grand pianoforte with the new action, and upstairs again to the new fire-escape, all things were in a state of high varnish and polish. And what was observable in the furniture, was observable in the Veneerings – the surface smelt a little too much of the workshop and was a trifle stickey.

(Charles Dickens, *Our Mutual Friend*)

Ah, the thick-witted old rogue of a giant! He threw down the golden apples, and received back the sky, from the head and shoulders of Hercules, upon his own, where it rightly belonged. And Hercules picked up the three golden apples, that were as big or bigger than pumpkins, and straightway set out on his journey homeward, without paying the slightest heed to the thundering tones of the giant, who bellowed after him to come back. Another forest sprang up around his feet, and grew ancient there; and again might be seen oak-trees, of six or seven centuries old, that had waxed thus aged betwixt his enormous toes.

(Nathaniel Hawthorne, *Tanglewood Tales*)

Questions

(a) Which of these passages gives the strongest impression of character?

(b)   Which do you think is the most subtle?

(c)   How does Dickens show that he is using the technique ironically?

(d)   Is the last passage representative of any re-telling of myth that you are familiar with? How do the objects work here to portray character? Is the scope of the myth enlarged or reduced?

———— Words and thoughts ————

Dialogue is of course a far more dramatic way to portray character. There is not only *what* is said: there are the implications of what is said, the tone of the speaker, the actual words he or she chooses.

Exercise 4

Read the following two extracts carefully, asking yourself:

(a)   Which of the two is the funnier?

(b)   What is it about the speaker's words in each case that gives a strong impression of her or his character?

(c)   What do you know about each character by the time she or he has finished speaking?

'[. . .] It is to be a morning scheme, you know, Knightley; quite a simple thing. I shall wear a large bonnet, and bring one of my little baskets hanging on my arm. Here, – probably this basket with pink ribbon. Nothing can be more simple, you see. And Jane will have such another. There is to be no form or parade – a sort of gipsy party. – We are to walk about your gardens, and gather the strawberries ourselves, and sit under trees; – and whatever else you may like to provide, it is to be all out of doors – a table spread in the shade, you know. Every thing as natural and simple as possible. Is not that your idea?'

(Jane Austen, *Emma*)

Before a silence could fall, Margaret said 'Are you down here for long, Mr Welch?' [. . .]

Bertrand's jaws snatched successfully at a piece of food which had been within an ace of eluding them. He went on chewing for a moment, pondering. 'I doubt it,' he said at last. 'Upon consideration I feel it incumbent upon me to doubt it. I have miscellaneous concerns in London that need my guiding hand.' He smiled among his beard, from which he now began brushing crumbs. 'But it's very pleasant to come down here and to know that the torch of culture is still in a state of combustion in the provinces. Profoundly reassuring, too.'

'And how's your work going?' Margaret asked.

[. . .]

'What work do you do?' Dixon asked flatly.

'I am a painter. Not, alas, a painter of houses, or I should have been able to make my pile and retire by now. No no; I paint pictures. Not, alas again, pictures of trade unionists or town halls or naked women, or I should be squatting on an even larger pile. No no; just pictures, mere pictures, pictures *tout court*, or, as our American cousins would say, pictures period. And what work do you do? always provided, of course, that I have permission to ask.'

(Kingsley Amis, *Lucky Jim*)

(d)   Think again about all these impressions. Does there seem to be any connection between the way these two mini-portraits are produced and the humour attached to them?

Exercise 5

We have already touched on the relationship between character and plot. Some of the most effective uses of dialogue to portray character are also highly dramatic. The words of the speaker not only reveal something but do something. They act on the interlocutor to generate a reaction; this second speaker also reveals something, and provokes yet another response. Dialogue in some of the best and most serious novels is sometimes quite unrealistically significant. In our real lives we rarely speak significantly. Most of our words are used up in functional questions and answers or banal exchanges. One of the underlying assumptions of the greatest fictional dialogue seems to be that it need not be realistic to the point of being banal. Characters betray themselves in a dialogue charged with meanings far too sophisticated, or at least too concentrated, for ordinary human speakers to interpret. Almost every character in Henry James must surely have a brain the size of a pumpkin! Yet, yearning as we often do for meaningful exchanges in our own lives, it is a convention which most readers accept without difficulty, and often find deeply truthful.

Read the following passages of dialogue:

'You have as good as informed me, sir, that you are going shortly to be married?'

'Yes; what then?'

'In that case, sir, Adèle ought to go to school: I am sure you will perceive the necessity of it.'

'To get her out of my bride's way, who might otherwise walk over her rather too emphatically? There's some sense in the suggestion; not a doubt of it, Adèle, as you say, must go to school; and you, of course, must march straight to – the devil?'

'I hope not, sir; but I must seek another situation somewhere.'

'In course!' he exclaimed, with a twang of voice and a distortion of features equally fantastic and ludicrous. He looked at me some minutes.

'And old Madam Reed, or the Misses, her daughters, will be solicited by you to seek a place, I suppose?'

'No, sir; I am not on such terms with my relatives as would justify me in asking favours of them – but I shall advertise.'

'You shall walk up the pyramids of Egypt!' he growled. 'At your peril you advertise! I wish I had only offered you a sovereign instead of ten pounds. Give me back nine pounds, Jane; I've a use for it.'

'And so have I, sir,' I returned, putting my hands and my purse behind me. 'I could not spare the money on any account.'

'Little niggard!' said he, 'refusing me a pecuniary request! Give me five pounds, Jane.'

'Not five shillings, sir; not five pence.'

'Just let me look at the cash.'

'No, sir; you are not to be trusted.'

'Jane!'

'Sir?'

— 53 —

'Promise me one thing.'

'I'll promise you anything, sir, that I think I am likely to perform.'

(Charlotte Brontë, *Jane Eyre*)

'[. . .] Are you really in love with her?' Maria threw off.

'It's of no importance I should know,' he replied. 'It matters so little – has nothing to do, practically, with either of us.'

'All the same' – Maria continued to smile – 'they go, the five, as I understand you, and you and Madame de Vionnet stay.'

'Oh and Chad.' To which Strether added: 'And you.'

'Ah "me"!' – she gave a small impatient wail again, in which something of the unreconciled seemed suddenly to break out. '*I* don't stay, it somehow seems to me, much to my advantage. In the presence of all you cause to pass before me I've a tremendous sense of privation.'

Strether hesitated. 'But your privation, your keeping out of everything, has been – hasn't it? – by your own choice.'

'Oh yes; it has been necessary – that is it has been better for you. What I mean is only that I seem to have ceased to serve you.'

'How can you tell that?' he asked. 'You don't know how you served me. When you cease – '

'Well?' she said as he dropped.

'Well, I'll *let* you know. Be quiet till then.'

She thought a moment. 'Then you positively like me to stay?'

'Don't I treat you as if I did?'

(Henry James, *The Ambassadors*)

Choose one of these passages to study in more detail. Try to answer these questions in relation to this *one* passage:

(a) Is the impression of character that the reader gains from this dialogue stronger or weaker than it was in the extracts from *Emma* and *Lucky Jim* you studied in **Exercise 4**?

(b) What do we learn about these characters?

(c) Are there qualities in them we suspect but are not sure of?

(d) Where in the text are these suspicions coming from?

(e) Does any remark made by either character seem to have more meaning than you would expect from this apparently fairly ordinary conversation?

Re-read the extract you chose, thinking about your answers. Has the meaning of the passage as a whole changed for you in any way?

Now re-read the extract you didn't choose. Has the meaning of this passage now become any clearer?

Mystery

Sometimes, especially in late 19th- and 20th-century fiction, a writer very consciously ignores some of the tools of character-portrayal at his or her disposal. Descriptions of characters, direct or indirect, may be vague and impressionistic. Sometimes they may not be present at all. Direct access to a character's thoughts may be denied us. Conversations may be ambiguous, or even misleading. Curiosity may be more important than vividness. Even if we read attentively, we may find ourselves falling through apparent *holes* in the narrative and at a loss to interpret a character's behaviour.

If we are at ease with the more generous conventions of 19th-century Realism, we may find ourselves frustrated by characters as slippery and elusive as some of our more casual acquaintances. On the other hand, we may find this very lack of easy insights exciting and convincing in a way that a more completely comprehensible character can never be. The cryptic glimpses we are allowed of Lolita, in her banal marriage, or of Cordelia, the absent heroine of Margaret Atwood's *Cat's Eye*, in her psychiatric hospital, are tantalising but *real*. They give us a sudden unexpected view of character which seems to fight the knowledge we have so far managed to glean in other cirumstances. They work to give us a new understanding, but at the cost of the understanding we already have. They can surprise us and undermine our confidence, and move us unexpectedly if we let them. They make us question the picture we had previously built up. We look at the features in the blurred photograph and wonder when and in what circumstances it was taken. We also wonder how good the photographer was.

Exercise 6

Take time to think back over all the novels and stories you have read and remember. This is something you can do best over a longer period, say a week or a fortnight. Jot down the names of any characters who have seemed to you powerful or fascinating in that they were genuinely mysterious.

Then, refreshing your memory if you can by going back and looking at the books in which they appeared, try to work out what it was that generated this illusion of mystery. (It is, after all, an illusion.) How far is it due to the author's decision to show a character's behaviour without accounting for its motives? How far is it due to ambiguities in the dialogue? How far is it due to sudden unexpected changes of perspective?

———————— It's a . . . ————————

The turn-of-the-century French writer, André Gide, wrote disparagingly of Balzac's characters. They reminded him of an American cartoon about a maternity home for hens, where the matron-hen breaks her news to the pacing, chain-smoking father-to-be cockerel in the words, 'It's an egg!' The reader knew they were eggs. Nothing they could say or do would make them in any way surprising.

This is of course absurdly dismissive. Yet there is a grain of truth in it. Perhaps it was above all the influence of Dostoyevsky and his strange, contradictory, passionate characters which made more modern novelists reassess not only the techniques they were using to portray human personalities in the novel but also their interpretation of what 'character' meant. There was Freud, too. As the echoes of his researches penetrated to the remoter corners of Europe, a nice rounded fictional character with unity and consistency began to look less and less satisfying. If the unconscious mind could astonish and betray, then any fictional character worth his or her salt should astonish and betray too. The eggs began to be chipped open from the inside. Even the ones that never hatched were photographed from different angles and in artistic lighting.

Exercise 7

One of the most innovative character-creators of all time was Marcel Proust, the author of the monumental 16-volume novel, *Remembrance of Things Past*. If you have never read any Proust, try reading the second section, *Swann in Love*, which is in some ways self-contained and so a good way in to this extraordinary book.

But first, to focus clearly on how Proust's character-portrayal functions, read the following two passages and compare them. In the first, Proust's narrator, Marcel, is an adolescent, and is meeting M. de Charlus for the first time. In the second passage (which comes almost at the end of this vast novel), he has returned to Paris about 30 years later, towards the end of the First World War, and meets him again in very different circumstances. If we have read the whole book, we shall have met Charlus several times, yet we shall never feel we know him well. Each meeting brings us an apparently unfamiliar character, as different and unpredictable in each new set of circumstances as the people we meet in real life.

[. . .] as I was passing the Casino alone on my way back to the hotel, I had the sensation of being watched by somebody who was not far off. I turned my head and saw a man of about forty, very tall and rather stout, with a very black moustache, who, nervously slapping the leg of his trousers with a switch, was staring at me, his eyes dilated with extreme attentiveness. From time to time these eyes were shot through by a look of restless activity such as the sight of a person they do not know excites only in men in whom, for whatever reason, it inspires thoughts that would not occur to anyone else – madmen, for instance, or spies. He darted a final glance at me that was at once bold, prudent, rapid and profound, like a last shot which one fires at an enemy as one turns to flee, and, after first looking all round him, suddenly adopting an absent and lofty air, with an abrupt revolution of his whole person he turned towards a playbill in the reading of which he became absorbed, while he hummed a tune and fingered the moss-rose in his buttonhole. [. . .] He gave me the impression of a hotel crook who, having been watching my grandmother and myself for some days, and planning to rob us, had just discovered that I had caught him in the act of spying on me.

M de Charlus for an instant raise[d] his eyes to heaven, but soon he brought them back to earth. "I admire all the heroes of this war," he said. "Why, my dear boy, those English soldiers whom at the beginning I rather thoughtlessly dismissed as mere football players presumptuous enough to measure themselves against professionals – and what professionals! – well, purely from the aesthetic point of view they are quite simply Greek athletes, you understand me, my boy, Greek athletes, they are the young men of Plato, or rather they are Spartans. I have a friend who has been to Rouen where their base is, he has seen marvels, marvels almost unimaginable. [. . .] And the boys from the provinces, how amusing and nice they are, with the way they roll their *r*'s and their regional dialects! I have always lived a lot in the country, I have slept in farms, I know how to talk to them. Still, our admiration for the French must not make us deprecate our enemies, that would only be to disparage ourselves. And you don't know what a soldier the German soldier is; you haven't seen him, as I have, march past on parade, doing the goose-step, *unter den Linden.*"

(Marcel Proust, *Remembrance of Things Past*)

(a)   These two passages occur hundreds of pages apart. They are both about the same character, M de Charlus, the most notorious character in the entire 3,300-page novel. Do the two portraits seem to you to be of the same personality?

(b)   If we juxtapose these two portraits, are there contradictions?

(c)   Does the second passage give us any insight into the first?

(d)   If we go back and look at the first, does it help us to understand the second?

(e)   How far might the circumstances of the observer (Proust's narrator, Marcel) explain the way in which the first portrait has developed into the second?

(f)   Proust has opened our eyes to a different kind of fictional character – one that is not built up *logically* by a process which is cumulative, but one which is built in fits and starts and sudden illuminating insights, in a series of conflicting portraits. How do you yourself react?

(g)   In what sense could this kind of fragmentation be called realistic?

Like the less subtle tools of character-creation, Proust's magic-lantern-show is a technique. But it implies a view of character and personality which is fundamental to some of the greatest of 20th-century fiction: character is no longer something fixed and stable, to be described and labelled, and pinned out in a glass case; it is something which squirms and wriggles, demanding and devouring our attention, until it is ready to emerge . . . as something barely recognisable.

Commentary

Exercise 2

How you respond to this exercise is of course highly individual. There can be no absolute standard to help us decide which fictional characters are memorable. Possibly our personal reactions are so different that even some kind of opinion-poll would show no clear favourites. I have a sneaking suspicion, though, that a large proportion of us, if interviewed at random in the street, would plump for a character from Dickens, partly because of their long television and film exposure. Dickens' characters are usually described fully at the time of the reader's first meeting with them. Television, of course, defines a character's physical characteristics even more clearly.

We undoubtedly react differently to fictional characters whose physical appearance is described and those who are left to our imagination. The first may follow us around like the Cheshire cat's grin. The second may haunt us like its unseen body. We only have to think of the visual media, such as film, television, or theatre, to realise that the absent character can be a powerful focus of desire or irritation: Frank Churchill and Jane Fairfax are almost as *real* to us before they enter Emma's existence at Highbury as after; we wait a whole play, and perhaps even longer, for Beckett's elusive Godot.

Readers' preferences differ, of course. Some of us may find descriptions necessary and satisfying – may feel that a film or television adaptation of a novel makes the characters suddenly more vivid and comprehensible. Others of us may feel disappointed and impatient, preferring our own interpretation of character to a director's. These are the readers who are likely to find the whole Realist descriptive convention limiting and perhaps in the end expendable.

Exercise 3

(a)   Again, the answer to this must be subjective, but I would guess that for most readers, in general, the impression conveyed by the first passage is the most striking and immediate. It is detailed enough, without being over-meticulous. It is not undercut by any kind of humour. It has very little real ambiguity to deepen and qualify our impression of character while at the same time inevitably blurring its outlines. I would judge that for most readers this particular fictional character would be at least as present to the imagination as his function in the thriller intrigue demands. He might even linger to give us an extra few moments of unease!

(b)   It is the Flaubert passage which is undoubtedly the most subtle. Charles' astonishing hat is full of pitiful and grotesque implications for its wearer. Yet it is never obviously a symbol, never simply an excuse. Flaubert's technique here works through association rather than through complete substitution: Charles Bovary is as ridiculous as his hat; but he is also the person who has to live with it, not only stupid but also pathetic – as impotent as we would be with a hat like that, and as sad.

(c)   Dickens' ironic use of the technique is very obvious in the seemingly endless (and many would say, heavy) repetition of the two words 'bran new' throughout the paragraph. It is also clear that he has opted for a simple enumeration of the Veneerings' possessions, a kind of catalogue, rather than for any more developed description. There is no mistaking the caricature here. As caricature, it is bold and at times very funny.

(d)   The last passage here seems to me to be an unusual re-telling of mythical material. Classically, we are given far less detail about people and objects than Hawthorne gives us here. The result is a very thought-provoking one. The whimsical details (apples as big as pumpkins, forest between the toes) have a strong imaginative appeal. They are concrete and yet surprising, in the same way that poetry is often concrete and yet surprising. They do undoubtedly enable us to *see* Hercules and the giant as we might not have seen them in another kind of telling. But in doing so, the author pulls us away from the domain of myth into that of the fairy-tale, and perhaps even further – towards the place where 'real' characters live. The universality of the myth begins to be lost. It is no longer as complete in itself and satisfying as myth should be. We stop looking to it for answers, and begin to look at it with questions.

Exercise 4

(a)   No one can tell you what to find funny, and it is all too easy to let yourself become unresponsive to the humour in a book you are studying. All the same, I think few readers would be completely untouched by either of these extracts, read in context (though out of context they might conceivably seem more puzzling than funny). Framed by the deeper seriousness of Emma's growth and understanding, the first extract seems to me to be the funnier of the two in context. When the two passages are read in isolation, the effect is certainly altered, and I should imagine many readers would smile more readily here for Kingsley Amis than for Jane Austen.

(b)   Jane Austen projects Mrs Elton's tone of voice wonderfully in a combination of breathless syntax (look at all the dashes!), repetition (simplicity seems to be her *idée fixe!*), and the wealth of detail which belies it. In very few words, Jane Austen can open up a chasm between a character's self-image and her actual identity. Add to this the patronising familiarity of 'Knightley' (not 'Mr Knightley') and poor Mrs Elton has damned herself hopelessly in a matter of a few seconds!
Bertrand's manner is unmistakably pompous. Most of his words are unnecessary and serve only to invest what has already been said with a spurious importance. On the surface, he is self-deprecating. What he *says* is self-deprecating. But stylistically he gives himself away. We can imagine his *mere pictures*: they must be dripping with pomposity, affectation, and a certain limited fashionable success.

(c)   We soon know that both these characters are very different from how they imagine themselves to be. Because we have direct access to them through their own words, we have a sudden insight into weaknesses they are not aware of. In fact we know little about either Mrs Elton or Bertrand Welch, but what we know is extraordinarily suggestive.

(d)   This ironic use of dialogue to portray character is a device which can be used to serious or even uncomfortable effect in other contexts, but it does seem to have a special affinity with comedy. Obviously it establishes a bond of complicity between narrator and reader which excludes the character in question. This could be a scenario for animosity or threat, but in real life we are surely more used to it as the necessary condition of laughter at someone else's expense.

Exercise 5

(a)   I would guess that for almost every reader the impression of character gained from either of these two passages would inevitably be less vivid and immediate than the portraits of **Exercise 4**. This is not to say that it would be less interesting.

(b)   From the *Jane Eyre* passage we learn that Mr Rochester is bitter, aggressive, at the same time angry and provocative, and that Jane herself is honest, fiercely independent and determined to live up to the standards of integrity she has set herself. We also learn that both are quick-witted, natural fighters, and that the struggle between them is a struggle between equals.

From the passage from *The Ambassadors* we learn that Maria Gostrey is hiding something, and that she is good at concealment; that her motives are unselfish. Strether is not impervious to her needs, or unaware of the ambiguity of her position, but he is also very much preoccupied by his own.

(c)   We are not sure of the direction of Mr Rochester's anger. His tone to Jane seems to oscillate between aggression and teasing. Could he be bitter towards her, or is she the present target of anger against someone else? We are not sure whether the suspicion of violence and cruelty is 'intrinsic' in his nature or the product of circumstances.

We suspect from Maria's question and from Strether's evasive answer that he is indeed in some sense *in love with* Mme de Vionnet. We also suspect, from Maria's own reactions and evasions, that she may be deeply emotionally involved with Strether. If she is, she is almost superhumanly controlled, and the reader surely admires her for it.

(d)   There are many small ambiguities one could pick out. Perhaps the most revealing are Mr Rochester's sarcastic 'march straight to – the devil?' and 'You shall walk up the pyramids of Egypt!', Maria's 'Ah me!' and Strether's at first unfinished 'When you cease – '. Strether's 'When you cease – ' is a particularly striking example. When he goes on to complete the sentence it is in a way we may not have expected. We might have been waiting for something more on the lines of, 'When you cease, I shall . . . ' For a fraction of a second we are touched by the suspicion that Maria herself matters to him in a way even he has not yet fully understood.

(e)   All these remarks seem to carry more than their fair weight of meaning.

Exercise 6

The answers to this suggestion will again be personal and to some extent subjective ones. Rosamond Lehmann seems to me to do this well: when Jennifer, one of the central characters in *Dusty Answer* misses the final rendezvous, we never really understand why. Yet our whole judgement of her character hinges on it.

If you drew a blank with this question, you could turn to Dostoyevsky's *The Idiot* and ask yourself about character and mystery as you read. Dostoyevsky is almost always fertile ground for a study of characterisation built on ambiguous or unstated motivation.

Exercise 7

(a)   I suspect that most readers would answer 'no' to this. The subject of the first portrait is shifty, secretive, almost criminal or deranged. The subject of the second is sociable, articulate, expansive, enthusiastic. What he says is not straightforward, though: there seem to be contradictions lying just below the surface.

(b)   There seem to be obvious anomalies here. The silent watcher of the first passage is not easy to reconcile with the smooth talker of the second. But real people may change like this with time and circumstances. It is only the unvarying, well-lit 'photographs' we have become familiar with through novels written in the Realist tradition that have allowed us conveniently to forget the fact as soon as we pick up a work of fiction.

(c)   Once you have become familiar with Proust's 'world', you will find that it is almost as difficult to remember your initial reactions to his characters as it is to remember your initial reactions to people you meet and subsequently get to know intimately. Yet it seems to me that there are deductions about Charlus' sexual tastes which can be made from the second passage and which suddenly illuminate in retrospect his peculiar behaviour in the first.

(d)   In this light, the intensity, secrecy and apparent hostility of the initial portrait surely becomes suddenly more comprehensible and so possibly more sympathetic. Charlus is no longer a maniac; he is a tormented and sensitive enthusiast. Yet that first impression of threat and dislocation still lingers.

(e)   If you have only these extracts to work from, this must be conjecture, but may have yielded interesting results. In fact in *Remembrance of Things Past,* the difference in perspective between the two portraits is amply justified, from the point of view of realism, by the passage of time. Proust's narrator, Marcel, has grown up and aged. He is no longer a boy on a beach, but a mature man in a society drawing-room. Insight into M de Charlus' strange identity has come to him with insight into the apparently irreconciliable choices of life, society and self.

(f)   No one can legislate about this, obviously. But the more you meet characters who develop in unexpected ways, the more you will appreciate the fictional techniques which can help you to make sense of their development.

(g)   The realism here has more to do with human *relationships* than with an intrinsic human 'identity'. It is not so much that we *are* fragmented, but that we meet and know each other in a fragmentary way. This distinction between complexity and viewpoint should become clearer as you work through the following chapter.

3

VOICE
AND VISION

Choices

When we open a novel, we are presented, even in the first paragraph, with a way of looking and a way of telling. At the very beginning, an author chooses how big a swathe to cut into the formless material we call *reality*. And with that first decision comes another crucial choice: a story must be told, and telling implies a teller, with a voice, a tone, a set of morals.

If we are not used to studying novels seriously, it is all too easy to assume that the 'truth' we are given is 'the whole truth' and that the voice we hear in our heads is, simply, the author's own voice. But the voice we hear on the first page of a novel is never entirely the author's. It never completely makes sense to say that an *author* is telling a story, recounting its incidents or describing its characters. Even in the most impersonal, transparent of narratives, there are choices of perspective which are not obvious. And there is a narrator's voice which may belong recognisably to a certain author, but which is still distinct, distanced from that author's real, everyday voice and chosen for the way it colours and illuminates the story that is being told.

For this reason, it is always revealing to give particular attention to a novel's opening: what do we see, what do we hear, and in what tone do we hear it? Through these few opening paragraphs, a novelist establishes a relationship with us. He or she is setting up a pattern of expectation which will be satisfied or frustrated in the chapters to come. If we look closely, we shall find clues not only about what is coming, but about *how* it is going to come and how we can best meet it.

Exercise 1

Go back to three novels you know reasonably well and which have made a particularly strong impression on you. Try to write down the one thing you remember most about each. Your answers need not be long – a single sentence will probably be enough. Then look at the opening paragraphs of the three novels in question. Imagine you were trying to 'sell' your three novels to a friend by studying only their opening pages together. What could you pick out as a preview of what is to come? Is there already a hint of story or characters? Is there a choice of viewpoint? What about the voice you 'hear'? Is it already establishing the kind of relationship with you that you remember? Can you put your finger on where, and how?

———— Look, no blinkers ————

In the 18th century, when the novel was still a comparatively young genre, there was often a feeling that the story-telling had to be *justified*. It was not enough simply to draw back imaginary curtains and confront the reader directly with a story which seemed almost to tell itself before his or her eyes. It was not convincing. How did that story come to be told? If we were to accept on some level that the events we were hearing about were 'real', then we also had to understand how all these fascinating 'facts' came to be in the author's possession. What these earlier readers of novels apparently demanded, and what novelists often bent over backwards to provide, were feasible explanations of the actual act of telling. There were re-tellings of stories told to friends and acquaintances, there were wonderful finds of revealing or even incriminating personal correspondence, there were important narrative documents fallen into strange hands after a character's death. When the story is simply *told* to us, without any of these subterfuges to justify it, the narrator often very self-consciously intruded into the narrative to comment on and distance his or her material. Fielding's *Tom Jones*, published in 1749, is probably the most famous novel of all time for this kind of narrative intervention and the complex ironies it sets up.

We are familiar with all this and yet not familiar. We all smile at being addressed as 'dear reader', just as we laugh at the intrusive conventions of silent film. A modern reader, confronted with a novel which purports to be a collection of authentic documents or letters, may well be puzzled and ask whether this is truly fiction. The 19th century ambition for a more photographic kind of imitation of reality and the transparent narrative conventions it demanded have become so very familiar to us that we still tend to regard anything else as an interesting deviation. Yet our ancestors needed these fictional guarantees.

Most fiction writers in the 19th century threw off this 'pretence', in the name of an ideal often called *mimesis*. Developments in the visual arts – in painting and in early photographic techniques – undoubtedly influenced the way writers felt about what was *worth* portraying in art, and this in turn changed our way of seeing. An almost photographic reproduction of an agricultural worker or a death-bed scene had as much artistic validity as a harmonious symbolic representation of shepherds and angels. To see well was to see perfectly and not flinch, to see the warts of a society as well as its aspirations. The novel could rival science in its exciting new discoveries, and it could be as rigorous. The novelist could look straight into the hearts and minds of all his or her characters. There was no longer any need to make excuses for playing God.

Exercise 2

Omniscience usually refers to a novelist's decision to see, without barriers or limitation, into the thoughts and motivation of his or her characters. Read the following passages carefully and answer the questions that follow:

> The day of the races was a very busy one for Karenin; but in the morning when he made his plans for the day he decided that immediately after an early dinner he would go to see his wife at their

country house and from there to the races, at which the whole Court would be present and where he ought to appear. He was going to see his wife because he was determined to do so once a week to keep up appearances. Besides, it was the fifteenth – the day he gave her money for the house-keeping expenses.

With his habitual mental control, having once deliberated these matters to do with his wife, he did not let his thoughts stray further in regard to her.

(Tolstoy, *Anna Karenin*)

Upon receipt of the news Mrs Hardy retired to bed for a week, during which time Christine, by now extremely frightened, was obliged to wait on her. Grim-faced [. . .] Mrs Hardy was not communicative, although when the bridge cronies came to pay visits of condolence she would reveal herself as a woman of sorrows, and murmur, 'Don't ask me what I've been through.' 'I can imagine,' one or other of the visitors would respond sympathetically. 'No,' she would reply. 'No words can express . . . ', and would let her hand fall in a noble gesture of despair. Christine had an inkling that she was referring to the marriage rather than the bereavement, but of course did not allow the thought to take root. She herself was in a state of loneliness compounded by a terrible fear, fear that she might have to spend the rest of her life ministering to Mrs Hardy who would never get up again.

(Anita Brookner, *Latecomers*)

The excessive feeling manifested would alone have been highly disturbing to Mr Casaubon, but there were other reasons why Dorothea's words were among the most cutting and irritating to him that she could have been impelled to use. She was as blind to his inward troubles as he to hers; she had not yet learned those hidden conflicts in her husband which claim our pity. She had not yet listened patiently to his heart-beats, but only felt that her own was beating violently. In Mr Casaubon's ear, Dorothea's voice gave loud emphatic iteration to those muffled suggestions of consciousness which it was possible to explain as mere fancy, the illusion of exaggerated sensitiveness: always when such suggestions are unmistakably repeated from without, they are resisted as cruel and unjust.

(George Eliot, *Middlemarch*)

Garinati leaves his room, locks the door behind him, and begins walking down the long spiral of the staircase.

Along a canal. The blocks of granite that line the quay; under the dust gleam occasional crystals, black, white, and pinkish. To the right, a little further down, is the water.

A rubber-coated electric wire makes a vertical line against the wall.
Below, to pass over a cornice, it makes a right angle, once, twice. But afterwards, instead of following the inner surface, it stands away from the wall and hangs free for about a foot and a half.
Below, fastened again against the vertical wall, it describes another two or three sinusoidal arcs before finally resuming its straight descent.

The little glass door has creaked loudly. In his hurry to get away, Garinati has opened it a little more than he should have.

(Alain Robbe-Grillet, *The Erasers*)

Questions

(a) In how many of these passages is the narrator really omniscient?

(b) What is it in the text that tells you whether the narrative viewpoint is omniscient or limited?

(c) How does the breadth and scope of the viewpoint affect the reader's reactions in each case?

Exercise 3

With this last exercise still in mind, look closely at the two extracts which follow. Are these examples of omniscient narration, or not? With which of the preceding four passages does each of these seem to have most in common?

Madame Bovary made for the kitchen fireplace. With the tips of her fingers she took hold of her dress at the knees, lifted it over her ankles and stretched out her black-booted foot to the fire, above the leg of mutton on the spit. The flames lit up her whole body. The texture of her dress, the smooth pores of her clear skin, even her eyelids, which she blinked from time to time, were penetrated by the glare; and when the wind blew in through the open door, a warm glow spread all over her.

On the other side of the fireplace a young man with fair hair stood watching her in silence.

(Flaubert, *Madame Bovary*)

The lovers were standing together at one of the windows. It had a most favourable aspect; and, for half a minute, Emma felt the glory of having schemed successfully. But it would not do; he had not come to the point. He had been most agreeable, most delightful; he had told Harriet that he had seen them go by, and had purposely followed them; other little gallantries and allusions had been dropt, but nothing serious.

(Jane Austen, *Emma*)

I, he, she, you

Another crucial narrative choice is closely linked with this one. Whether or not a novelist opts for omniscience or a more limited set of insights, the third-person verb-forms are a tried and tested part of his or her equipment. 'He', 'she' and 'they' are so common with omniscient narration that what the reader usually experiences is a kind of transparency, a narrative which lets us slip through into the story almost without noticing there is a story-teller at all. As we have seen, the third-person narrative viewpoint can also be used where the fictional narrator is very definitely *not* omniscient.

But if a writer chooses a limited insight rather than a theoretically boundless one, the choices that follow are sometimes even more interesting. We are all used to 'I', but does a fictional 'I' always carry the same kind of conviction? What about two, or even several, first-person narratives? Should they corroborate or contradict each other? What are the narrative possibilities of 'we'? And how do we feel when we come face to face with 'you'?

Exercise 4

Read the following passages, asking yourself as you read how the grammatical person (i.e. first, second or third person) in which each is written is modifying the meaning of what is said and affecting your reactions to it:

Carrie, left alone by Drouet, listened to his retreating steps, scarcely realizing what had happened. She knew that he had stormed out. It was some moments before she questioned whether he would return – not now exactly, but ever. She looked around her upon the rooms, out of which the evening light was dying, and wondered why she did not feel quite the same towards them. She went over to the dresser and struck a match, lighting the gas. Then she went back to her rocker to think.

It was some time before she could collect her thoughts, but when she did, this truth began to take on importance. She was quite alone. Suppose Drouet did not come back. Suppose she should never hear anything more of him.

(Theodore Dreiser, *Sister Carrie*)

Waiting at the buffet for orangeade, she watched him take out his silver case and a matchbox and light his cigarette, slowly and carefully. Then he smoothed his hair, adjusted his tie, brushed his sleeve, his shoulders. In case I've left any mark, powder, a hair or anything. He's afraid of looking slovenly, neglected, ridiculous, and not knowing it. That's why he's neater, more polished up than anybody else. He didn't smoke his cigarette, but let it burn away between his long fingers. He sat back, his head slightly bent, the muscles taut in his face, waiting.

Now he looks like a blind man.

(Rosamond Lehmann, *Invitation to the Waltz*)

1945: Your father comes home from his war work. He gives you a piggyback ride around the broad yellow thatch of your yard, the dead window in the turret, dark as a wound, watching you. He gives you wordless pushes on the swing.

Your brother has new friends, acts older and distant, even while you wait for the school bus together.

You spend too much time alone. You tell your mother that when you grow up you will bring your babies to Australia to see the kangaroos.

Forty thousand people are killed in Nagasaki.

1944: Dress and cuddle a tiny babydoll you have named "the Sue." Bring her everywhere. Get lost in the Wilson Creek fruit market, and call softly, "Mom, where are you?" Watch other children picking grapes, but never dare yourself. Your eyes are small, dark throats, your hand clutches the Sue.

1943: Ask your mother about babies. Have her read to you only the stories about babies. Ask her if she is going to have a baby. Ask her about the baby that died. Cry into her arm.

(Lorrie Moore, 'How to Talk to Your Mother (Notes)' from *Self-Help*)

Try to answer these questions:

(a)   In which of these passages is the narrative viewpoint consistent?

(b)   At what point exactly do we become aware of the 'I' voice in the second extract?

(c)   Is it the 'I' or the 'she' which is the more intimate here?

(d)   At what point in the third extract do you feel closest to the narrative voice?

(e)   With which of these three characters is it easiest to identify?

(f)   In your ordinary thoughts and speech, how many different meanings can you find for the word 'you'?

Reading minds

Most readers have probably already given some thought to what 'I' or 'he/she' can mean in a narrative and how we tend to react to them. The possibilities of 'you' are not so frequently exploited, but can be just as exciting. The grammatical 'you' is not a single, simple viewpoint, but a mixture of several. As we can see from the last extract above, 'you' conceals several possible meanings. Just as 'he' or 'she' can be a consciousness a narrator moves fluently in and out of, 'you' can be at least three things. It can be 'one'. It can be the narrator himself or herself. Or it can be ourselves, as readers. Or it can oscillate between the various possibilities, while still in a sense containing them all.

If 'he' and 'she' and 'you' can do all this, what about 'I'? The first-person narrative viewpoint is perhaps the most familiar to us of all. When tales were told orally, rather than written and read, the 'I' was a real *flesh-and-blood* presence. The medieval tale-tellers who enthralled whole courts and marketplaces with their 'he' and 'they' were visibly and tangibly necessary to their narrative with an immediacy we 20th-century readers have lost sight of. But even the stories we read suppose a teller. In even the most impersonal of narratives an 'I' is implicit.

Sometimes the 'I' is overt. We are used to stories in the form of first-person narratives. Probably they still carry a hint of that striving for authenticity that we recognise in 18th-century epistolary novels. The immense popularity of the diary-novels ostensibly written by Adrian Mole is proof of the way in which a very strongly dramatised narrative *persona* can shape our pleasure in the story. As we follow the development of the events we are encouraged to side with or against the voice that is relating them. If we identify with that voice, and through the voice with its owner, we may become involved very directly. But the author may use that voice to create distance between us and its owner and we may smile or even laugh at what is being said. First-person narratives can be wonderful sources of comedy.

But in spite of this ironic potential, the first and most immediate use of the first-person narrative is to create intimacy. When one of our friends tells us a story about a third party and says 'he' or 'she', that friend is implicitly asking us to adopt his or her viewpoint. But when someone says 'I' to us, he or she is asking us to accept something more than a viewpoint: an 'I' brings with it a personality, a set of values, an emotional response; it claims attention and makes implicit demands on us. What we hear is the tip of the iceberg.

Once we see the whole iceberg, the comic possibilities are lost. What was funny was the discrepancy between the narrator's interpretation of events and our own. When we see *everything*, this discrepancy tends to disappear. The deeper we are allowed to go into the narrator's thoughts and feelings, the more we begin to see extenuating circumstances behind his or her errors of judgement. There may still be ironies, but they are more likely to be painful than comic. They may even seem to threaten us personally in our own image of ourselves.

Perhaps the most notorious use of the first-person narrative in all of our fiction is the *interior monologue* or *stream of consciousness* technique closely associated with certain currents of experimental fiction of the 1920s, and with James Joyce and Virginia Woolf in particular. In fact, this technique may just as well be framed by a third-person narrative. As the barriers between reader and character disappear, the grammatical person itself ceases to matter.

Exercise 5

Read the following passages through one by one, as fluently as you can. After reading each one, stop for a minute and try to collect your impressions of what is happening and who is thinking. Then go back and read them all for a second time, more carefully.

The bed was heaving up and down and I lay there thinking, 'It can't be that. Pull yourself together. It can't be that. Didn't I always . . . And all those things they say you can do. I know when it happened. The lamp over the bed had a blue shade. It was that one I went back with just after Carl left.' Counting back days and dates and thinking, 'No, I don't think it was that time. I think it was when . . .'

Of course, as soon as a thing has happened it isn't fantastic any longer, it's inevitable. The inevitable is what you're doing or have done. The fantastic is simply what you didn't do. That goes for everybody.

The inevitable, the obvious, the experienced . . . They watch you, their faces like masks, set in the eternal grimace of disapproval. I always knew that girl was . . . Why didn't you bloody well make a hole in the water?

(Jean Rhys, *Voyage in the Dark*)

What business had the Bradshaws to talk of death at her party? A young man had killed himself. And they talked of it at her party – the Bradshaws talked of death. He had killed himself – but how? Always her body went through it, when she was told, first, suddenly, of an accident; her dress flamed, her body burnt. He had thrown himself from a window. Up had flashed the ground; through him, blundering, bruising, went the rusty spikes. There he lay with a thud, thud, thud in his brain, and then a suffocation of blackness. So she saw it. But why had he done it? And the Bradshaws talked of it at her party!

(Virginia Woolf, *Mrs Dalloway*)

His smile faded as he walked, a heavy cloud hiding the sun slowly, shadowing Trinity's surly front. Trams passed one another, ingoing, outgoing, clanging. Useless words. Things go on same, day after day: squads of police marching out, back: trams in, out. Those two loonies mooching about. Dignam carted off. Mina Purefoy swollen belly on a bed groaning to have a child tugged out of her. One born every second somewhere. Other dying every second. Since I fed the birds five minutes. Three hundred kicked the bucket. Other three hundred born, washing the blood off, all are washed in the blood of the lamb, bawling maaaaaa.

Cityful passing away, other cityful coming, passing away too: other coming on, passing on. Houses, lines of houses, streets, miles of pavements, piledup bricks, stones. Changing hands. This owner, that. Landlord never dies they say. Other steps into his shoes when he gets his notice to quit. They buy the place up with gold and still they have all the gold. Swindle in it somewhere. Piled up in cities, worn away age after age. Pyramids in sand. Built on bread and onions. Slaves Chinese wall. Babylon. Big stones left. Round towers. Rest rubble, sprawling suburbs, jerrybuilt. Kerwan's mushroom houses built of breeze. Shelter, for the night.

No-one is anything.

This is the very worst hour of the day. Vitality. Dull, gloomy: hate this hour. Feel as if I had been eaten and spewed.

(James Joyce, *Ulysses*)

When you have digested the three passages as well as you can, answer the following questions:

(a) Only one of these passages is in fact an extract from what may technically be called a first-person narrative. Can you tell which it is?

(b) All of them have features which are normally associated with first-person narration. Try to pinpoint what it is in each passage that creates the illusion that we are looking directly into someone else's mind.

(c) To which of the three do you respond with the most immediacy? Can you say why?

(d) Many critics and writers have seen James Joyce's *stream of consciousness* as an imaginative and admirable experiment which could not be taken further or convincingly repeated. With these three passages still in mind, can you think of any reasons why this might be true?

Do I know you?

Even now, in the 1990s, it seems almost impossible to talk about narrative voice and narrative distance in fiction without reference to Wayne C Booth's enormously important book, *The Rhetoric of Fiction*, first published in America in 1961. Few critical works talk of the mechanics and implications of narration with such a combination of clarity and intelligence and few demonstrate so persuasively that to study an author's basic narrative choices is not simply to study technique, but to qualify and illuminate a novel's whole meaning.

A narrative may seem impersonal and yet build a kind of intimacy. A narrative may seem intimate and yet repel us. A narrator who says 'I' is taking us into his or her confidence, and yet we may not welcome that confidence. We may like and trust the voice, or we may feel irritated by it and wary. The possible ways in which narrative voice may colour a story are endless. All this seems obvious now, but has really become current in critical thinking only since Wayne Booth's book seemed, in the 1960s and 1970s, to tell critics what they did not know they knew.

One of the most effective principles of depth in fiction is irony. We have seen how, in a third-person narrative, the use of the indirect inside view can convey a double set of information: an event filtered through a character's mind is at the same time both itself and a reflection of the character who is interpreting it; we can see what *really* happened, and we can see how the character who is struggling to come to grips with the 'truth' may be deluded.

In a first-person narrative, these ironic possibilities are even greater. There is surely a naturalness in the 'I' form of the narrative which works to establish intimacy. Whether we like it or not, this voice is addressing us directly, and we are called upon to respond to it, not just in its capacity as a story-teller, but, first of all, in all the ordinary human ways in which we usually react to a human speaker. If a speaker talks to us at length of his or her own life and experience, we usually respond with sympathy or boredom. In fiction, if we are not to put the book down at the first page, an 'I' narrative must intrigue and beguile us into some state of ready collusion. If there are ironies, if there is distance between author and narrator, and between narrator and reader, it is against this background of almost automatic collusion that it begins to take shape.

Exercise 6

Read the following extracts and try to decide:-

(a)   Which of the four narrative voices do you feel closest to?

(b)   Which of the four do you feel the most distanced from?

(c)   Can you give any reasons for your choices?

I have been told that in one of our neighbour nations, whether it be in France or where else I know not, they have an order from the king that when any criminal is condemned, either to die, or to the galleys, or to be transported, if they leave any children, as such are generally unprovided for by the forfeiture of their parents, so they are immediately taken into the care of the government and put into an hospital called the House of Orphans, where they are bred up, clothed, fed, taught, and, when fit to go out, are placed to trades or to services, so as to be well able to provide for themselves by an honest, industrious labour.

Had this been the custom in our country, I had not been left a poor desolate girl without friends, without clothes, without help or helper, as was my fate; and by which I was not only exposed to very great distresses even before I was capable either of understanding my case or how to amend it, but brought into a course of life scandalous in itself and which in its ordinary course tended to the swift destruction both of soul and body.

(Daniel Defoe, *Moll Flanders*)

It was really summer, but the rain had fallen all day and was still falling. The weather can best be described by saying it was the kind reserved for church fêtes. The green leaves were being beaten off the trees by the steady downpour and were drifting about in the puddles. Now and then there would come a gust of wind so that the trees moaned and tossed their arms imploringly, though they had been rooted in our soil long enough to know better. Darkness fell early – indeed there had seemed little light all day, so that the process was slow and imperceptible. But when it was complete, the darkness was intense beyond the street lights and the rain still fell through it. I had played the piano until my head sang – pounded savagely and unavailingly at the C Minor Study of Chopin which had seemed, when Moisewitch played, to express all the width and power of my own love, my own hopeless infatuation. But Imogen was engaged to be married, that was the end.

(William Golding, *The Pyramid*)

I don't remember my mother's hair being anything but white. My mother went white in her twenties, and never saved any of her young hair, which had been brown. I used to try to get her to tell what color brown.

'Dark.'

'Like Brent, or like Dolly?' Those were two workhorses we had, a team.

'I don't know. It wasn't horsehair.'

'Was it like chocolate?'

'Something like.'

'Weren't you sad when it went white?'

'No. I was glad.'

'Why?'

'I was glad that I wouldn't have hair anymore that was the same color as my father's.'

Hatred is always a sin, my mother told me. Remember that. One drop of hatred in your soul will spread and discolor everything like a drop of black ink in white milk. I was struck by that and meant to try it, but knew I shouldn't waste the milk.

(Alice Munro, The Progress of Love)

(d)   Can you put your finger on anything in the second passage which creates intimacy?

(e)   Can you put your finger on anything in the same passage which is undermining or destroying the potential intimacy between reader and narrator?

(f)   Which of these last two questions (d and e) was the more difficult to answer?

Exercise 7

Sometimes, in a first-person narrative, the question of distance is more problematic than this. There may be few, if any, clues, and little overt irony. The first-person viewpoint is allowed to work as it will towards the establishment of a sympathy against which the reader initially has little defence. But as the story unfolds, it gradually becomes clear that the behaviour of the 'I' character is morally suspect. Already, by taking the first-person *persona* at face value, we have in some sense given our consent, we have acquiesced in his or her behaviour. And yet this behaviour, we come to realise with growing alarm, is something we cannot condone, must not collude in, should perhaps not even be listening to. Here the handling of the first-person viewpoint may be a genuine *tour de force*. Of all the narrative options at the novelist's disposal, this kind of ambivalent use of first-person narration is possibly the most likely to raise moral questions, rather than to suggest moral answers. It is at the same time insinuating and uncomfortable.

Read the following two passages, trying to absorb all you can of the voice which is narrating and of the fictional *persona* behind the voice. Then answer the questions which follow:-

Granted: I am an inmate of a mental hospital; my keeper is watching me, he never lets me out of his sight; there's a peephole in the door, and my keeper's eye is the shade of brown that can never see through a blue-eyed type like me.

So you see, my keeper can't be an enemy. I've come to be very fond of him; when he stops looking at me from behind the door and comes into the room, I tell him incidents from my life, so he can get to know me in spite of the peephole between us. He seems to treasure my stories, because every time I tell him some fairy tale, he shows his gratitude by bringing out his latest knot construction. I wouldn't swear that he's an artist. But I am certain that an exhibition of his creations would be well received by the press and attract a few purchasers. He picks up common pieces of string in the patients' rooms after visiting hours, disentangles them, and works them up into elaborate contorted spooks; then he dips them in plaster, lets them harden, and mounts them on knitting needles that he fastens to little wooden pedestals.

(Günter Grass, *The Tin Drum*)

May I, Monsieur, offer my services without running the risk of intruding? I fear you may not be able to make yourself understood by the worthy gorilla who presides over the fate of this establishment. In fact, he speaks nothing but Dutch. Unless you authorize me to plead your case, he will not guess that you want gin. There, I dare hope he understands me; that nod must mean that he yields to my arguments. He's on the move; indeed, he is making haste with a sort of careful deliberateness. You are lucky; he didn't grunt. When he refuses to serve someone, he merely grunts. No one insists. Being master of one's moods is the privilege of the larger animals. Now I shall withdraw, Monsieur, happy to have been of help to you. Thank you; I'd accept if I were sure of not being a nuisance. You are too kind. Then I shall bring my glass over beside yours.

(Albert Camus, *The Fall*)

Questions

(a) Which of these two voices did you *like* best?

(b) How far do you trust these two characters? Does one seem to you to be more trustworthy than the other?

(c) Do liking and trustworthiness seem to coincide?

(d) Is there anything in the texts which seems to trigger dislike?

(e) What is there to warn you that either voice might be untrustworthy?

We have no choice here but to think, and weigh up, and make our own decisions. If we read passively, refusing to create for ourselves the distance which the author seems at first to withhold from us, we are buying comfort at the price of something far more important.

———————— Commentary ————————

Exercise 2

(a) Of these four passages, the extract from *Middlemarch* seems to me to be the best example of omniscient narration. The passage from *Anna Karenin* is also a good candidate. The second and last of these extracts on the other hand, offer a more qualified set of insights. In the last extract in particular we are not entirely sure whether insight is being offered or refused to us.

(b) The third extract balances insights into both partners in this unsuitable marriage in a way that is surely almost Godlike. The author's decision to allow us access into the thoughts and vulnerabilities of both parties seems to promise equal access to the workings of opposing forces in any of Middlemarch's conflicts.

In context, the first extract, with its invitation to share the hopes and fears of one of the book's least sympathetic characters, seems to promise the same generous vision. Out of context, though, it is indistinguishable from the option of a limited inside view confined to the intimate thoughts of one character.

The narrator of the second extract is patently not omniscient. She may well allow herself insight into characters other than Christine, but here, at least, we are given access only to Christine's reactions. This is clear in the way we are denied access to Mrs Hardy's and so forced to share Christine's own uncertainty and uneasiness.

The last extract is a characteristic example of Robbe-Grillet's peculiar 'now you see it, now you don't' technique. Are we seeing what we are seeing through the mind of one of the characters? – or are we not? The incomplete syntax of 'Along a canal' is reminiscent of a *stream of consciousness* narrative, with all its implications of sympathy and identification. The order of the description in the third section implies a seeing eye which moves from one detail to the next in sequence. How can we escape the intimation in the 'once, twice' of a mind which counts, in the 'instead of following the inner surface' of a mind which has expectations? Yet the inside view is never made explicit, and the hard, impersonal, geometrical precision of 'sinusoidal arcs' is very disconcerting.

(c)   The answer to this is inevitably subjective and reflects all the reading experience which has gone into making you the kind of critic you are. Some readers will see omniscience as a truer tool for the revelation of reality, and some will see a limited viewpoint as a closer reflection of the kind of reality we all experience in our day-to-day lives. We may find that the words we use to justify our preferences are words with strong moral connotations, words like *honesty, generosity,* and *fairness*. It seems to me that this *technical* option does in fact throw up a series of questions about the moral status of the novel, involving our expectations of fiction at the very deepest level.

Exercise 3

On the face of it, the second passage seems to offer insights more unambiguously than the first. The first is apparently offering us none. In the passage from *Emma* we are told explicitly of Emma's thoughts and feelings. In the first passage we are apparently told of no one's thoughts at all. In fact, both passages are marked by what the French call *style indirect libre* and what in English is also known as indirect free speech. If we look closely at the *Madame Bovary* passage, we gradually become aware that what we are seeing is not simply Emma Bovary herself, but Emma Bovary through the eyes of a watcher, and a sensuous watcher at that. If we then turn back to Jane Austen, we can see that the first 1½ sentences of that passage use exactly the same unstated coincidence with the viewpoint and values of a single observing character. Here the viewpoint becomes more and more explicit as we go on, but initially the uncertainties it generates are the same as in the Flaubert passage. Strange as it may seem, this ambiguous use of the third-person narrative to give and at the same time half withhold insight, is closer to the experimental fiction of Robbe-Grillet than to any of the other passages in **Exercise 2**.

Exercise 4

(a)   The viewpoint itself is consistent in all three extracts. The grammatical person which expresses it is consistent in the first and last extracts.

(b)   In the third sentence: not only does the grammatical person change, but the tense of the narrative as well.

(c)   The 'I' voice is by far the more intimate. The 'she' voice, although it sticks closely to the vision of one individual, limits itself to what can be *seen*. It is the 'I' voice which breaks in to question, interpret, and above all to *feel*.

(d)   It is impossible to legislate about this, but in questioning your own sympathies, you will probably also have had to think about your reactions to shifts in the narrative. It *does* shift. The apparent unity of the second-person narration welds together two very different forms: the statements, which are almost all about what 'you' do and experience in 1945, and the imperatives, which are used to describe the even more emotive happenings of 1944 and 1943. The very odd mixture of identification ('Things just like that happened to me when I was four or five.') and alienation ('Who is this voice telling me what to do and feel?') can hardly fail to produce a strong and very complex emotional response.

(e)   This again must be personal, but an awareness of how you reacted to these three passages may give you fresh insights.

(f)   'You' can be another person who is being addressed. It may stand for more than one person. It may mean 'one'. It may be a disguised way of saying 'I'. Which is it in the Lorrie Moore extract? Do 'he', 'she', 'I' and 'we' carry a similarly mixed charge of associatons?

Exercise 5

(a)   The first passage is unambiguously part of a first-person narrative. The second passage sticks to the third person and past tenses we usually associate with reported speech. The third passage is almost impossible to place in this respect, shifting as it does from third person and past tense to present and, ultimately, to the 'I' we have surely been expecting.

(b)   The Jean Rhys passage, like the extract from *Ulysses*, contains a series of associative leaps, giving the impression of a 'real', surprisingly irrational mind at work. The impression in both cases is reinforced by incomplete or compressed sentences and fragments of sentences ('Counting back days and dates and thinking.'; 'This owner, that. [. . .] Swindle in it somewhere. [. . .] Pyramids in sand.'), and in the case of the Jean Rhys extract, by direct questions. In this extract, inverted commas are less telling than the actual voice which bridges thought and 'speech'. In the second passage, Virginia Woolf adheres rigorously to the more rational narrative mode she has established. But that third-person narration is flexible enough to hold intimate personal reactions expressed with a 'first-person' kind of immediacy (' . . . through him, blundering, bruising, went the rusty spikes. There he lay with a thud, thud, thud in his brain . . .'), questions ('But why had he done it?') and exclamations ('And the Bradshaws talked of it at her party!').

(c)   Again, this is a matter of personal experience and personal values, but I should imagine that many readers would react very immediately to the first extract. We are carefully prepared for the brief fall into Anna's stream of consciousness, led as it were by the hand from the bed to the 'I', to explicit thoughts and questions and ultimately to the disjointed fragments of thought-processes very like our own. The fact that the stream of consciousness technique coincides here with a moment of extreme experience will surely justify it dramatically, even if we are unused to the effort it is asking of us.

(d)   If we see the novel as the fictional reflection of a *social* world, then a stream of consciousness is not the most obvious way to render it. The single viewpoint is here more rigorous and so in a sense more limited than it is in more conventional first-person narratives. As the reader's vision is allowed to coincide with the narrator's more and more intimately, the possibilities of irony are, it seems to me, gradually squeezed out. The more we look *in*, the less we can look *through*, and it is above all the looking *through* which until the experiments of the 20th-century, gave the novel its recognisably rich texture. *Ulysses* is, of course, vast. But it is arguable whether the vastness is due to, or *in spite of*, Joyce's chosen technique.

Exercise 6

(a) and (b)   The fact that the answers to both these questions are inevitably subjective needn't prevent us from noticing which features of the narrative are working to win or undermine our sympathy.

(c)   The second passage has touches of humour, which may elicit a slightly patronising kind of affection in the reader, who may well recognise his or her younger, sillier, more vulnerable self. The extract from *Moll Flanders* (first passage) is probably a good example of the pure power of first-person narration: how easy it is to overlook those few words, 'a course of life scandalous in itself' and dwell with premature sympathy on the 'very great distresses' the 'I' persona naturally prepares us for! The third extract, with its snatch of dramatic dialogue, is more complicated. We are presented already with a clash of vision between two characters and there is a natural tendency to side with one or the other of them. The first-person narrative predisposes us to prefer the protagonist's own judgements, even while we are touched and intrigued by her mother's.

(d)   The second sentence creates intimacy: we are all in this little joke (against English weather and English rural society) together.

(e)   An ironic distance seems to me to creep in in the last two sentences. 'All the width and power of my own love, my own hopeless infatuation' is a bit too rhetorical to be entirely convincing, especially when it is coupled with 'had seemed'. The romantic name, Imogen, the Romantic connotations of the music, and the starkness of 'that was the end' are funny. We stand back and smile at the melodrama of this character's view of himself. At the same time, paradoxically, we feel affection for him at this sudden revelation of vulnerability. Perhaps *identification with* a character and *feeling for* a character are two very different things.

(f)   The first-person narrative, even at its most neutral; works naturally to establish closeness. Empathy in this context is usually invisible. I would expect the distancing techniques which you focused on in (e) to be easier to pinpoint and talk about.

Exercise 7

(a)   Surely most readers would opt for the voice they hear in the first passage?

(b)   Again, there can be no rules about our subjective reactions. However, it seems to me that most readers would feel wary of the voice in the second passage. In the first passage, it is perhaps the facts of the case, rather than the voice itself, which are disquieting.

(c)   Liking and trustworthiness may or may not coincide. In real life, for practical purposes, they usually do, though we may withdraw our sympathy only some time after our trust has been abused. In fiction the coupling of liking with distrust may be an extraordinarily potent mixture, and one which generates complex moral and psychological questions. In contexts which are also politically suggestive, as here in *The Tin Drum* or in a novel like Michel Tournier's *Erl King*, the granting of sympathy to a morally ambiguous narrator may be particularly devastating.

(d)   We surely dislike the voice of the second extract for its style as much as anything else. It is unnecessarily formal, pedantic, over-courteous, insinuating, with its 'May I, Monsieur' and 'I dare hope'. The voice of the first extract is very different: ostensibly direct, open, generous.

(e)   The distrust we feel for the voice which speaks to us in the second passage, because it is generated by stylistic means, probably feels very much like a gut reaction. Coupled with the speech tics mentioned above is the sheer claustrophobia which results from the narrative situation: we are being addressed directly and we are replying, yet we have no power over the replies we are evidently making – our answers are not even heard. It is nightmarish: as every nerve in our body shrieked '*Go Away!*' what we evidently actually said was, 'Yes, please do join me.' – here this man is, in spite of everything, making himself comfortable at our elbow!

In the first passage the distrust comes at first from knowing that the fictional narrator is in a closed mental hospital and so, by society at least, judged to be insane and/or a criminal. We begin to question what follows, asking ourselves whether or not it is reasonable. Would the warder's willingness to show off his knot-creations really betoken gratitude, or would it have another meaning? Isn't this description of his work just a little obsessive? Isn't the reasonableness of all this a little too carefully rational? And through it all, do we hear yet another voice? Is *The Tin Drum* itself a *knot-creation* of some kind?

II

POETRY

4
LANGUAGE
AND ATTENTION

—— Who does a poem belong to? ——

Of the three major literary genres, poetry has traditionally been seen as the most problematic, the most elusive. No one would deny that a poem is a very difficult thing to define. And yet we are being called on to respond to a piece of poetic writing with a subtly different set of reactions and criteria from those which we normally use to respond to a piece of prose. How are we to know when to 'switch on' this special response? How can we analyse a piece of writing which seems to make virtues of secrecy and indirectness?

Dictionary definitions are not very helpful. The Chambers Twentieth-century Dictionary defines a poem as 'a composition of high beauty of thought or language and artistic form, typically, but not necessarily, in verse.' We can see that the compilers of dictionaries have run up against the same problems as the student or ordinary reader: a poem is already, not *very* beautiful, but *highly* beautiful; its beauty lies in a mixture of form and *either* thought *or* language; it may well be in verse, but it is not *necessary* that it should be.

In practice, we tend to accept that a poem is a poem because, in one way or another, we are told it is a poem. We have found it in an anthology, or a poetry magazine, or a collection of poetry; someone calls it a poem when they give it to us to read, a poet stands up in front of a room full of people to read – presumably – his or her own poetry. When we are dealing with a poem on a page, the way it is printed usually announces to us that this is something special we are reading. When we attend a reading, the pace at which the poet reads his or her work, the tone of voice in which he or she reads, the value he or she places on individual words and sounds, all signal to us that we are to react differently from how we would react to a speech or an announcement.

Exercise 1

Try to make the opportunity to listen to poetry read by an actor or actress on the radio or television. Make notes on the way in which the poem is read. Then listen to poetry read, on radio or television or, better still, in the flesh, by the poet who wrote it. (If no opportunity is forthcoming, your local library may have recordings of poetry in both actors' and poets' voices.) Again, make notes on the *way* in which that poet chose to read his or her poems. Compare your two sets of notes, asking yourself the possible reasons for any differences.

Exercise 2

Each of the following short extracts is taken either from a poem or a piece of prose writing. In the case of the poems, the line-breaks have been removed and punctuation and capitalisation normalised, so that, initially, we can approach each with a more neutral set of expectations. Try to decide in each case whether what you are reading is a fragment of prose or a fragment of poetry. Make a record of your decisions: the point of this exercise is not to test *you* to see if you are a subtle critic, but to see whether it is in fact *possible* to react properly to poetry when we have few or no obvious signals that it is a poem we are reading, and then to draw conclusions.

(a)   Our brains ache, in the merciless iced east winds that knive us . . .

(b)   I can imagine, in some otherworld primeval-dumb, far back in that most awful stillness, that only gasped and hummed, humming-birds raced down the avenues.

(c)   In sunlight, in shadow, by moonlight, by candlelight. In the long afternoons when the house was empty. Only the sun was there to keep us company.

(d)   I sought a theme and sought for it in vain, I sought it daily for six weeks or so.

(e)   Enter the throat of darkness. Follow the word winding to the heart of the stone.

(f)   A single bird call began the day. Each day the same bird, the same call.

(g)   This book is the record of a struggle between two temperaments, two consciences and almost two epochs.

(h)   Here lies a most beautiful lady, light of step and heart was she; I think she was the most beautiful lady that ever was in the West Country.

(i)   At the end of a long-walled garden in a red provincial town, a brick path led to a mulberry, scanty grass at its feet.

(j)   The eye is drawn to it as to a great sun fallen from the marbled sky through boughs of trees and rolled across ribbed fields to wait pulsating in the shadow of the house.

Some of these extracts, even in this amputated form, are undoubtedly calling up a poetic response. Either we give the poem which follows a particular quality of attention, or we put that poem aside. Others are more like what we expect of prose, and so, it seems fair to assume, more dependent on the positioning of the words on the page to achieve their effect, which may, ultimately, be just as powerful and just as *poetic*. Some poems start in quiet ways – or even in downright prosaic ways. Others, which may flash their poem-identity-cards at us much more obviously, may turn out in the end not to be poems at all. But however they do it, whether by typography, rhythm, rhyme, or by a mixture of meaning or language which in other contexts we should see as bizarre, a poem has to create in us an expectation of poetry in order to survive.

Closely allied to this expectation, are a host of uneasy and uncomfortable questions: If a special quality of attention is necessary, how do I know I am not 'over-reading'? How do I know *my* meaning is the poet's meaning? Shouldn't I go and look him up and see what kind of life he lived and whether he wrote anything about the poem and how he came to write it? Shouldn't I know the social and political circumstances? Shouldn't I know whether he was in love and how he felt about dying? Shouldn't I know whether he rides a bicycle or has a new collection coming out in February?

All these are serious questions, and they are all related. But together they raise another, even more fundamental issue: the issue of who a poem belongs to. A little poem (which is not in fact a little poem in anything but length!) by Emily Dickinson, written probably in 1872, puts this more tellingly than I can:

> A word is dead
> When it is said,
> Some say.
>
> I say it just
> Begins to live
> That day.

We, the individual readers are necessary to the existence of a poem just as surely as we are necessary to a play. The poem, once written, can exist quite well without its author to explain or perform it. But it cannot exist without a reader's attention and life-experience to fill its silences.

This does not mean that a poem can mean *anything*, or that when we are asked to discuss a piece of poetry we are justified in reminiscing about when and how our children were born, or why our most recent relationship went so terribly wrong. Part of *experiencing* the poem (and a good poem must surely be moving) is probably to relate it inwardly to these or similarly personal things. But to discuss it sensibly we have to be able to recognise and talk about the mechanics of suggestion without rushing in to fill the silences with something obviously our own. Good poems leave us space. We have to be able to talk about how that space is created without explaining it away.

———— Reading and readings ————

The medium through which a poem comes to us makes this kind of attention more or less easy. There is a great difference between the way one responds to a poem on hearing it read and the way one responds to a poem on the page. In any but academic circles, it has come to seem almost old-fashioned to read poetry on the page, for oneself, at one's own pace. Much modern poetry is not written with this kind of treatment in mind, and we are perhaps falsifying it and reducing its impact by studying it in this way. After all, poetry has always been something to be *heard*, concerned no less with sound than with how it looked on the page, and of course it is by hearing a poem read that we can best appreciate the sound it makes. But if we hear a poem rather than see it for ourselves, we are emphasising its dramatic qualities. We experience it in the same way we experience a drama or a piece of music. It unfolds to us *on the run*, as it were. We catch at meanings and images. We have no chance to go back and make less obvious connections. If we read a poem on the page, we are aware of its patterns almost before we are aware of its development. We are looking at a tapestry which may or may not have a story woven into it. It is the colour and design that appeal to us initially and we look more closely at it to find meaning.

It seems to me that when we are confronted with a poem we can appreciate it best by trying to take the best from both these responses. We can read it aloud to ourselves, or find a way of having it read to us, and we will do well to try to *catch* this initial response, since it can never entirely be repeated. We can look at the poem on the page, read it several times over a period of days or even weeks and wait for other meanings to surface.

Usually, if it is a good poem and worth studying, other meaning will surface without our having to force anything, though living with a half-understood poem can be uncomfortable at first if we are not used to literature which is ambiguous or elusive. The turn of the century French poet Paul Valéry claimed that a real poem would never entirely give up all its meaning to its readers, and that this explained why the actual words of a poem continue to haunt us.

Exercise 3

There must be at least one snatch of poetry which you have not been able to forget. It could be a single line, or a few lines of a poem you have read quite recently, or you may have to go back as far as your childhood for some rhyme that has *stuck* inexplicably. Write down your fragment of a poem. Does it look as you remembered it? Can you think of anything special *about the words themselves* which can partly account for their memorability? Do you understand them fully, or is there a margin of strangeness which can never quite be explained away?

Go back and find the whole poem. Read it again. How do your remembered lines appear to you in context?

Poetic language

One of the many ways in which a poet can signal to his or her readers that what they are reading is a poem is by using a special kind of language. He or she can use unexpected words, or put them together in an unexpected way. Even without being 'poetic' in the conventional sense, he or she can signal in all sorts of ways that the language we have in front of us is potentially richer and denser than ordinary functional prose. The changes may be minimal – a suppressed *the* here, a suppressed *and* there, a present tense where in ordinary narrative we would expect a past, but they can buy the poet considerable freedom. At least part of the function of formal rhymes and rhythms in poetry is to alert the reader so that he or she is ready to give the quality of attention which will call the poem into existence. If a poet uses language in special ways, he or she no longer needs formal sound-effects for this purpose. One could argue that he or she no longer needs even a special 'poetic' layout for his or her words on the page.

Twentieth-century English poetry has tended to play down these linguistic signals. A language which simply *is* dense without having 'Look at me, I am a poem' written all over it seems to us nowadays to be somehow more satisfying. Poets who use language as subtly as Auden and Larkin make a lot of the poetry which came before them read as if its author had highlighted every line in day-glow pink. Many modern poets have carried on this current of unemphatic 'everyday' language, making ordinary words and ordinary conjunctions of words so discreetly rhythmical that they sometimes feel closer to real speech than they do to written prose. The *signalling* here is done by something else.

Some poets use language in an obviously un-functional way. It is apparent to us, even when we read only a small snatch of one of their poems, that had they wanted to get an ordinary functional message across to us, the words they would have chosen would have been quite different. Logically, the more the language itself signals to us that what we are reading is poetry, the freer the poet is to dispense with conventional poetic metre. The logical extension of this is the prose poem, where ideally the poetic density of the language should tell us just as clearly as rhyme and typography that this is poetry we are reading. In Britain the prose poem has been virtually ignored, while in certain European countries and in North America it has been a rich and fertile area of exploration. This is surely connected to our respective attitudes to poetic language.

Exercise 4

Read the following two poems. Which of them says to you the more loudly: 'I am a poem. Read me with attention.'? Now read them again, more carefully. Then answer the questions which follow.

Buzzard

our connection is silence
   the plunge in the blood

what music he moves to –
   he plays me
from the bed of the lane
he reels out my sight
he turns round the hills
eddies   splits air
lounges like paper
he drops the whole sky

a comet too near the earth
   rabid he crashes
   yellow eye glittering
   savage his absence
   scoring the fields

leaves hang in stillness
a breath drawn   suspended
our connection is silence
   the plunge in the blood

Frances Horovitz

New Car

Doesn't, when we touch it, that sheen of infinitesimally
                                        pebbled steel, doesn't it, perhaps,
give just a bit, yes, the subtlest yielding, yes, much less
                                        than flesh would, we realize,
but still, as though it were intending in some formal way
                                        that at last we were to be in contact
with the world of inorganics, as though, after all we've
                                        been through with it, cuts, falls, blows,
that world, the realm of carbon, iron, earth, the all-ungiving,
                                        was attempting, gently, patiently,
to reach across, respond, and mightn't we find now, not
                                        to our horror or even our discomfort,
that our tongue, as though in answer, had wandered gently
                                        from the mouth, as though it, too,
shriven of its limits, bud and duct, would sanctify this
                                        unit, would touch, stroke, cling, fuse?

                                                            C K Williams

Questions

(a)   What is it that signals to you in each case that this is a poem?

(b)   What is special about the language of the first poem? Can you point to examples? How does the language affect the way you read? What difference does the lack of punctuation make?

(c)   How would you describe the language of the second poem? Is there any variation in that language? How does it make you read?

Exercise 5

Another special use of language which is often associated with poetry is the kind of playing with words which we find in a lot of poems written for children. Just why we tend to see verbal play as belonging so much to childhood is not obvious. We seem not to expect adults to delight in language with quite so much obvious gusto. In my opinion this is a pity, because with the ability to delight in wordplay goes the ability to *fend off* the need for secure, comfortable, *single* meanings. The Surrealist poets thought children were special, that their vision and the connections they made naturally were something which was in danger of being lost to the rational, utilitarian world in which adults lived. The Surrealist poets of the 1920s and 1930s were, of course, searching for something much deeper than the meanings suggested in most playful poems. Yet the unexpected conjunctions of meaning which word-games like these throw up sometimes go far deeper than we give them credit for.

Try not to tighten up mentally as you read the next three passages of poetry. Enjoy the verbal play for what it is, without at first scrutinising it for meaning:

> Oh, do not tease the Bluffalo
> With quick-step or with shuffalo
> When you are in a scuffalo
> in Bluffalo's back-yard.
>
> For it has quite enoughalo
> Of people playing toughalo
> And when it gives a cuffalo
> It gives it very hard.
>
> (from 'The Bluffalo' by Jane Yolen)

> anyone lived in a pretty how town
> (with up so floating many bells down)
> spring summer autumn winter
> he sang his didn't he danced his did.
>
> Women and men (both little and small)
> cared for anyone not at all
> they sowed their isn't they reaped their same
> sun moon stars rain
>
> (from 'anyone lived in a pretty how town' by e e cummings)

Genesis

> In the beginning, God crusted
> the earth and He watered it. And He
> made the swallows fly
> and said unto them, Swallow flies!

And unto man He said, Man,
thou shalt walk as the fly crows, yea
even as the cry flows! And He beheld
the students of Divinity and lo!
He saw that they were no good. And
He said unto them, Publish, or
no parish! – And the end began
at the beginning, and eternity passed
swiftly, and forever took time out
never to stop.

Felix Pollak

Questions

(a)   Which of these examples seems to you to be the most playful?

(b)   What does the verbal play in this case consist of?

(c)   Which seems to you to be the most serious?

(d)   How do you account for this seriousness?

(e)   Can you analyse what the poet of the last extract is doing in lines 6 and 7? What effect do the transpositions of words and sounds have?

Many contemporary poets would regard this kind of delight in experimenting with words as a fairly superficial poetic tool. But if we think about the reaction it elicits at its least threatening (usually in humorous poetry and/or poems written specifically for children), we can see how far it goes towards breaking down our conventional, *reasoned*, approach to language and demand for instant meaning, in favour of something else. If we are to respond to this kind of poetry at all, we are forced to respond to it in a way which would be inappropriate for a passage of prose. If we search for an immediate, *single* message, we shall be disappointed. The only way to relate at all to this kind of language play is to let it wash over us and simply enjoy it. As we enjoy it, the meanings of this spicy, unexpected verbal mixture begin to come to us. 'Toughalo' does not mean at all the same thing as 'tough'. We all show, as soon as we laugh, that we are aware that its meaning is quite different. That meaning cannot be found in any dictionary, or taught by any teacher: it is made again each time a new reader – child or adult – sees the incongruity and finds it funny.

This is very overt verbal play. It puts us in a position where we *cannot* read only ordinary meanings into words. But most poets play with words in a less extravagant sense. Rhyme, rhythm, alliteration and assonance are all forms of word-play. The difference is that they do not actually make us question the accepted meanings of words. We have only to look at some of Gerard Manley Hopkins' poetry to understand how intensely serious a poet's playing with the relationship between sound and meaning can be. But in a sense it is still play. It helps us to approach a poem with an openness that obviously logical and functional language has no use for.

Poetry and tone

When we look at the question of verbal play in poetry, we cannot avoid talking about humour and seriousness, and seeing that, in some poems at least, the line between them is very thin indeed. Poems, like narratives, have a tone, and in good poems that tone is often very elusive. The poem may be superficially comic. But because in poetry we are almost always dealing with more than one level of meaning, there may be a seriousness which underlies the comedy. A poem may appear gentle, yet its meaning may be savage. A poem may be overtly angry, yet its meaning may be comprehensive and generous.

The best poetry is surprising, and one of the forms that surprise can take is a shift in tone which suddenly changes or qualifies the poem's meaning. We look back (or strain to remember) the poem's beginning and find it has opened out into something quite different from what it was at first. The patterns of sound, or typography, or imagery may all be tending towards unity, making us see the poem as a very tightly-made, harmonious thing – while the tone suddenly (or perhaps not so suddenly) lets us *fall through* this tight structure to a glimpse of something no more harmonious or reassuring than the world we live in.

Exercise 6

Read the following poems several times. Then try to answer the questions:

The Heart's Location

all my plans for suicide are ridiculous
I can never remember the heart's location
too cheap to smash the car
too queasy to slash a wrist
once jumped off a bridge
almost scared myself to death
then spent two foggy weeks
waiting for new glasses

of course I really want to live
continuing my lifelong search
for the world's greatest unknown cheap restaurant
and a poem full of ordinary words
about simple things
in the inconsolable rhythms of the heart.

Peter Meinke

For a Five-Year-Old

A snail is climbing up the window-sill
Into your room, after a night of rain.
You call me in to see, and I explain
That it would be unkind to leave it there:
It might crawl to the floor; we must take care
That no one squashes it. You understand,
And carry it outside, with careful hand,
To eat a daffodil.

I see, then, that a kind of faith prevails:
Your gentleness is moulded still by words
From me, who have trapped mice and shot wild birds,
From me, who drowned your kittens, who betrayed
Your closest relatives, and who purveyed
The harshest kind of truth to many another.
But that is how things are: I am your mother,
And we are kind to snails.

Fleur Adcock

The Second Coming

Turning and turning in the widening gyre
The falcon cannot hear the falconer;
Things fall apart; the centre cannot hold;
Mere anarchy is loosed upon the world,
The blood-dimmed tide is loosed, and everywhere
The ceremony of innocence is drowned;
The best lack all conviction, while the worst
Are full of passionate intensity.
Surely some revelation is at hand;
Surely the Second Coming is at hand.
The Second Coming! Hardly are those words out
When a vast image out of *Spiritus Mundi*
Troubles my sight: somewhere in sands of the desert
A shape with lion body and the head of a man,
A gaze blank and pitiless as the sun,
Is moving its slow thighs, while all about it
Reel shadows of the indignant desert birds.
The darkness drops again; but now I know
That twenty centuries of stony sleep
Were vexed to nightmare by a rocking cradle,
And what rough beast, its hour come round at last,
Slouches towards Bethlehem to be born?

W B Yeats

Questions

(a) Read each of the three poems again to yourself, this time aloud. Do you hear a voice which is distinct from your own? Can you hear a distinct tone of voice in each?

(b) In 'The Heart's Location' does the tone remain consistent?

(c) If it seems to you to change, where exactly does the change take place?

(d) Can you account for that shift in the kind of words the poet is using?

(e) In 'For a Five-Year-Old' how and where does the language of the poem change?

(f) How does this change modify the tone of the poem?

(g) What elements of the poem *are* consistent?

(h) In the light of your answers to questions (e), (f) and (g), how do you interpret the poem?

(i) Try to look at 'The Second Coming' in the same way. How are modulations in language and tone modifying the meaning here?

Paying attention

In the case of poetry, the phrase *paying attention* seems almost a pun. If we are not used to it, the kind of intense listening and scrutiny we are asked to give to a poem may often feel as painful as reaching into our pockets to buy some commodity which may or may not prove to be worth the initial outlay. But if there is any definition of poetry which is as applicable to the low-key, un-ornamented, seemingly informal modern poem as it is to Milton or Wordsworth, it is perhaps this: that if we consent to grant the poem our full attention, at every level we are capable of, then the poem will in the end give us our money's-worth: a poem is a piece of writing suggestive and fertile enough to reward the special kind of attention poetry demands. If this definition of poetry seems circular, it is perhaps because we have not yet come to terms fully with what we ourselves are asking of a poem. But in practice, it seems to work. The more poetry we learn to read carefully, the more poems we are able to appreciate. The more we look, the more we see that there are very good, tangible reasons for a given poem's having the effect it does. The more we learn about the surprising ways in which vastly different poems can transform themselves under our attention, and still reward it, the more we shall in the end be confident enough to say – whether or not we can define poetry – , 'That is a poem, and I'm afraid this isn't.'

Emily Dickinson's brave definition of poetry is one which still stands today:

If I read a book and it makes my whole body so cold no fire can ever warm me, I know that is poetry. If I feel physically as if the top of my head were taken off, I know that is poetry. These are the only ways I know it. Is there any other way?

The subjective response, in an attentive reader, is as reliable a way as any to recognise a poem. But the attention and the emotion themselves will teach us, if we let them, to talk about our convictions, to look again at the poem and recognise what is triggering that enormously important subjective response. We can all, thank goodness, have the top of our heads taken off. We can all, also, describe the knife or the explosion that did it.

Exercise 7

This is an exercise which needs to be done over a longer period of time. In my experience, a week seems to be adequate, but if you have more time at your disposal, you could easily stretch the different parts of the exercise out over a fortnight or even longer. It is worth spending as long as you can over this particular exercise at this stage, to build a critical awareness which will be worth its weight in gold later. What we are trying to do, is to produce by the artificial means of *slowing up* the reader's initial response to the poem, the more searching kind of attention which later you will be able to give more quickly. Try to stick as closely as you can to the instructions given:

(a)   Day 1: Read the following three poems once. Choose one of them to study in more depth.

Miners

There was a whispering in my hearth,
    A sigh of the coal,
Grown wistful of a former earth
    It might recall.

I listened for a tale of leaves
    And smothered ferns;
Frond-forests; and the low, sly lives
    Before the fawns.

My fire might show steam-phantoms simmer
    From Time's old cauldron,
Before the birds made nests in summer,
    Or men had children.

But the coals were murmuring of their mine,
    And moans down there
Of boys that slept wry sleep, and men
    Writhing for air.

And I saw white bones in the cinder-shard,
    Bones without number;
For many hearts with coal are charred;
    And few remember.

I thought of some who worked dark pits
    Of war, and died
Digging the rock where Death reputes
    Peace lies indeed.

Comforted years will sit soft-chaired
    In rooms of amber:
The years will stretch their hands, well-cheered
    By our lives' ember.

The centuries will burn rich loads
    With which we groaned,
Whose warmth shall lull their dreaming lids
    While songs are crooned.
But they will not dream of us poor lads,
    Lost in the ground.

                    Wilfred Owen

I Shall Paint My Nails Red

Because a bit of colour is a public service.

Because I am proud of my hands.

Because it will remind me I'm a woman.

Because I will look like a survivor.

Because I can admire them in terrific jams.

Because my daughter will say ugh.

Because my lover will be surprised.

Because it is quicker than dyeing my hair.

Because it is a ten-minute moratorium.

Because it is reversible.

Carole Satyamurti

An Otter

Underwater eyes, an eel's
Oil of water body, neither fish nor beast is the otter:
  Four-legged yet water-gifted, to outfish fish;
    With webbed feet and long ruddering tail
    And a rounded head like an old tomcat.

Brings the legend of himself
From before wars or burials, in spite of hounds and vermin-poles;
  Does not take root like the badger. Wanders, cries;
    Gallops along land he no longer belongs to;
    Re-enters the water by melting.

Of neither water nor land. Seeking
Some world lost when first he dived, that he cannot come at since,
  Takes his changed body into the holes of lakes;
    As if blind, cleaves the stream's push till he licks
    The pebbles of the source; from sea

To sea crosses in three nights
Like a king in hiding. Crying to the old shape of the starlit land,
  Over sunken farms where the bats go round,
    Without answer. Till light and birdsong come
    Walloping up roads with the milk wagon.

Ted Hughes

(b) Day 2: Read your chosen poem again. What is it about? Write down your answer briefly (one sentence will be enough) and keep the piece of paper on which you wrote your answer for reference.

(c) Day 3: Read your chosen poem again.

(d) Day 4: Read your chosen poem again.

(e) Day 5: Read your chosen poem again.

(f)   Day 6: Read your chosen poem again. What is it about? Write down your answer, again in a single sentence, on the same piece of paper. Are your two answers identical? Think about any differences which may have surfaced.

(g)   Day 7: Read your chosen poem again. Think again about its meaning and where in the poem itself that meaning seems to come from. In note form, or more fully if you prefer, write down *everything you can* about the poem. If you have kept strictly to the format of the exercise and allowed yourself to write hardly anything at all about the poem until now, there should be plenty to say. Your answer to this could easily run into several pages, or be the basis for a full-length (1,500-word) essay.

(h)   If you have time, go back now and study the other 2 poems in the same way. You may be able now to reduce the time-scale of the exercise slightly. As you do this, you will be learning the kind of critical attention that, I firmly believe, is appropriate to the study of poetry.

Commentary

Exercise 1

Reactions to this exercise will obviously vary with each individual reader's experience. It is impossible to generalise convincingly about the ways in which actors and poets read. However, you may have been lucky enough to catch an actor reading *dramatically*, or at least reading a poem in such a way as to give its first, most obvious meaning the best possible chance to be understood. When I have heard un-rhymed poems read by actors, I have noticed that they are often seemingly *clearer* than on the page, the reading tending to carry the sense across line-breaks, following punctuation rather than the visual pattern, as we are taught to when we learn to sing hymns at school. Many poets, on the other hand, try to compensate for what the eye cannot see, making a point of hesitating slightly at the ends of their lines, as the eye would, using the small silence to *disturb* the first, most obvious meaning, and creating ambiguities. Poets often read their own work in a more monotonous voice than an actor would. 'He isn't much of a reader,' we sometimes say. 'He doesn't do his own work justice.' But perhaps this kind of *colourless* delivery is letting the words *work* for us in more than the simple expected way.

Exercise 2

Only three of these ten extracts are in fact taken from a piece of prose. Extract (c), which is taken from Jean Rhys's novel, *Wide Sargasso Sea*, is possibly the most surprising. To me, this piece seems to proclaim itself unmistakably as poetry: its subtle modulations and near-repetitions, the way it balances one word or one sentence against another, its density of meaning, even the suspicion of rhyme it contains at the ends of the second and third sentences, all surely call for a 'poetic' response. Extract (g) (from Edmund Gosse's autobiographical *Father and Son*), surely proclaims itself at the outset by its subject. Extract (f), which is from Isaac Bashevis Singer's novel, *The Slave*, is closer to poetry. Its simplicity, repetitions and rhythms probably make it indistinguishable from the poetry in this exercise.

Obviously, I have the advantage – or disadvantage – of knowing where these extracts all came from! In some of them the poetic signals are extremely subtle and, if the poem were not typographically and commercially set apart as poetry, might at first go unrecognised. But it seems to me they are there. In all these cases, the language is *special* – unmistakably special in extracts (a), (b), (d), (e) and (h), and very subtly special in extracts (c), (i) and (j).

In extract (i), that specialness is a matter of balance and rhythm, rather than of vocabulary: the words actually sound very different when read aloud – what is banal on paper may not be banal to the ear.

The final extract seems to me to announce that it is prose. The sheer length and complexity of this sentence (even as my punctuation has shortened it) seem to tell us that we are reading something large and leisurely – perhaps a descriptive passage in a longish novel. What might first trigger a *poetic* expectation is the richness of its adjectives ('marbled', 'ribbed') which could well seem rather 'over the top' in a prose description: we might perhaps guess that they are there for poetic reasons. We might then become aware of the unobtrusive rhythms and rhymes or half-rhymes which are undoubtedly working on us, whether or not we are fully conscious of them.

Look, now, at how all these lines of poetry appear when they are printed properly. See how the visual signals and verbal signals reinforce each other to say, now, that each of these extracts *most certainly is* the beginning of a poem:

(a)

> Our brains ache, in the merciless iced east winds that knive us . . .
>
> (Wilfred Owen, 'Exposure')

(b)

> I can imagine, in some otherworld
> Primeval-dumb, far back
> In that most awful stillness, that only gasped and hummed,
> Humming-birds raced down the avenues.
>
> (D H Lawrence, 'Humming-Bird')

(d)

> I sought a theme and sought for it in vain,
> I sought it daily for six weeks or so.
>
> (W B Yeats, 'The Circus Animals' Desertion')

(e)

> enter the throat of darkness
>
> follow the word
>
>> winding to the heart of the stone
>
> (Frances Horovitz, 'West Kennet Long Barrow')

(h)

> Here lies a most beautiful lady:
> Light of step and heart was she;
> I think she was the most beautiful lady
> That ever was in the West Country.
>
> (Walter de la Mare, 'An Epitaph')

(i)

> At the end of a long-walled garden
>   in a red provincial town,
> A brick path led to a mulberry
>   scanty grass at its feet.
>
> (John Betjeman, 'The Cottage Hospital')

(j)

> The eye is drawn to it as to a great
> sun fallen from the marbled sky through boughs
> of trees and rolled across ribbed fields to wait
> pulsating in the shadow of the house:
>
> > (Caroline Price, 'The Heart of the Country')

Exercise 3

The response to this must be very individual. Nevertheless, I would expect your answer to the second part of the exercise to be yes, and I would expect you to have gained something from trying to analyse that linguistic strangeness to your own satisfaction. One of my personal favourites is a single line from a T S Eliot poem, 'New Hampshire' (*Landscapes*):

> Cover me over, light-in-leaves;

where the meanings of death, sleep, summer, autumn, down, up, ground, sky, blindness and seeing are all knotted together, pulled tight in the astonishing hyphenated word at the end of the line, and the balance and contrast between the sounds and rhythms of the line's two halves. I have said this one line over to myself thousands of times. It never ceases to be meaningful, yet still refuses to give its meaning up to me entirely.

Exercise 4

(a) In both cases it is firstly the fact that you have read them in a section of a book devoted to the study of poetry, and secondly that they are spaced on the page in such a way that they are visibly claiming to be poetry. In the case of 'Buzzard' this visual aspect is more clear-cut. The way certain lines are inset, the lack of punctuation and capitalisation all signal to us that this is an extraordinary use of language for a more than ordinary purpose. In 'New Car', the long lines momentarily cheat the eye into approaching the poem as prose. In the Frances Horovitz poem there are also very strong linguistic clues. The C K Williams poem, which at first seems more akin to the words of an ordinary speaker, also signals to us, perhaps in a more subtle way: its unnatural length (for a question), its insistent listings and repetitions, all pull from us a more intense kind of awareness. Here, too, there are patterns of sound. Embedded in the longer, more explicitly thoughtful lines, they may be hardly noticeable, but they are working on us all the same to slow our reading down, force us almost to adopt in our minds a certain tone of voice which makes the final question not just surprising, but also meaningful.

(b)   In 'the plunge in the blood', with its strange mixture of concrete and abstract meaning and its sound-echoes, language is all-important. It is telling us very clearly that we are here faced with something which we cannot read sensibly on a single, immediate level.

Frances Horovitz's decision not to punctuate is not just a visual clue that this is poetry. A poet who chooses to omit punctuation is inviting the reader to read ambiguously. If we put in an imaginary full stop after 'paper' at the end of line 9, line 10 attaches itself in meaning to lines 11 and 12: 'he drops the whole sky' is already a picture of a bird plummeting. But without that full stop (which is *not there*), 'he drops the whole sky' is still attached to 'eddies splits air/lounges like paper', and the image is – *what*? I begin to see a bird still hovering, powerful, full of *potential* attack, a sky falling from it (like a bomb? like leaflets? like sunlight?). The same kind of double effect is produced in the three lines:

> yellow eye glittering
> savage his absence
> scoring the fields

What we have here is the same absence of punctuation coupled with a new element: because of the line-breaks, 'savage his absence' seems at first to mean 'his absence is savage', and to be a rather self-conscious 'poetic' inversion. In fact it allows the reader space to play with meaning. We *do* understand 'his absence is savage', but as we look again, we *also* begin to see 'yellow eye glittering savage' and 'absence scoring the fields'. These meanings *are all* there. The initial strangeness is helping us to give the poem the kind of attention which will let us become aware of them.

(c)   In spite of a very different mood and technique, C K Williams uses some of the same linguistic devices to concentrate meaning in 'New Car'. Contemporary English and American poetry very often signals that it is poetry by omissions of some or all of the small, neutral, unnecessary words we would use in our speech. We have no 'and' or 'or' here. In such an enormously long question, isn't that rather peculiar? Like our own selves wandering out to greet the strange seduction of this metallic, painful world, the poem wanders, not through the expected conjunctions, but through an insistent series of 'as though . . . ' clauses, each reaching a bit further than the one that went before it.

The language of 'New Car' is more angular and uncomfortable than the language of 'Buzzard'. We have words like 'infinitesimally', 'intending', 'formal', 'organics' which are abstract and uncompromisingly unevocative. Yet we also have 'pebbled', 'earth', 'tongue', 'bud', 'duct', 'stroke', 'cling', and the astonishing 'shriven' and 'sanctify'. Just as the poet plays in the no-man's-land of his long, unwieldy lines, he also plays in the space between different registers of words. 'Fuse', the perfect last word of the poem, would be equally at home in either register.

The effect of syntax and language here is surely to make us read more and more slowly and then re-read, even possibly to break off and re-read. If we read too fast, we get lost. We are grateful for the repeated 'yes' and 'as though [. . .] as though' which guide us through the long question like an outstretched hand. We are led by a human voice through a difficult and uncompromising world.

Exercise 5

(a)   I imagine most readers would choose 'The Bluffalo'.

(b)   It consists of adding -'alo' or sometimes simply -'o' (with modified spellings to make pronunciation clear) to rhyming or potentially rhyming words so that they rhyme with 'bluffalo'. In several cases, these rhymes are not only startling and funny to the ear but also visually incongruous. The fact that 'bluffalo' rhymes with 'toughalo' makes us see afresh what a silly illogical language English is (and perhaps any language is) in some respects.

(c)   This is a matter of personal interpretation. I would say the Pollak poem, but many might put forward the cummings one equally convincingly.

(d)   The seriousness comes both from the frame of reference (*Genesis*) and from the meanings of the words playfully created. 'Swallow flies' is only a pun, and a funny pun at that, but if it is God's first command, it is also sad and frightening.

(e)   'the fly crows' is also funny, but the reader is disorientated: the image has something of the nightmare about it, 'the cry flows' is a variation on the Spoonerism, (a *muddling* of the initial sounds of the two words). The *muddle* suggests impotence; the meanings of the words themselves surely suggest universal desolation. But it is the constant metamorphosis of these images, and the feeling of inevitability generated by their strange logic, which is the most powerfully suggestive here.

Exercise 6

(a)   I would expect the answer to this to be *yes*, except perhaps in the case of the third poem, where language and density of meaning may make the poem difficult to *hear* for many modern readers.

(b)   No. There is a very definite change in tone.

(c)   It seems to me to begin to change in lines 12 and 13, and very obviously to have changed in line 14.

(d)   The poet is using the *ordinary words* and rhythms of everyday speech until he reaches lines 12 and 13. These two lines have a kind of neutrality which is not present in the first part of the poem. The words are still *ordinary*. We could still hear ourselves say them. But they would not be out of place in a more formal, written context: the very colloquial, immediate *heard* voice which is so noticeable in lines 3–11 is no longer in evidence. The short penultimate line makes us slow down. By the time we reach the end we are almost ready for the unexpected seriousness of the final metaphor (– a rhythm cannot *actually* be inconsolable: the poet is using 'rhythms' to stand for something far larger).

(e)   It seems to me that there is a distinct change to a more abstract and complex language at the beginning of the second stanza. Lines 3 and 4 of this second stanza and the last 1½ lines of the poem are exceptions to this general change.

(f)   The tone becomes more meditative and considered in stanza two. The voice is now no longer the voice of a mother talking to her child, but that of a woman talking to herself. Lines 11 and 12 are a startling interruption: the direct, emotive language, the few telling adjectives, the striking repetitions, all combine here in a kind of crescendo, to give an effect of disbelief, almost of shock. When the language reverts to the language of childhood in the last two lines of the poem, the tone cannot be recaptured. The effect is now at least partly ironic: the intrusion of violence has coloured the clear-cut morals of five-year-old childhood with all sorts of uncomfortable implications. We can still read gentleness into that last line, but it is a different kind of gentleness – wistful, defeated, vulnerable, bitter, ironic – ambiguous.

(g)   These changes of language and tone are all the more effective for taking place against a background of continuity. Look at how symmetrical the poem is formally. In shape, rhythm and rhyme-scheme the second stanza echoes the first almost exactly. Lines 11 and 12 stand out visually for their length and for their repeated beginning, but they do not stand out rhythmically. The effect is that of a surface, a gloss of convention covering painful experience. There is unity here, but it is precarious: this fragile bridging of adult and five-year-old experience may part under us and let us fall through.

(h)   There is no ideal answer to this. The important thing is to talk about what the poem is doing before you rush to interpret its meaning.

(i)   This is a much more difficult poem, and so my question becomes a more difficult question. It is not appropriate to answer it here in detail. I would only point to the very definite shift in language and tone which operates in the one word 'slouches' in the final line. This one word modifies the meaning of the whole poem retrospectively. Go back and read it again. The colon in line 13 now appears as a kind of pivot, and the language of the first and second halves of the poem have become quite separate, as if the word '*slouches*' were acting as some sort of developing agent. Try writing about the two halves of the poem as if they were in fact quite separate from each other. Then put what you have written together and see how the meaning of each of the two halves is modified.

Exercise 7

You have one possible answer to this question already in front of you. If you have worked through the chapter carefully, you should have a certain confidence in the statements you have written about *your* poem, and the discoveries you have made. This is the kind of reading you are going to need to use when we come to even closer grips with the resources of poetry in the next two chapters.

5

SIGHT
AND SOUND

Poem and pattern

Once we have given a poem our full attention, we become ever more aware that it is not a statement, but a pattern. Colours and textures are woven into it. They reinforce or modify one another. And if there is a sudden unexpected strand of magenta or kingfisher, then it is against the tones and textures of the whole that that vivid flash of colour is to be interpreted. The visual metaphors of painting or embroidery often come to mind when we are discussing poetry, but the 'colours' and patterns of a poem may have nothing to do with explicit references to what we see. When a poet uses patterns of sound to create relationships between the words he or she uses, he or she is giving them new meanings which play round the ordinary everyday meanings of the words themselves. When a poet uses metaphor, he or she is tying a knot with strands drawn from two different orders of experience, and making us think again about the separate meanings of each.

When two people in our acquaintance strike up a relationship, our attitude to each of them changes subtly. We begin to look at them both differently, imagining how their qualities and needs must dovetail or conflict. When a poet knots words, we begin to look at those words in a new way and understand them more completely.

'Form' in a poem is as infinitely variable as poems themselves. When we talk about poetry, we have to talk about form, whether it is primarily a matter of the visual or aural pattern a poem makes, whether it is the tight requirements of a conventional sonnet, or a sustained metaphor, with developments and modulations. But what we should be very careful not to do, is to talk about form in isolation. In a poem, 'form' and 'content' are indistinguishable. Imagine a mosaic-artist whose tiny coloured tiles or fragments of pottery also had words written on them: each tile already *means* something, and the mosaic itself, its lines, its textures, its subtle gradations of colour, also carry meaning. We could put together a picture of a rotten carcass with words about wind and music and water printed on each tile; we could put together a pattern of leaping dolphins in words which evoked violence and despair.

Another thing we must be careful not to do is to impose some arbitrary form on a poem as if it were a template. It makes no sense to look at a crazy quilt as if it were a quilt made up of hexagons which got cut out wrong. It makes no sense to look at the most irregular unrhymed modern poetry as if it were incapable of being in rhyming couplets. All this is very obvious. But many of us have a residual nostalgia for Shakespearian or Romantic forms which still makes us look at modern poetry rather wistfully, preventing us from seeing the alternative forms that do exist.

Part of the trouble is that *formal* poetry has obvious credentials. It is visibly difficult to write lines which have a tight, satisfying rhythmical pattern, and even more difficult – especially nowadays – to make them rhyme convincingly without slipping over into sentimentality or dog-gerel. If we are unsure how to discuss poetry, we may find it reassuring to talk about the very noticeable formal patterns of a vilanelle or a sonnet, rather than risk the devils we don't know in a seemingly formless, haphazard poem by a more modern poet. But whether they are visibly and audibly crying out for us to notice them, or whether we must go and look for them, it is pointless (except as an exercise) simply to *enumerate* the patterns a poem makes. If we talk about rhyme or shape on the page, or even about metaphor, *in isolation*, we are not saying very much. In the end, we must try to link the various things we are saying about a poem's patterns *all together*. It is only by doing this that we can begin to see how they function, and so work towards the poem's meaning.

Formal pattern in poetry is culturally relative. When we in England think *sonnet*, we think first of the Shakespearian sonnet, with its final satisfying rhyming-couplet flourish. In France or Italy a sonnet would be an Italian sonnet first – the final six lines all tied together by the interlocking rhymes – and the Shakespearian sonnet would be the variation. These distinctions are not so much historical as cultural: the relationship each reader has with the poem is affected by his or her cultural expectations. We can read translations of haiku. English and American poets may – and do – write in the haiku form and we approach these poems in the knowledge that they conform to certain formal requirements, but we shall never read them as a Japanese reader would.

Exercise 1

Read the following poem, and then look at it again more carefully:

The Sun Rising

     Busy old fool, unruly sun,
     Why dost thou thus,
Through windows, and through curtains call on us?
Must to thy motions lovers' seasons run?
     Saucy pedantic wretch, go chide
     Late school-boys, and sour prentices,
    Go tell court-huntsmen that the King will ride,
    Call country ants to harvest offices;
Love, all alike, no season knows, nor clime,
Not hours, days, months, which are the rags of time.

     Thy beams, so reverend, and strong
     Why shouldst thou think?
I could eclipse and cloud them with a wink,
But that I would not lose her sight so long:
     If her eyes have not blinded thine,
     Look, and tomorrow late, tell me,
    Whether both th'Indias of spice and mine
    Be where thou left'st them, or lie here with me.
Ask for those kings whom thou saw'st yesterday,
And thou shalt hear, All here in one bed lay.

     She'is all states, and all princes, I,
     Nothing else is.
Princes do but play us; compared to this,

All honour's mimic; all wealth alchemy.
    Thou sun art half as happy as we,
      In that the world's contracted thus;
    Thine age asks ease, and since thy duties be
    To warm the world, that's done in warming us.
Shine here to us, and thou art everywhere;
    This bed thy centre is, these walls, thy sphere.

John Donne

Now see if you can list the different ways in which the poet is creating a pattern in the poem. Try to say something about the effect of each. Would the poem suffer from being less formal?

How should a poem look?

If we are reading a poem on a page, the visual pattern it makes is obviously more immediate than any other. There is a natural tendency to think that the patterns which surface slightly later are more subtle ones, that patterns of sound, and more especially patterns of tone, language and imagery are in the end what counts in a poem. Often we ignore the look of a poem almost completely: once it has told us that this is a poem we are reading, we drop it behind us like orange-peel and suck at the poem's 'flesh'.

In fact, patterns for the eye and patterns for the ear work in conjunction with each other. They may reinforce each other. Or they may set up an interesting dynamic. If we are reading to ourselves, our eyes tell us when to pause, when to slow up, as surely as our ears do. A line may be not very noticeably irregular in rhythmical terms, yet stand out for its length or brevity.

Many of the features of poetry that we tend to label as '*sound-effects*' have a visual effect too. We hear rhymes, but we also see them. We see alliteration, and sometimes assonance. We see long words and short. When we see repetitions of words or phrases we are more aware of them as a pattern, momentarily freed of their immediate meaning. When a poet writes:

'From me, who have trapped mice and shot wild birds,
From me, who drowned your kittens, who betrayed
Your closest relatives'

we *hear* the repeated words as insistence, and that insistence carries an emotional charge, but when we first read them on the page, they say 'pattern' to us, they cry out 'balance' and beg us to weigh them against one another.

This all means that the look of the poem on the page is something which can usefully be talked about, and which contributes to the poem's meaning. Even where a poet's choice of form seems almost to have been dictated by the cultural climate in which he or she lived, the ways in which the different patterns in the poem cut across one another, reinforce one another, or interlock, are always worth studying and will always in the end bring us closer to understanding what a poem means.

Nowadays a poem can look more or less as it likes. Poets today can still choose formality (though we can argue about whether the old forms carry new, ironic meanings), or they can choose apparent informality. They may choose new and striking forms of their own. But they cannot – and surely would not want to – make their poems invisible. Irregular features make up just as memorable a face as regular ones. The superficial distinguishing marks on someone we love are in the end as intimately a part of that person as the way he or she speaks.

Exercise 2

Look at the following two poem-shapes. Then write down *quickly* and without too much self-criticism, all that each shape initially suggests to you. Any fleeting reaction, however superficial or illogical it may seem, will be interesting at this stage:-

Xxxx xxxxxxx xxxx xxx xxxxx xxxxx xx xxxxx xxxx,
Xxx xxx xx xxxx xxxxx xxxxxxxx xxx xxxxx?
Xx xxxxx xxxxx xxxxxxxx xx xxxxx xxxxxxx
Xxxx xx xxxxxxxxxxxx xxxx xxxxx xxxxxxxx

Xxxxxxx, xxxxxx, xxxxxxxx, xxxxxxxxxx xxxxxxxx,
Xx xxxxxxxxxx, x xxxx xxxx xxxxxxxxx xxxx xxxxx,
Xxxxx xx xx xxxxx xxxxxxx xxxxx xxxxx xx xxxxxxxx
Xxxxxxxxxx xxx xx xxxx xxxx xxxxx xxxxx.

Xxxxxxxx, xxxx xxxx xxxxxxx xx xxxxxxxxx,
Xxx xxxxx xxxxxxxxxx xxx xxxxxx xx xxxx xxxx,
X xxxxx xxxx xxxxxxx xxxxxx xxxxxx xxxx xxxxxx,

Xxx xxxxxx xxxx xxxxxxx, xxxxxxx xxx xxxxxx,
Xx xxxxx xx xxxxxx xxx xxxx xxxx xxxxxx xxxxx,
Xxxxxx; xx xxxxx xxxxxx, xx xxx xxxx xxxx xxxxxxxx.

Xx Xxxxxx Xxxxx Xxxxx xxxx xxx
                        x xxx xxx xxx xxxx xxxx xxxxx xxxxx
    xxxx xxx xxxxxxxx xxxxxx
                        xxxxx xxx xxx xxxxxx xx xxx xxxxx
Xx xxx xxxxxxx xxxxx xxxxxxxxxx
                        xxx xxxxxxxx xx xxx xxxxxx xxxxx
                                        xx xxx xxxx
    xxxxx xxx xxxx xxx x xxxxx xx xxxxxx
                        xxxxx xxx xxxx xxxxxx xxx
                                        xxxxxxxxxxxx
                        xx xxxxxxx xxxxxxxxx
                                        xx xx xxxx
                        xxxx x xxxxxx xxxx

—————— Exploring space ——————

One extreme strand of experiment with the way a poem can look is what
we usually refer to in English as concrete poetry. The concrete poet is
using space and the disposition of the words on the page so pictorially
that patterns of sound are obscured or even irrelevant. Often, it is
impossible even to read these poems aloud, though poets themselves
are sometimes highly inventive when it comes to translating these visual
patterns into the oral requirements of a live reading. The tendency
among most critics, poets and general readers is to regard the poem
which draws a visible picture as *gimmicky* and superficial. Of course, this
kind of verbal silhouette or fragmentation can only go so far, and may cut
a poem off from its other resources. Yet poems like these can remind us
of a visual dimension which is always present (except when a poem is

read *to* us) and which we may not usually be very aware of. Lewis Carroll in *Alice in Wonderland* and the French poet Guillaume Apollinaire, who was to have such an important influence on the development of Dada and Surrealism across Europe, both drew 'word-pictures' or *calligrammes*. The contemporary Scottish poet Edwin Morgan still uses a more discreet version of this kind of arrangement of words on the page in conjunction with other forms of word-play to suggest meanings quite as serious as those of more conventional poetry.

Exercise 3

Look at these two poem-shapes, and answer the questions:

```
            Xx xxxxxx xxx xx xxxxxx
            Xxxxxxxxxxx xx xxxxx
            Xx xxxxxx xxx xxxxxx
            Xxxx xxx xxxxxxxxxxxxxxx

              Xx xx xx
                       x
                       x
                       xx
                       xx
                       xxx
                        xxXXXX
                        XxXXXX

Xxx xxxxxx x xxx xx xxx xxxxxxxxx xxx xxxxxxxx
Xxx xxxxxxxx xxx xxxxxx xxx xxx xxxxx xxxxxxxxxx
Xxxx xx xxxxxxx xxxxx xxx xxxxxxx xxxxxxxxx
Xx xxxxxxx xxxxx xxxxxx xxx xxxxxx
Xx xxxx xxxx xxx xx xxxx xx xxxx xxx xxx xx xxxx
Xx xxxxxxx xxxxx xx xxxx xxxxxxx xxx xxxxxx
            Xx xxxxxxxx xxx xxxxxxx
            Xxxxx xxxxxxx x xxx xxxxx
            Xxx xxxxxxxxxxxxx xxxxxx
            Xxx xxxxxxxx xx xxxxxx
```

xxx xxxxxxxx xxxx xxxxxx xx xx xxxxxx
xxxxxx xx xx xxxxxx
xx xxxxxx
xxxx xx
xxx xxx xxxxxxxx
xxxx xx xxxxxx xx
xx xxx xxx xxxxxxxx xxxx xxx xxxxx xx

xxx xxxxxxxx xxxx xxx xxxxxx xx
xxxxxx xx xxx xxxxx
xxxxx xxxx
xxxx xx
xx xxxxx xxxxxxx
xxxxx xxxxxxx xxxx
xxxx xx xxxxx xxxxxxx xxxx x xxx xxxx

xxx xxxxxxxx xxxx xxxxxx xxxx x xxx xxxx
xxxxxx xxxx x xxx xxxx
xxx xxxx
xxxx xxxxx
xxxxx xx xxx xxxx
xx xxx xxxx xx xxx xxxxxxx
xx xxxxx xx xxx xxxx xx xxx xxxxxxx xxxxxx

Questions

(a) What do you think the first poem is about?

(b) If you were writing it, can you think of a good *alternative* subject for this word-picture? How would the shape of the poem on the page colour your subject?

(c) Can you think of an obviously unsuitable subject? Imagine that subject were in fact the subject of the poem. How would the reader react?

(d) Can you describe the shape of the second poem?

(e) Now look at the last poem printed correctly:

Vico's Song

the universe that turned in on itself
turned in on itself
on itself
self was
was the universe
that was turned in
it was the universe that was turned in

the universe that was turned in
turned in got seven
seven days
days it
it spent turning
spent turning over
days it spent turning over a new leaf

the universe that turned over a new leaf
turned over a new leaf
new leaf
leaf lived
lived in the arms
in the arms of the eternal
it lived in the arms of the eternal return

Edwin Morgan

How is the shape of the poem being used?

———————— **Hearing things** ————————

If the way a poem looks on the page has the power to arouse our
expectations of poetry and play on them in ways we may not even be fully
aware of, the sounds poems make are more powerful still. From its
origins, poetry has always been closely linked with songs, spells, prayers
– all forms which conjure up in us a state of heightened awareness by
their musical or almost musical patterns of language.

Even without being psychologists, we can easily understand that these repetitive, rhythmical patterns of sound can be deeply satisfying to us, at a level which may not even register in our everyday, utilitarian thinking. We knew what our mother said to us possibly four or five years before we could read words on the page. We heard her heartbeat before we saw anything of the world. Most of us heard songs and rhymes, and the formally repetitive stories of childhood, well before we ever met the word *poem*. Most of us begged for those rhymes and stories to be repeated, word for word, *ad nauseam*, for the deep sense of delight they gave us. In our adult lives, poetry is arguably the nearest we can come to this profound satisfaction in the heard patterns of language. Poetry is the closest literature can come to music. It can give us some of the sensuous delight music gives us. Our minds can delight in the patterns too. And woven into the pattern the sounds make is a pattern of meaning which stimulates us to see pattern and meaning in our own lives.

Patterns of sound in poetry, like other kinds of pattern-making, are based on our expectations. They reassure or surprise us. They remind us subliminally of rhythms we have heard in childhood, or, more obviously, of the rhythms of other poems we have been taught about at school or become acquainted with as young adults. They relate more or less obviously to the rhythms and echoes of our ordinary speech. Because they are using real words in a real language with its own peculiar vowels and consonants, intonation and stress, they are built on what that language is good at. In English, poetry tends to be strongly rhythmical, with lines built up of 'feet', each foot a cluster of one stressed and one or more unstressed syllables. In a language with weak or negligeable stress, the number or length of the syllables themselves might be more important. In a 'sing song' language where rising and falling tones of voice were attached to individual words, the actual 'music' of the spoken syllables would be a part of the pattern too.

We do not necessarily need to be able to attach labels to the patterns of sound in a poem in order to talk about them. It may be a helpful shorthand to say, when we are discussing a piece of poetry, 'This is written in iambic pentameter' or 'This is a sestina.' It is sometimes easier to do this than to describe it in less technical language. But the important thing is to recognise a regular pattern when it occurs, to notice variations in it, and to try to understand how it plays on our expectations to carry meaning. A line with a regular, easy-to-label rhythm may be made up of words which carry similar meanings to a line with a quite irregular, idiosyncratic rhythm, but the effect, and ultimately the meaning, will not be the same.

Much modern poetry still uses fairly conventional rhythms. As the language of poetry has become less and less 'flowery', those aspects of sound-patterning which are the patterns of our ordinary speech seem to become ever more necessary. They are at the same time authentic and satisfying to the ear. They may seem real to us in the same basic kind of way as heartbeats or waves breaking. They are not an obvious artifice like rhyme or alliteration. They can exert a subtle control over the pace at which we read without being too obviously 'poetic'.

But they also lull us. They are a background against which a poet can produce a surprise. Rhythms, like rules, are there to be broken – subtly or not so subtly – or at least to be bent.

Exercise 4

Read the following two pieces of poetry aloud to yourself several times. (The first is a complete poem, and the second is an extract from a longer poem.) Without distorting the way you read or losing sight of the fact that the words have meaning, try to be aware of where the stresses naturally fall, and what patterns the stressed and unstressed syllables are making.

What was Lost

I sing what was lost and dread what was won,
I walk in a battle fought over again,
My king a lost king, and lost soldiers my men;
Feet to the Rising and Setting may run,
They always beat on the same small stone.

W B Yeats

Simply, one must imagine what has been lost:
The light along the edge of the lake gone dark

As death, leftover leaves
Crumbled into mulch and ground

Underfoot, a cry
Like a bird's or a child's, imprinting the waxsoft sky

With its echo, mind with memory –
Lost, lost. One must imagine

What has been, what has been lost
Between the third line and the fifth

With its official *Recommandé*.
And night eats up the flowers of the day.

Kelly Cherry, 'Letter to a Censor'

Now try to answer the questions:

(a)   What is the most characteristic rhythmical group of syllables in each poem? Can you describe it?

(b)   How regular is the rhythm in the first poem?

(c)   Where and how does the rhythm in this poem change most noticeably?

(d)   Which parts of the first poem are *highlighted* by rhythm, and how does it add to their meaning?

(e)   Can you talk about the effects of rhythm in the second extract?

(f)   How might this closer study of rhythm add to a comparison of the two poems?

Echoes

It is still common, especially among older readers, to meet a great nostalgia for rhyming poetry. We are all familiar with the voice that says, 'I don't call this a poem. I want something that rhymes.' Sometimes, especially if we are not used to giving the right kind of attention to poetry, other patterns a poet has at her or his disposal can seem too easy, too immediate. We may still need a rich, musical effect of sound to convince us that our painful attention is really necessary.

If we recognise this kind of wistfulness in ourselves, it is chastening to be reminded that rhymed poetry represents only one strand – an important strand, admittedly – in the development of English verse. Chaucer uses rhyme, but the Milton of *Paradise Lost* does not. Shakespeare's sonnets rhyme, but the wonderful poetry of Shakespearian drama is almost all in blank verse – rhythmical, but depending for its sound-echoes on more subtle patterns than rhyme. Betjeman, Auden, Larkin use rhyme sometimes, but not invariably. T S Eliot used it intermittently, often to ironic effect. Many contemporary poets are exploring subtle variations on conventional rhyme and metre, but it is arguable whether the rhymes they use can carry the same meanings as similar rhymes would have done for their predecessors.

It is probably the great flowering of poetry connected with the development of Romanticism that was the most responsible for our tenacious love of rhyme. This is paradoxical, because in fact a significant volume of the poetry written by the Romantics is unrhymed. But when Keats or Wordsworth or Byron couples the use of rhyme with other riches, the cumulative effect can be extremely potent. In critical terms, the nineteenth century is still very close, in poetry as it is in the novel and in drama. To us in the late twentieth century it may still seem to represent a norm to react against. Romantic poetry is so visibly and audibly poetic, so obviously rich in appeal to our senses, that even a hundred and fifty years on, we can hardly ignore it, any more than we can ignore Ibsen or Tolstoy. But if we define poetry as something which delights our ears and inner eyes in this way, we may be tempted to overlook other perhaps equally important resources which the poet has at his or her disposal. There is no point in lamenting the lack of rhyme in a poem, any more than there is in lamenting its lumpy silhouette on the page, or its determinedly colloquial diction.

That being said, a study of rhyme, where rhyme is a major element in the poem, can be very rewarding. Even where the rhyme is perfectly regular and conforms to some recognised poetic form which is common currency, there is interest in looking to see how rhyme reinforces or even changes meaning. Sometimes, if the poet does not use rhyme very well, there can be interest in recognising exactly how and why a rhymed poem has failed.

Exercise 5

Find a piece of rhymed doggerel. Greetings cards and calendars are obvious sources. Force yourself to give it the attention you might give to a piece of serious poetry. Describe the rhymes and notice which words they fall on. Do they help or hinder the 'poem'? If they fail to create a genuine poetic response, how and why do they fail?

The usual way to talk about rhyme in a poem with a regular rhyme-scheme is by using letters of the alphabet. When the rhymed lines occur in pairs, we say a poem is written in rhyming couplets. Or we could describe the rhyme with letters: AABB, CCDD, EEFF, GGHH. But as always, what we must be careful *not* to do, is merely to describe the rhyme-scheme without saying what it is doing. If we can't think what it is doing, we would do better not to talk about it and look at the poem again.

A poet may rhyme stressed syllables, or a combination of stressed and unstressed syllables, and, whether we are aware of it or not, we cannot help reacting to them in slightly different ways. 'Stone' and 'bone' are quite distinct as sounds from 'pillow' and 'willow'. How that difference affects meaning is something which varies with each individual poem and each individual reader. The half-rhymes pioneered by Wilfred Owen have a different effect again, an effect full of unstated questions and ambiguities.

Exercise 6

Read each of the following extracts several times. Describe the pattern of rhyme in each as simply and briefly as you can. Make notes (a short paragraph for each extract should be enough) on the *effect* of those rhymes.

> Leave her alone,
> She is the Island's daughter.
> Sleek heads, dark heads
> Are risen from the water:
> Leave her the company
> Her songs have brought her.
>
> (from L A G Strong, 'The Seals')

> Lend him to stroke these blind, blunt bullet-leads
> Which long to nuzzle in the hearts of lads,
> Or give him cartridges of fine zinc teeth,
> Sharp with the sharpness of grief and death.
>
> (from Wilfred Owen, 'Arms and the Boy')

— **129** —

Learning Chinese

Bronze fallen chestnut leaves   dulled by rain
mice overheard suddenly flurry   dumb night again
unwritten letters books closed   screened faces fled
     cold journey to make   a cold bed

Libby Houston

Exercise 7

Effects not unlike those of rhyme can also be produced by patterns of alliteration and assonance. These may be coupled with rhyming lines, or with internal rhymes, to produce a tight web of sound. But a poet does not have to choose these woven sound-effects: he or she may well make a conscious decision not to underline his or her patterns of metaphor or juxtaposition with these very obviously artificial echoes.

Read these closely:

My aspens dear, whose airy cages quelled,
Quelled or quenched in leaves the leaping sun,
All felled, felled, are all felled;
   Of a fresh and following folded rank
         Not spared, not one
         That dandled a sandalled
    Shadow that swam or sank
On meadow and river and wind-wandering weed-winding bank.

(from Gerard Manley Hopkins, 'Binsey Poplars')

Aunt Emily

Squat, dark and sallow, my adopted aunt
who always rinsed her hair in vinegar
to keep its colour true to life as if
she had some reason to preserve herself,
has died innumerable deaths for my sake,
most recently this morning, in her sleep.

We'll never see her like again; she worked
her fingers to the bone. I blame myself,
though she was ancient. Still, it always hurts.
I'm sobbing even as I'm writing this
in readiness to phone and say I can't
turn up to lecture on Proust today (*Time Lost*).

This time I'll bury her in Aldershot.
People understand bereavement, I must
make arrangements for a decent send-off,
travel, choose the hymns, compose an epitaph.
'At Rest' sounds suspect. 'Merciful Release'?
(Sometimes they nose into such niceties.)

Condolences will drop onto the mat
in my absence if I get the details right.
You have to have them at your fingertips,
though in the end what really counts is just
that whiff of vinegar, Aunt Emily says.
She sits four-square, arms folded, catching breath.

Sylvia Kantaris

Questions

(a)   How would you describe the patterns of sound in the first extract?

(b)   Pick out three specific sound *features* and describe them as well as you can. What is the effect of each.

(c)   Why do you think the author of 'Aunt Emily' has opted against conventional rhyme and obvious sound patterns?

(d)   Has she opted *for* something else?

Commentary

Exercise 1

It seems to me quite difficult to imagine a poem with more patterns in it than this one. Even before we try to come to grips with the meanings expressed explicitly in the words and the sometimes difficult syntax, we can be aware of the patterns, and the way in which they reinforce or cut across one another.

The first and most obvious pattern is the poem's visible shape on the page. We have no need even to count the stanzas, the lines in the stanzas, the long lines and the short ones. Our eyes tell us immediately that there is a repeated typographical design here. Our eyes also alert us to the poem's development through something as simple and immediate as its punctuation. Almost before we read it, we register the question-marks, the hyphens of lines 6 and 7, the commas of the first two stanzas, the change of emphasis to semicolons in the third. Our eyes are drawn to line 22, the shortest line of the poem, with its full stop.

If we count stresses, we find a pattern there too. As we should expect, it tends to echo and reinforce the poem's pattern on the page. The rhyme cuts across both, linking long lines with shorter ones, balancing apparent contrasts – except at the end of each stanza, where line-length, rhythm and rhyme are all momentarily working towards some kind of resolution.

There are also sound-patterns operating on a smaller scale, and they are subtle. Think about the balance between the two halves of line 28: 'To warm the world, that's done in warming us'. Think how the two w-sounds of the first half and the repeated 'warm'/'warming' set us up to expect another w at the end of the line. 'Us' does not begin with a *w*. 'Us' is special, perhaps more special even than warmth and world.

Syntax has its patterns too. The poet uses imperatives repeatedly in the first two stanzas, and again at the end of the poem, addressing the sun directly in a way which is at first provocative and even humorous. But if we look at the later 'imperatives', we see that they are deceptive. 'Ask for those kings [. . .]/ And thou shalt hear' is an imperative which is beginning to turn into something else. 'Shine here to us and thou art everywhere' may strike us initially as a command, but it is really a conditional ('If thou shinest here to us, thou art everywhere'). Perhaps the most important conditional 'command' is the one which occurs at the centre of the poem:

'If her eyes have not blinded thine,
Look, and tomorrow late, tell me [. . .]'.

It is no accident that here the 'if' is explicit. Patterns which repeat imperfectly can be a way of focusing our attention on what is beginning to change.

There are patterns of inversion which we, with our present-day liking for *natural* speech rhythms, even in poetry, may find off-putting. We can argue about how far the strangeness of structures like: 'Love, all alike, no season knows' or 'Thy beams, so reverend, and strong/ Why shouldst thou think?' would have been invisible to contemporary readers. Nowadays we are quite simply unable not to react to it, and notice it, as we would notice a regular twist of cable in a piece of knitting.

Certain important words recur in the design. It is interesting, even before trying to analyse their meaning, to notice when and where. How many times does the word 'sun' occur, and where? What about the words 'love' or 'lover'? What about 'thou' and 'thy', and the other personal pronouns and possessive adjectives? The word 'all' occurs four times in the third stanza. Does it occur anywhere else in the poem?

The patterns of reference and imagery we can trace here take us even further in, towards the poem's meaning. At first we have calling, then seeing, then being. We have a social hierarchy of school-boys, apprentices, court-huntsmen, kings and princes. We are moving from a low-status world to one in which even the highest status is irrelevant. We are moving inwards from the window to the bed, from the exotic geography of spice-routes to the inner geography of two human beings in a room. The poem is in some ways like those word-games where you must get from 'GAUNT' to 'PSALM' in so many lines, changing only one letter at a time. Look at the first line of the poem. Look at its last line. See how far Donne has travelled, and how far we have come with him. Think how the space we have covered – perhaps the vastly different tones of the opening and closing lines are the best gauge of this – is making us feel the reality of this journey into an ever more intimate (smaller or larger?) space.

In my opinion this poem is inconceivable without its form. Any good poem is inconceivable without its form.

Exercise 2

The first poem is a regular Italian sonnet. It could be about anything. If it were a meditation on love, it would not be surprising. If it were a meditation on lumpy gravy it would be much more so, and inevitably come to us with a baggage of humorous expectation. Line 7 sticks out, and lines 3 and 8 are shorter than the rest. Can we stop our eyes from being drawn to those?

The second poem is fragmented. We are looking at something airy and spacious, with loose strands which may or may not be tied together. Perhaps we ourselves are following a thread from one side of the page to the other. Perhaps we are not sure, even from looking at it, whether we shall lose our way before reaching the end of the poem.

Exercise 3

(a)   All answers here are the 'right' answer. In fact, the actual poem is, on one level at least, about smoking in war-time. As soon as we know this, we start seeing a pipe, a peaked cap, an oustretched arm – or, alternatively, a larger pipe and a wisp of smoke rising to make a cloud.

(b)   The poem could be about people straggling between two separate places, or about water running from one level to another. It could be about anything. The shape would always have implications – about the water and the people, about the smaller place and the larger, asymmetrical place. The white spaces surrounding people or water, and the bite of space in the lower left-hand corner of the page, would always do *something* to qualify how we felt about the words themselves and their meaning.

(c)   It could be about butterflies, or dough-nuts, or the circularity of human experience. If it *were* about one of these, its shape would surely make it suspect and ironic, if not downright funny. We should be nonplussed, or we should laugh. Perhaps the whole idea of using space on the page so blatantly in a serious context is ironic and provocative in this way.

(d)   The second poem has a very definite shape which is repeated in each stanza. To me it looks like two arms reaching out on either side of an empty centre. You could see it as waves on the sand, or crescents.

(e)   With the words of stanza 1, it is surely this image of limbs reaching out round an empty centre which predominates. Then, as the pattern is repeated, we may begin to see waves receding and breaking one after the other. By the end, it may be the crescent shape which seems the most immediate. The words themselves have changed, causing us to look at the visual pattern each stanza makes in a new way. And the pattern is versatile enough to support all three meanings – and so underline the basic paradox of a repetition which engenders change, a change which is itself repetitive.

Exercise 4

(a)   In the first poem, the characteristic rhythmical group is made up of one stressed syllable and two unstressed syllables. Occasionally, the sense of one group runs into the next in such a way that the groups become continuous, and instead of the pattern of one unstressed syllable followed by one stressed syllable we hear at first we begin to feel a different pattern emerging – one stressed syllable followed by one unstressed syllable. Whether or not we can give technical names to these two rhythms does not matter. What matters is that we should be aware of the way in which the changing rhythms influence our reading of the poem.

In the second fragment, stressed and unstressed syllables tend to alternate. Sometimes a three-syllable group makes us register (consciously or unconsciously) a small extra something, an extra step in the dance, a suspicion that something has been quietly slipped in – or perhaps that something in the body of the poem has been suppressed.

(b)   It is not completely regular. It seems to me to be seriously *irregular* in three places.

(c)   I would say that the last line itself is where the change in rhythm is most noticeable. Reading it aloud, we almost stumble. We are forced suddenly, uncomfortably, to read more slowly.

(d)   The first line is different from the others, in that the *missed* syllable (between 'lost' and 'dread') creates a perfect balance between the two halves of the line. Try reading it as the more regular 'I sing what was lost and I dread what was won,' and ask yourself what difference the omitted syllable makes. Lines 4 and 5 are irregular at the beginning. 'Feet' at the beginning of line 4 is also 'highlighted'. But the last line is ambivalent from the point of view of rhythm in a way none of the others is. The pattern of the rest of the poem is asking for us to read it with four stresses. Yet the pattern is very definitely broken at the beginning of the line and by the time we reach the end we are able to read 'same small stone' in a different and more questionable way. 'Small' (is it stressed or unstressed?) becomes, simply through the patterns of rhythm established and broken in what has led up to it, the most important and ambiguous word in the poem.

(e) There are many things that could be said here. Look for instance at the way the particularly *regular* rhythm of line 4 works with the stanza break to give 'ground' a second meaning (which is destroyed as soon as we reach 'Underfoot' but not entirely erased.) Look how the two-syllable rhythm of lines 4 and 5 *open out* into the three-syllable rhythms of line 6. Look at the freak single repeated stress of 'Lost, lost' and ask yourself what it is doing. Look at line 9, and how 'been' is at first stressed, then unstressed (in 'been *lost*' (my italics)). Look at the way the irregular and uncertain patterns of line 11 are rendered down into the uncompromising two-syllable finality of line 12.

(f) Both poems are in a sense about loss. Their rhythms are one way into them. Look at them again closely and try to decide whether or not it would be far-fetched to see the Yeats poem as a poem which, even in its sound, gives us a sense of something missing, and the Kelly Cherry fragment as a part of a poem which gives us something and witholds something intermittently.

Exercise 5

Obviously, I am not in a position to talk about your chosen piece of doggerel! The questions and their answers may seem frivolous, but they can surely teach us something about how rhyme in modern poetry works when it works well. Some of the best of the rhymed poetry written now uses rhyme or half-rhyme so inconspicuously that it is possible to read the poem on the page (or even hear it) without being consciously aware that it is in rhyme. Underneath, though, we do notice. Something in us responds to the pattern we hear, and subtly adds to its meaning. If we are not aware of the background music in a film, can we assume that the director might just as well have left it out? Aren't we more likely to wish that when the music impinges on us *too much*?

Exercise 6

'The Seals': The second, fourth and sixth lines rhyme with one another. The result is repetitive, almost like a spell or incantation. No matter what the words actually mean, their sound is drugging us with a kind of magic. 'Arms and the Boy': The effects of half-rhyme, like those of full rhyme, vary with each poem. This poem is in rhyming couplets, but the half-rhymes Owen uses give us none of the comfortable, predictable resolution we normally expect of regular rhymes. When a composer introduces a faint suggestion of discord into a traditionally structured piece of music, we react to it very differently from a piece in which discords are 'normal'. Perhaps the effect here is to underline the meanings of the rhymed words and make us think twice about why they should be linked.

'Learning Chinese': Here again we have a variation on traditional rhyming couplets (AABBCC). The rhymes work together with the internal break in the lines to produce a question-and-answer effect. What we have is not *exactly* rhyming couplets, but a series of longer half-lines which do not rhyme, and a series of shorter half-lines which do. The line-length here is an important element, which works in conjunction with the rhyme to make us feel that something is finally and appropriately (if sadly) resolved. If the poet had written 'a cold empty bed' instead of 'a cold bed', the force of the rhyme and its final 'answer' would have been lost.

The whole effect of rhyme in the poem is to make us aware of the tight control. Rhyme here is perhaps standing in for an oriental poet's rigorous paring-down to essentials. This poem is not a haiku. Haiku are shorter and do not use rhyme. Yet something of the oriental flavour of haiku is present here, and it surely has as much to do with the way the poet has used rhyme as with the poem's title.

If you have found yourself intrigued by this exercise and by the *many* possible, serious and ironic, uses of rhyme, have a look at T S Eliot's 'The Love Song of J Alfred Prufrock': Pick a couple of rhyming lines and carry them round with you (in your head or on a scrap of paper) for a fortnight. How does the rhyme you have chosen contribute to *meaning*? Then go back and read the whole poem again.

Exercise 7

(a)   They are extraordinarily rich. The ABACB(A)CC end-rhymes are echoed by repetition – of whole words and of sounds – inside the lines. We could use words like 'lush' to describe them. We could see their tight internal patterns as representative of a kind of necessity surrounding the trees themselves.

The repetitions surely do give us the feeling of something's continuing, something's being perpetuated – when the words of the poem are apparently saying the opposite.

(b)   'All felled, felled, are all felled;' is a repeated lament, almost a bell tolling. The fact that this repetition takes up the sounds of 'quelled,/ Quelled or quenched' not only points up the ironies (the trees who were themselves so powerful have now been reduced to nothing) but also has the effect of *adding* the extra words 'quell' and 'quench' to the meaning of 'felled'.

The 'fresh and following folded rank' in line 4 uses alliteration to build coherence from words which are in fact very different both in meaning and in frame of reference. What are we seeing here – soldiers? laundry? Only the alliteration can make us feel the vision *does* momentarily hold together, *does* add up to a fragile kind of meaning with its strange separate touches of colour.

The 'dandled a sandalled/ Shadow' in lines 6 and 7 is using internal rhyme to give substance to a new and elusive element: at the centre of this section there is an invisible child who claims our attention.

(c)   She has determinedly chosen the idiom of contemporary speech, complete with asides and clichés. I think she has done it because it is our unemphatic, unrhetorical language which, at its best, allows real emotion to surface. She is playing death down rather than building it up, because building it up doesn't work. Just as Aunt Emily's death is the last and smallest in the first stanza, death is sufficiently important to be tossed off casually after the more interesting business of living. There is a real presence here, and real emotion, in the discipline of ordinary words.

Yet if we look closely at the end-words of each line, we can see that she has in fact opted for the suggestion of a pattern of assonance: if you look at the poem in couplets, you will find a shared sound in each (except in stanza 2, where the pattern changes briefly to alternate lines).

The poet has opted for the faintest whiff of something tart and vaguely unsatisfactory, a poetic *vinegar* which leaves us wondering about the peculiar mixture of guilt, grief and self-preservation it triggers, in the poet and in the reader. This is a *tart* poem, not only in tone and language, but even in the patterns of sound it half-makes.

6
—— THE IMAGE ——

—————— Match-making ——————

The speciality of poetry is to bring together things drawn from different orders of experience. Whether the poet is comparing love and death, or a bus ticket with a potato, a good poem will make us look at both or all of its terms in a different light. Love will never be innocuous again; the potato will show us something about the way we travel, and the bus-ticket will somehow nourish us, even as it makes us laugh.

In many ways a poem is like a marriage. There are no perfect marriages. If there were we should not be able to tell where the bride began and the groom ended in wedding photographs. Yet in poetry we do sometimes have the feeling that a comparison – explicit or implicit – is 'made in heaven'. The poet is not simply pulling together two elements because they have certain readily defined qualities in common; the comparison genuinely reveals a shared centre which we recognise, even though we have not been fully aware of it until now. When this happens in a poem, the feeling the linking brings us is one of necessity: the poem is like that because it has to be like that. Although we have never seen it before, a bus-ticket really *is* a potato. Show your potato to the ticket-inspector and you will find you can travel to unexpected places.

The best comparisons in poetry are probably, at first sight, unlikely relationships. If two things are too obviously comparable, we shall have heard them compared so often in our ordinary lives that we shall probably not react to the comparison at all. 'How is Tom getting on at school?' we might ask a friend. 'Oh, fine. He's really blossoming,' the friend might tell us. We waste no time imagining Tom with opening petals. We cut straight through to the *real* meaning. Our ordinary speech is full of *dead* metaphors and similes of this kind. If the poet is to make us look again at our world, he or she must begin by uniting two apparent strangers, or at least by uniting old friends in a way which makes us aware of their very real differences.

Comparisons in poetry can take enormously different forms. They may be decorative, or they may be genuinely revealing. They may be small, bright touches on a more sober background, or they may provide the whole structure of a poem. They may use the words 'like', or 'as' or 'as if' as pointers, or they may use nothing so obvious. Increasingly with contemporary poetry it has become difficult to label the two elements which are being compared. Often the reader is left with the suspicion that a metaphor has been blown up and explored so completely that the first term of the comparison is almost lost. Here there is no 'like' or 'as' to help us. There is not really even anything we can point to as a metaphor. Yet we still have the feeling that the poet is talking about more than the subject he or she seems to be giving us. Metaphor has become so intimately connected with the poet's conception of what a poem is that it has become almost a starting-point, not just for the poet him- or herself, but also for the reader. The poet may give us very few clear signposts, yet we find ourselves still looking for 'extra' meanings. The distinction between metaphor and symbol was always a tricky one. With the development of modern poetry and its ever more concealed metaphors, that distinction often becomes impossible. But a symbol, like a metaphor, still has its root in language. If we come back to the words themselves and the way they are used, we shall not find ourselves drifting off into conjecture. If the trail of honey across the poet's kitchen table is standing for something larger, there will be something in her language to tell us so. We are not asked to invent the poem, only to read it with humility and see what it contains.

Exercise 1

Look at the following examples of different kinds of comparison, taken from very different poems. Read each one carefully several times, and then answer the questions which follow.

>   As when the potent rod
> of Amram's Son in Egypt's evil day
> wav'd round the Coast, upcall'd a pitchy cloud
> Of Locusts, warping on the Eastern Wind,
> That o'er the Realm of impious Pharoah hung
> Like Night, and darken'd all the land of Nile:
> So numberless were those bad Angels seen
> Hovering on wing under the Cope of Hell
> 'Twixt upper, nether, and surrounding fires;

(Milton, *Paradise Lose*)

> The eggplants have pins and needles.
> Long dreams have plagued their sleep.
> By the redbrick garden wall
> Cucumbers droop like whips.
> The poppylamps blow out in the wind.
> Petals flock and settle
> Like coloured reflections.
> The sun, like sea-drowned amber, peers
> Through a dense silt of cloud.
> But nettles go on being nettles
> And roosters go on being roosters.

(Novella Matveyeva, 'The Eggplants have Pins and Needles')

Break

> We put the puzzle together piece
> by piece, loving how one curved
> notch fits so sweetly with another.
> A yellow smudge becomes
> the brush of a broom, and two blue arms
> fill in the last of the sky.

We patch together porch swings and autumn
trees, matching gold to gold. We hold
the eyes of deer in our palms, a pair
of brown shoes. We do this as the child
circles her room, impatient
with her blossoming, tired
of the neat house, the made bed,
the good food. We let her brood
as we shuffle through the pieces,
setting each one into place with a satisfied
tap, our backs turned for a few hours
to a world that is crumbling, a sky
that is falling, the pieces
we are required to return to.

Dorianne Laux

Questions

(a)   Who or what is being compared to what in the first extract?

(b)   List the comparisons in the second extract. Can you say what is being compared to what in each case? Does the form the comparison takes vary?

(c)   What is the force of the last two lines of the Matveyeva extract?

(d)   What is being compared to what in 'Break'?

(e)   What are the mechanics of the comparison?

(f)   Which of the two terms of the comparison is the more haunting?

(g)   Which do you think is more important to the poet herself?

(h)   Can you say why?

Simile

Most of us, if we have studied literature at all, can recognise a simile and a metaphor, and already know the difference between them. At school we have probably been taught that a simile draws a comparison explicitly by using words like 'like' or 'as'. With metaphor, the mechanics are less clear-cut.

The tendency of most contemporary poetry has been to swing further and further away from simile and explore the subtle effects open to metaphor. At the time when C Day Lewis wrote his influential book, *The Poetic Image* (first published in 1947), it began to seem as if poetry almost *was* metaphor. The conventional view of simile is as a figure of speech which is rather like metaphor, in that it does manage to draw comparisons, but as metaphor's poor cousin, in that it is inevitably rather pedestrian: it has to spell out to us what is like what, instead of deftly circling the ostensible subject of a poem with a ring of suggestive fire.

But many poets, especially in America, are making us rediscover the real richness of simile. Winifred Nowottny was already aware of this in her wonderfully intelligent book, published in the 1960s, *The Language Poets Use*:

> 'Suggestion [. . .] is one potentiality of metaphor. It may, however, well be true that suggestion is usually better done by simile. Simile (when simple) does not indicate the respect in which one thing is like another thing. It says the things are alike; it is up to us to see why; the things may be alike in a number of ways. Thus simile in turn has its own advantages. It may be a considerable advantage to the poet to claim that likeness exists without indicating where it lies.'

Far from closing down possibilities of suggestion, the best similes function as the very opposite of metaphor: they are not a bit coy about what is like what, but they may not tell us why. The Chambers Twentieth Century Dictionary definition of simile is 'an explicit likening of one thing to another.' The poet may say that a sunset is like blood or that his or her state of mind is like the state of mind of someone who has drunk poison. But the form the likeness takes may be less expected. Because we are not asked to puzzle out *what* is like *what*, our attention is freed to concentrate on the *why* – and perhaps to work out and balance our different and even conflicting versions of the *why*. Similes can call on us to flesh out the comparison with our own experience in a way a metaphor rarely does. (So A is like B. How and why is A like B? What do I know of A and B?) A strong simile at the end of a poem can close a poem without closing it, exploding into the territory of our own complicated emotions.

Exercise 2

Look at the following two examples. The first is an extract from a poem.
(It is the last stanza of a five-stanza poem.) The other is a whole poem.

> The sky leans on me, me, the one upright
> Among all horizontals.
> The grass is beating its head distractedly.
> It is too delicate
> For a life in such company;
> Darkness terrifies it.
> Now, in valleys narrow
> And black as purses, the house lights
> Gleam like small change.

> (Sylvia Plath, 'Wuthering Heights')

Where I Came From

My father put me in my mother
but he didn't pick me out.
I am my own quick woman.
What drew him to my mother?
Beating his drumsticks
he thought – why not?
And he gave her an umbrella.
Their marriage was like that.
She hid ironically in her apron.
Sometimes she cried into the biscuit dough.
When she wanted to make a point
she would sing a hymn or an old song.
He was loose-footed. He couldn't be counted on
until his pockets were empty.
When he was home the kettle drums,
the snare drum, the celeste,
the triangle throbbed.
While he changed their heads,
the drum skins soaked in the bathtub.
Collapsed and wrinkled, they floated
like huge used condoms.

Ruth Stone

Questions

(a)   How many metaphors can you find in the Sylvia Plath extract?

(b)   How many similes are there?

(c)   Which come first, the metaphors or the similes?

(d)   Can you suggest why?

(e)   Compare the effect of the final simile in the first extract to that of the last two lines of the Ruth Stone poem.

——— Metaphor ———

Metaphor is perhaps still the poet's greatest freedom. If the business of poetry is to see and to make us see that two or more superficially very different things are in fact intimately alike, then metaphor gives the poet the most versatile means of doing it. Occasionally we are, quite simply, told that one thing *is* something else (which, on a purely literal level, it obviously is not.) More often we are not 'told' anything. It is left up to the different usages of the descriptive words to imply that two separate things are at some level the same. A vapour-trail cuts the sky. Knives cut. So a vapour-trail is like a knife. Grammatically, metaphors may take almost any form – a verb, an adjective, an adverb, a prepositional phrase – and create effects as various as the words themselves. There are sustained metaphors, metaphors which set up a series of echoes, provocatively mixed metaphors, metaphors within metaphors. Once the poet decides to suppress the explicit linking words and make other words take over that function, the scope is seemingly unlimited.

Nathalie Goldberg, in her generous and inspiring book, *Writing Down the Bones*, captures something of the sheer energy of metaphor when she says, 'We can step through moons right into bears.' Perhaps in our real lives we do perpetually step through moons right into bears. Perhaps a kind of comparison flexible enough to say this in dramatic, surprising ways will actually help us not only to express what we feel to be the truth, but even, initially, to *see* that it is true:

'We are all connected. Metaphor knows this and therefore is religious. There is no separation between ants and elephants. All boundaries disappear, as though we were looking through rain or squinting our eyes at city lights.'

Here, of course, the power of metaphor is seen primarily from the point of view of the writer. But from the reader's point of view, the function of the comparison may not be very different. The very mechanics of metaphor force us to integrate the two terms of the comparison more completely than we would tend to do for a simile. If it is to make any sense to us, we are forced to see one object in terms of another, even as we first read it. We probably experience it immediately with a mixture of surprise, discomfort and delight in varying proportions. Sometimes the metaphor will seem lovely and decorative. Sometimes it will seem, quite simply, inappropriate. But in the best poetry we jump the gaps metaphor opens up in front of us with a kind of recognition: as we make the leap the gap itself seems to grow smaller.

Exercise 3

Look at the following metaphors taken from poems (or, in one case, a play) which are enormously different in length and context. Then answer the questions.

>   – Come, seeling night,
> Scarf up the eye of pitiful day;
> And with thy bloody and invisible hand
> Cancel and tear to pieces that great bond
> Which keeps me pale! – Light thickens; and the crow
> Makes wing to th'rooky wood:
> Good things of day begin to droop and drowse;
> Whiles night's black agents to their preys do rouse. –

>   (Shakespeare, *Macbeth*)

>   I thought of wedding presents,
>   white tea things
>
>   grouped on a dresser,
>   as we entered the cloud

and were nowhere –
a bride in a veil, laughing

at the sense of event, only
half afraid of an empty house

with its curtains boiling
from the bedroom window.

(Craig Raine, 'Flying to Belfast', 1977)

The weightless mosquito touches
her tiny shadow on the stone,
and with how like, how infinite
a lightness, man and shadow meet.
They fuse. A shadow is a man
when the mosquito death approaches.

(Keith Douglas, 'How to Kill')

Questions

(a)   What is the force of the metaphors in the first extract?

(b)   How many metaphors can you find in the Craig Raine extract?

(c)   Which of them leaves the most powerful impression?

(d)   Look at the last extract. There is a simile here, followed by a metaphor. Which is the stronger? Can you explain why?

Exercise 4

Study the following two poems as attentively as you can – if possible, over a period of time. It may take a few days for the images in the poems to take on their full resonance. Then choose one of the poems and write as much as you can about any metaphors you can find in it and the way in which they lead the reader in towards the poem's meaning.

Love in a New Language

She is upstairs learning the language.
He must pause on the landing, give her time.
They have come through borders,
by accident saying the right thing, hitching
over danger, walking along motorways;
soon they will breakfast on the *Terasse*
be again rich without money.
Nearing the fourth floor, little flag
of achievement ready, he discounts
others who gained high ground before him
returning without fanfare: a trick
to limit custom to the regulars.
The pack on his back shifts, settles
on a too-recent bruise of caution:
she will prove a slow learner, halting him
on the stairs for years, decades. That
little joke they will share
when she has showered, and donned the language.

Then, with a slip of the tongue, she will unbuckle him.

E A Markham

The Drowned Children

You see, they have no judgement.
So it is natural that they should drown,
first the ice taking them in
and then, all winter, their wool scarves
floating behind them as they sink
until at last they are quiet.
And the pond lifts them in its manifold dark arms.

But death must come to them differently,
so close to the beginning.
As though they had always been
blind and weightless. Therefore
the rest is dreamed, the lamp,
the good white cloth that covered the table,
their bodies.

And yet they hear the names they used
like lures slipping over the pond:
What are you waiting for
come home, come home, lost
in the waters, blue and permanent.

(Louise Glück from *Descending Figure*)

When you have finished, read your chosen poem again. Is it clearer now, or is it less clear? Is it richer? Go back and read the other poem once more.

How far did your choice of poem here depend on the images you saw in it? Are the images in the other poem achieving an effect which is similar, or are they doing something quite different?

Metaphor as pattern

Sometimes a poem does not have to be based on a single extended metaphor for its images to form a pattern. The pattern may not be immediately obvious. It may strike us quite suddenly near the end of the poem and then work retrospectively on *all* the images and other relationships the poem sets up. From being something we perceive as decorative, the metaphor has grown to become the real backbone of the poem. The poem develops as the metaphor develops. The poem moves us and asks us implicit questions and suggests answers as the pattern gradually becomes comprehensible.

Exercise 5

Study the following poem and answer the questions:

The Moment

When I saw the dark Egyptian stain,
I went down into the house to find you, Mother —
past the grandfather clock, with its huge
ochre moon, past the burnt
sienna woodwork, rubbed and glazed.

I went deeper and deeper down into the
body of house, down below the
level of the earth. It must have been
the maid's day off, for I found you there
where I had never found you, by the wash tubs,
your hands thrust deep in soapy water,
and above your head, the blazing windows
at the surface of the ground.
You looked up from the iron sink,
a small haggard pretty woman
of 40, one week divorced.
'I've got my period, Mom,' I said,
and saw your face abruptly break open and
glow with joy. 'Baby,' you said,
coming towards me, hands out and
covered with tiny delicate bubbles like seeds.

Sharon Olds

Questions

(a) How do you react to the simile in line 21: How unexpected is it?

(b) How many other images can you find in the poem which prepare us for this one, and reinforce it when we go back and read it again?

(c) Which of the other words or pictures the poem gives us are contributions to the effect of this final comparison?

(d) Pick out one of them and say how it works.

Jumping the gap

It was the Surrealists, with their conception of metaphor as exploration, who probably did most to give us our modern view of metaphor in poetry. Sometimes the creative mind would free itself from all the baggage of convention and rationalisation, and when it did the images and comparisons it produced were genuinely astonishing – as astonishingly vivid and memorable as dream-images or the visions of childhood. They were also truthful: they revealed what the ordinariness of life habitually kept hidden and comfortable. The freer the poetic imagination, the more likely it was to come up with images which would show us the real nature of reality. If we can step right through moons into bears, it may be because moons and bears do actually exist in some deep truthful place together.

The very strangeness of a metaphor may work in the same way as some of the *games* with language that we looked at in **Chapter 7**. A 'far-fetched' comparison may actually prevent us from reading a poem with the ordinary, rational tools we use to interpret prose. We may be expected to let our minds play round the incongruous conjunction of two very unlikely things, and if we can do that without feeling threatened we may indeed come from the poem with something like a kind of truth.

Exercise 6

Look at the following poem:

Do You Remember

Do you remember the sweet scent of plantains
How strange familiar things can be after a departure
The dreariness of food
A dismal bed
And the cats
Do you recall the cats with shrill claws
Shrieking on the roof as your tongue explored me
And arching their backs as your nails scored me
They vibrated when I yielded
I have forgotten how to love
The doleful bubbles of delirium have vanished from my lips
I have abandoned my mask of leaves
A rose-bush is dying under the bed
I no longer sway my hips among the rubble
The cats have deserted the roof

Joyce Mansour (translated by Sylvia Kantaris)

———— Falling through the hole ————

In some of the very best and most emotive of twentieth-century poetry, the reader is somehow given the conviction that the poem is based on an extended metaphor, yet without being at all sure what that metaphor is. What we are being given is being compared to something else, but the something else is left half-hidden. Perhaps there *is* no something else which can be coherently fitted together. There is still metaphor in the air, but it is a metaphor which has no obvious other term: the poet's whole house smells subtly of curry and we sniff at it in appreciation, but when we go to the stove there is nothing there, or perhaps only the barest suggestion of spices spilled yesterday.

Yet the smell must be there, or we wouldn't smell it: somewhere in the words of the poem there are words or connotations of words which help lead us through to the possibility of a second level of meaning. Very often it is a metaphor, with its sudden by-passing of our expected channels of reasoning, which does this. We have to be careful not to block out what strikes us as incongruous in the poems we read. Very often it is the incongruous *detail* that can help us find the key to the poem's meaning.

Let's look back at the Ted Hughes poem we quoted already on page 107, 'An Otter'. You may have chosen to look closely at this poem, or you may have chosen one of the others. But even if you chose it, you may well have talked quite extensively about the 'otteriness' of the description, without ever mentioning its incongruities. If you look closely again, you will see there are all sorts of words and images here which cannot literally be applied to an otter's perception of its world, and barely even to a man's perception of an otter's world. The otter *is* – miraculously – as man sees him, and yet also as man sees himself. The 'holes of lakes' are holes to us even more than to him. The mystery of his transitions becomes the myth of our own. The pain and isolation of his world become the pain and isolation of ours.

If we have escaped the incongruities, the human time-agony that underlies the whole poem, we surely cannot ignore its ending. The word 'walloping' can leave us in no doubt. With the arrival of the milk wagon, the human world bursts in ironically on the only half-human landscape of lines 17 to 19. The poet is suddenly omni-present in his poem, and sleepless. Now we can hardly go back and re-read the poem without being aware of his presence. Yet because the metaphor is unstated it is still open, questioning, pointing even deeper inwards. And, miraculously, the otter still *is an otter*, 'outfishing' us even as we begin to think we understand him!

Exercise 7

Read the following poem several times and write down in a single sentence what you think it is about. Then answer the questions.

Mushrooms

Overnight, very
Whitely, discreetly,
Very quietly

Our toes, our noses
Take hold on the loam,
Acquire the air.

Nobody sees us,
Stops us, betrays us;
The small grains make room.

Soft fists insist on
Heaving the needles,
The leafy bedding,

Even the paving.
Our hammers, our rams,
Earless and eyeless,

Perfectly voiceless,
Widen the crannies,
Shoulder through holes. We

Diet on water,
On crumbs of shadow,
Bland-mannered, asking

Little or nothing.
So many of us!
So many of us!

We are shelves, we are
Tables, we are meek,
We are edible,

Nudgers and shovers
In spite of ourselves.
Our kind multiplies:

We shall by morning
Inherit the earth.
Our foot's in the door.

Sylvia Plath

Questions

(a)　What is the subject of the poem?

(b)　List the metaphors you can find in it.

(c)　Do any of the metaphors seem to fit together to suggest a wider interpretation?

(d)　Do any of them conflict, colouring that interpretation?

(e)　How far are the mushrooms still '*just*' mushrooms?

(f)　Drawing on the whole poem – its shape and sound as well as its images – write as much as you can about its meaning.

—— Is there life after metaphor? ——

Is it possible for a poet to ignore the riches of metaphor and yet still write poems which move us? Is it possible to make the reader feel that there is more at stake without needing to fall back on comparisons? Can metaphors be so subtle that they only haunt a poem without ever really existing grammatically? Are there other devices to link different realms of experience and so take the place of metaphor?

Many contemporary poets seem at times almost to have turned their backs on the conventional poetic use of imagery. Their language seems straightforward and even colloquial. It sometimes has a starkness which impresses us by the very fact that it does *not* seem in the slightest lyrical or 'poetic'. Then even metaphors begin to look suspect. Perhaps 'poetry' itself begins to seem a little bit romantic and embarrassing.

Yet if we look closely, very few modern poems are in fact without metaphor entirely. Where it is used sparingly, its effects are often all the more powerful.

Exercise 8

Metaphor and simile are not the only ways of making comparisons. Sometimes, in a taut poem, the simple fact that two things are mentioned together is enough to make each of them reflect something of the colour of the other.

Search for poems without a single overt comparison. You will be surprised how few contemporary poems you find. When you do find one, ask yourself if anything else in the poem is taking on the job of linking two different registers of human experience. Are there different voices in it? Are there incongruous juxtapositions? Are there traces of a historical or fictional persona which might comment obliquely on the time and state of mind from which the poem was written?

The aim of the exercises in this chapter – and also of those in the two chapters that went before – has been to encourage you to see metaphor and its relations as part of the close meaningful pattern within a poem. In our century, metaphor has come to be the dominant pattern. In other centuries, other, more obviously formal relationships have often predominated. In the next century, the emphasis will be different again.

But what continues to be special about the language of poetry is that the words invariably mean *more than once*, and in the best poetry, the whole meaning that eventually comes to us is more than just a sum of its parts. If you can relate the different ways in which a new poem speaks to you, you are already halfway to understanding what the poem is 'saying'. And what it is 'saying' can always be discussed more meaningfully by looking closely at the patterns it makes and how they act and react on one another, than by trying to paraphrase what the poet is 'trying to express'. If the poet had been 'trying to express' something which could have been expressed quite simply without making a formal pattern with words, he or she would probably not have written a poem at all.

———————— **Commentary** ————————

Exercise 1

(a)   The fallen angels are being compared to the swarm of locusts called up by Moses over Egypt.

(b)   The eggplants are being compared to limbs which have 'gone to sleep', and then to sleeping people, perhaps even to sick people ('plagued'). Cucumbers are compared to inert whips. Poppies are compared to extinguished lamps. Petals are compared to birds or insects reflected in water (although the explicit comparison is to *reflections*, and the further metaphor is only implicit in the word 'settle'. The sun, in a double comparison, is amber under the sea in a simile and at the same time an eye in the metaphor of the verb 'peers'. The metaphor which links cloud to silt reinforces the original under-water simile. In these nine short lines, it is possible to count as many as ten comparisons.

(c)   After such a firework display of metaphor and simile, lines 10 and 11 bring us up short. We are not called upon simply to embrace the poet's metaphorical vision, but to think about what metaphor itself means. The comparions are rich, mixed, colourful, vividly visual – and all in some way tinged with destruction. The nettles and the roosters somehow 'survive' to be themselves. Nettles sting. Roosters are intrusive and raucous. Yet we are still seeing them exactly as they are. In spite of the pain implicit in all the images and in the idea of the nettles, there is something here which lives as itself, quite simply – something tenacious which meets another day.

(d)   The jigsaw puzzle is compared to the fragmentation of our ordinary lives, and by extension to the adolescent girl's growing perception of it. It is a kind of inverse comparison: the jigsaw is a jumble which is being carefully pieced together, while 'the neat house, the made bed,/ the good food' are already in a sense complete, but always threatening to crumble. The final twist of the comparison brings them together again, as the perpetually disintegrating puzzle that is life is seen as something we have to go on working on, to put together over and over again.

(e)   In lines 3–6, we are already prepared for the metaphorical meaning of the jigsaw. The word 'sweetly' in line 3 is unexpected and allows us to glimpse a more serious kind of emotion than the excitement of doing jigsaws. 'Becomes' in line 4 makes us think that perhaps an actual transformation is taking place. The subsidiary metaphor of 'two blue arms' opens up into the suggestion of something human, of two arms reaching, the expanse of blue that is our real sky, perhaps the coldness of the act of reaching. Lines 7–10 seem to me to be the centre of the metaphor. 'We patch together porch swings' is indistinguishable from the real, ordinary, repeated human actions of mending real broken porch swings for a family which breaks them, season after season. The deer's eyes become real deer's eyes. The shoes are suddenly real shoes. Only the little, hackneyed, inconspicuous metaphor of the young girl's 'blossoming' in line 12 is in opposition to this blue and gold autumn which is in pieces. At the end of the poem, the metaphor is finally made clear: the jigsaw is reassuring and manageable; it is the real world that is in pieces – 'the pieces/ we are required to return to.'

The title is important too. By suggesting not only the 'break' in the puzzle and the breaking of life itself, but also a break between the perceptions and emotions of the different generations in one family, it gives the basic metaphor yet another dimension.

(f)   The answer to this must be subjective, but for me it is the jigsaw itself with the 'eyes of deer in our palms, a pair/ of brown shoes.' The miracle of metaphor is that the jigsaw *does* still exist as something quite humble, that we have all probably done, perhaps even in circumstances similar to these, and yet it is also more than itself. The jigsaw has *become* something more than itself, and has the power to move us.

(g)   This is of course an impossible question to answer, but nevertheless a question which deserves to be thought about.

(h)   There is considerable pain, it seems to me, in the cold, almost official word 'required' in the last line, which gives us an intuitive glimpse of the life that she is not describing directly.

Exercise 2

(a)   Grammatically, there are at least four metaphors, though the last three (lines 3–6) could all be seen as a single more extended metaphor, since they all contribute in their separate ways to what we might describe as a kind of personification of the grass, or a projection of a part of the poet's own emotions on to the grass.

(b) Grammatically, there are two ('black as purses'; 'Gleam like small change') but again they fit readily together into a single picture.

(c) The metaphors come first. It is the final complex simile which ends the poem.

(d) It seems to me that the poet is moving out into even greater ambiguity. If we try, we can begin to analyse why the grass is humanised, what qualities it is which link it to the poet's own standing figure and the complex emotions which surround her. But the images are becoming ever more cryptic. It is as if the poet's desires are somehow split between the *vertical* world and the *horizontal* one. The darkness is terrifying, and yet the dark valleys hold something. In the end 'like small change' is an open image which throws us back on ourselves. It seems obvious. Visually it compels us. Yet the 'small change' is inscrutable – attractive and yet disappointing. The whole poem is building towards this marvellous, exasperating image. A metaphor here would have destroyed the poem, by half telling us what we should *do* with the change. As it is we can only keep looking at it and wondering.

(e) The way the two similes are used here is similar, though poem b). is perhaps easier to talk about. We are told the drum skins floated 'like huge used condoms'. We are not told *how* they were like condoms. Obviously the picture here is a visual – and even humorous – one. Yet an uneasiness remains. The simile somehow also holds the suggestion of a comment on this marriage as a whole, on the quality of its sexual relationship with its hint of betrayal, and on the face it turned towards the adolescent daughter growing up inside it. This simile is also ambivalent, but not as enigmatic as Sylvia Plath's. Again, because it is in a position of prominance at the very end of the poem, it works retrospectively to make us question and reassess everything that has gone before.

Exercise 3

(a) These metaphors 'describe' the transition from day to night. Yet their violence is less a reflection on the night itself than on Macbeth's state of mind. As night falls and action comes closer, the metaphors fade. (The transition is marked by rhyme.) The metaphorical language here is contained within and justified by Shakespeare's whole conception of his principal character.

(b)   There is certainly at least one ('curtains boiling/ from the bedroom window.') 'Were nowhere' could also be seen as a kind of metaphor: it is at least obviously untrue on a literal level. The punctuation at the end of this line creates ambiguity at the end of the poem. The bride in the veil could be one of the things the poet was thinking of – a continuation of the train of thought he began with the wedding presents. But the dash makes us see her also as somehow part of the nowhere we are lost in. Our common sense tells us that she is part of what the poet is flying towards, but as we read the poem she is also the cloud, the sense of strained expectation, the suspension of being the poet feels as he flies over Northern Ireland. The final metaphor is a reflection of the state of mind of a bride, perhaps. But it is surely also a metaphor for Belfast itself.

(c)   It is this last unmistakable metaphor which leaves the most power-ful impression. If you turn to the poem and read it from the beginning, you will find that this metaphor is linked with the poem's first two-line stanza by another 'boiling' image. What is boiling here is something larger than a bride's curtains.

(d)   This is partly a matter of personal taste. The simile is vivid and easy to grasp; the metaphor is much more abstract. I would say that the force of both comes from the transition from one to the other. Man, shadow, mosquito and shadow are interwoven. The two pairs are linked in something like a kind of dance. The shock of the end is that the mosquito's shadow-partner has revealed his true identity. The literal meaning ('man is a shadow') is not half as powerful as this sudden unexpected conjunction of mosquito and death at the end of the poem.

Exercise 4

I do not propose to give my own account of the functioning of metaphor in these two poems. The comments on the exercises which you have done already should be detailed enough for you to be your own critic by now! It seems to me, though, that neither of these poems would – or should – ultimately become *clear*. If we have managed by line 18 to give a reasoned meaning to the extended metaphor in the first poem, the last line may well 'unbuckle' us, as it does 'him'. In the second poem, the last line, with its faint suggestion of ink on the page, is equally, or more, unfathomable. Nevertheless, the two poems are very different, the first using the strange conjunctions of real life to suggest a metaphor, and the second using the conjectural world of metaphor to cast doubt on the poet's own claim on life. The second poem seems to me to be haunting in a way few poems can be. There is the basic, implicit comparison – between the children's drowning and the poet's emotional drowning, between their death and hers – and there are the smaller, easier to pin down, comparisons, the 'manifold dark arms' and the 'lures slipping over the pond'. Perhaps these smaller images are the key to the larger one?

Exercise 5

(a)   We probably all react differently. For me, this final image is unexpected, and yet has a peculiar rightness about it. The interesting thing is that both the surprise and the appropriateness of this final simile can be accounted for in the development of metaphor in the poem as a whole.

(b)   There are obvious metaphors in the poem: the 'Egyptian stain' in line 1, the 'ochre moon' of the clock-face in line 4, the 'body of the house' in line 7, and the 'saw your face abruptly break open' in line 18. They set up a complex pattern of metaphor (excavation and burial, the body as earth) which at the same time prepares us for the seed image and makes the continuation of life a kind of miracle.

(c)   The colours, which are not the colours of life, but of ancient pigments ('ochre', 'burnt/ sienna woodwork') and the vision of the house as a deep, buried place ('deeper and deeper down', 'below the/ level of the earth', 'thrust deep', 'the surface of the ground') all contribute to the 'Egyptian' metaphor. We are excavating this house and expect to find death. We do, in a sense, find a kind of death in the 'small haggard pretty woman/ of 40, one week divorced.' But we also find joy and the possibility of new growth. The earth we had thought of as a tomb 'break[s] open' and retrospectively all the words which had reinforced the idea of burial become words about earth covering a handful of seeds.

(d)   You will choose your own example. My own favourite is the clock's 'ochre moon', which seems to change as we read the poem, from the inscrutable face of buried Egyptian time to the new real time of the menstrual cycle with its own new-old colour and its own 'hugeness'.

Exercise 6

(a) Strictly speaking, there is hardly anything in this poem which declares itself as metaphor. The cats' 'shrill claws' and the 'doleful bubbles' are perhaps the nearest we come grammatically to imagery, and these are not difficult to understand as what we call 'transferred epithets' (i.e. 'shrill' and 'doleful' are really to be interpreted as going with something else). We have no way of knowing if the 'mask of leaves' is real or imaginary, no way of knowing about the rubble or the rose-bush – except what our common sense tells us.

(b) Certainly, cats, rubble and rose-bush all cohere into something that has human meaning, if we can suspend our disbelief and let them. The key is the line, 'I have forgotten how to love' (and the title, 'Do You Remember . . .'). If we begin to see lines 12–15 as alternative ways of making this direct statement, then we begin to understand the behaviour of the cats as well.

(c) The last line brings ordinary existence and poetic statement together. It is simple and apparently matter-of-fact. Probably real cats *have* deserted a real roof. But it is also one of the ways of restating line 10. It throws us back to lines 5–9, where cats dominate the centre of the poem. If we look at the behaviour of the cats we shall learn about the nature of love. 'Remembering' is remembering how to love. The departure we are asked to remember is perhaps not only the departure of someone we love, but also the departure into strangeness and disorientation that comes with love itself.

Exercise 7

(a) The subject of the poem is mushrooms growing.

(b) There are almost too many to list: the poem is full of them – 'Our toes, our noses/ Take hold'; 'Soft fists insist on/ Heaving'; 'The leafy bedding'; 'Shoulder through holes'; 'Diet on water'; 'Bland-mannered'; 'meek'; 'Nudgers and shovers/ In spite of ourselves'; 'Inherit'; 'Our foot's in the door.'

There is the apparently contradictory pair of paired metaphors: 'Our hammers, our rams' (line 14) and 'We are shelves, we are/ Tables' (lines 25–6).

There is also the suggestion of metaphor contained in the negatives:

'Nobody [. . .]/ [. . .] betrays us'; 'Earless and eyeless,// Perfectly voiceless'; 'asking// Little or nothing.'

(c)   I have already arranged my list to suggest a pattern. There are the personification metaphors which fit together to form a picture of embryonic human life. There are the two pairs of images which are set against each other, but which also fit very well (and with an element of incongruity and humour) into the extended metaphor of pregnancy. There are the *un-metaphors* which set up a background expectation of violence, dominance, betrayal.

(d)   There *is* conflict here, latent in the poet's use of metaphor. The two paired metaphors, in particular, open up very different worlds, the one suggesting violence, the other a funny domestic world which reminds us of our childhood fairy-tales.

(e)   The answer to this is necessarily subjective. For me they are not actually very 'mushroomy' at all, though I can feel the leaves and pine-needles and smell the damp wood smell in stanzas 2–4. This doesn't necesssarily mean that the poem is in any way flawed.

(f)   I can't do this for you. But I can hope you also said something about the last line. Why have the mushrooms got toes and noses but only one foot?

Exercise 8

It is surprisingly difficult to find a contemporary poem which doesn't contain a single metaphor, but Craig Raine's 'Mother Dressmaking' (from *A Martian Sends a Postcard Home*) is interesting from this point of view. The poem does contain similes and metaphors, but they are not the most important source of meaning in the poem. The fundamental relationship here (in the last three lines) is based not on metaphor, but on something we could call *metonymy*. A mother dressmaking, a budgerigar's tongue, and children drawing on a steamy window, are brought together, not because they are fundamentally in some way alike, but because they occur next to one another in the poet's memory. The implied comparison is inviting the reader to provide a meaningful *missing link*.

III

THEATRE

———

7
FILLING THE SPACE

———— Seeing and reading ————

It is all too easy, when we begin to study a play as literature, to forget that it is written not to be read, but to be *seen*. Too often, we find ourselves reading plays as if they were novels which somehow got written in dialogue form. We look for the story and try to build up coherent fictional characters from a collection of the speeches they make and the actions they are given to perform. We go back and analyse the words on the page for intellectual or poetic 'meat', and lose sight of the fact that when we are in the audience we hear the dialogue only once, and must move from it to the meaning of the drama as a whole.

But the literature of the theatre is always theatre first and 'literature' second. If it is not dramatic, it is nothing. If we fail to experience it in its own right as a complete spectacle, with spatial and visual and other non-verbal elements as well as with all its verbal meanings, we are allowing ourselves to be sensitive to less than half of what it really gives us. If we lose sight of the fact that a theatrical performance takes place in a time which ticks away its two or three hours and cannot stop or go into reverse, then we are cutting ourselves off from one of theatre's most poignant constraints, one of its richest resources.

Theatre is, in the way the novel is not, a microcosm. The final curtain is final. We shall feel less involved in what happens on the stage if we let ourselves forget that for a real audience in a real theatre a play is a linear development which happens in a certain chosen order *once*.

This does not mean of course that to make sense of any play we have to go and see it. Obviously, seeing it is the ideal. If we can go to a performance we are putting ourselves in the vulnerable position of guinea-pigs. We can observe ourselves reacting to what happens on the stage and feel the tension or the shock of events almost as if we were living them. But it is not possible to go to see every play. Even specialist critics writing on dramatic authors admit that some works are so rarely performed that they have never had the opportunity to see them on stage. What we can try to do is reproduce as well as we can in our imaginations the conditions of the theatrical experience. We can allow ourselves a two- or three-hour space in which to read through a play in its entirety. We can imagine a set, a physical space for the action, the actors' voices, gestures, costumes. We can try to be aware of the interplay of the text and our own reactions, and when we come back to look again at where the sense of drama is coming from, we can begin to study it, not in a *literary* way, but by putting ourselves momentarily in the position of director. In our minds we can play with interpretation and space and lighting, before we look at the text in other ways. If we rush to abstract and analyse the less dramatic qualities of a play, we may find ourselves with a very dead play on our hands.

Perhaps to study a play properly we have still got to be able to feel we can *walk out* of it. It is not enough for a play to surround us in poetry if the poetry leaves us untouched. It is not enough for a play to present us with a serious ideological question if what we are experiencing bores us. In a play, perhaps more than in any other literary genre, the literary and intellectual qualities are functional. If a novel tells a story and a poem 'takes the top of our heads off', a play which is dramatic always *puts us through it* in some way. When we turn back the pages to examine the serious things a playwright has *said* we should not lose sight of how we felt about them as something we were initially *put through*. For drama is necessarily manipulative. The audience follows the play at the end of a taut thread of attention, and while the thread is still taut, the dramatist can pull us through pain or hilarity. But when the thread breaks, it is well and truly broken. If a play ceases to engage us, it may still be literature in some sense, but it is no longer drama and we are no longer able to look at it as such.

Exercise 1

Cast your mind back to plays you have walked out of. (If you have not been a theatre-goer, perhaps you can substitute your memories of films you have seen for plays in this exercise.) Why did you walk out of them, and at what point? If you didn't actually walk out but felt a repressed desire to, why did you feel you wanted to, and why did you repress it? If you have never even considered walking out, ask yourself what this tells you about yourself as member of a theatre audience.

In some ways the text of a play is like a musical score. In itself it is incomplete. It is waiting to be interpreted. It needs all the paraphernalia of stage and actors and scenery, or concert-platform and orchestra and instruments, to exist fully. Yet no one performance can ever be definitive. There is always an extra ingredient, something the performance itself brings. A good director is not dismayed by the sparseness of the stage-directions in a play by Shakespeare or Molière: the silence itself offers him or her an opportunity. Whether lost or never written, it is these spaces which theatre itself exploits, to become a truly lived experience. Every play is in a sense unfinished and provisional.

Exercise 2

Radio drama is in this sense halfway between stage or television drama and the novel. We hear the voices and the sound-effects, but the rest we are left to see in our mind's eye, as we would the places described to us in a piece of fiction.

Listen to a play on the radio and ask yourself:

(a)   How must the written text of the play you have heard differ from what the text of the same play would be like if it were to be re-written for the stage?

(b)   How do the responsibilities of author and director differ in the theatre and on the radio?

(c)   Which of the two texts would be the more 'literary'?

The stage as space

The stage is first and foremost a space, a physical space in which something *happens*. Perhaps it has taken the critical insights of a gifted director to make us see this. Peter Brook's book, *The Empty Space*, is remarkable for cutting the ground from under the feet of much over-academic drama and criticism, and showing us what we should already have been all too aware of – that if we look at theatre as just another branch of written literature, we are killing something: theatre starts when *a theatre* opens its doors, when the area for the action is empty and waiting, when the audience begins to file in, expecting that space to be filled.

Playwrights, unlike readers and critics, have rarely ignored this fact. A play must be produced to become whole. A dramatic author must surely constantly bear in mind the circumstances in which his or her play is likely to be produced. A novelist or poet can write as if never to be heard, or at least can see what he or she writes as something like a message in a bottle, thrown to the mercy of the tides and currents, but a dramatist cannot afford that luxury. A play has a tangible, physical reality which it cannot attain without outside help.

So it is hardly surprising that the development of drama through the ages is intimately connected to the physical realities of stage production, to geography and climatic conditions, to scientific advances, and to the theories of stage reality, stage design and acting styles that went with them. The open-air theatres of ancient Greece would dampen most plays in our British winter climate. The vast arenas of ancient Rome fostered a certain kind of popular spectacle, probably more akin to pop-concerts or football matches or stunts with heavy goods vehicles in the function they performed than to what we call 'serious drama' today. From those open-air spaces even to the makeshift stages and modified farm-waggons and street theatre of medieval drama is an enormous jump. From the physical spaces of the morality plays to the fixed stage in a designated building is a huge jump again. The end of the patent system in the mid 19th-century, in opening the way towards the unrestricted use of buildings for theatrical purposes, is arguably as crucial to the development of contemporary British drama as the great theorists from Aristotle to Bertold Brecht.

This need not mean that when we read a play and do our best to visualise and experience it as if we were members of a real audience, we have to know every single fact about the conditions for which it was written. The accepted criterion of all great literature, whether poetry, prose or drama, is its survival *despite* changing conditions: no matter how historically ignorant we are, it still has the power to communicate with us and move us. What it does mean is that we should be aware of the words and spaces in the text which tell us something about staging the play: we should use all the information we are given to make the play complete in our minds; whether we decide to go for authenticity or a new daring interpretation, we should always try to be as attentive and creative as the ideal director. We should work at keeping our feet on the ground as he or she does, conscious of the play as a lived, shared experience which takes place in a given space at a given time.

Exercise 3

Read the following extract from the stage directions of Michael Frayn's play, *Noises Off*, and answer the questions:

The living-room of the Brents' country home. Wednesday afternoon. (Grand Theatre, Weston-Super-Mare, Monday January 14).

A delightful 16th-century posset mill, 25 miles from London. Lovingly converted, old-world atmosphere, many period features. Fully equipped with every aid to modern living, and beautifully furnished throughout by owner now resident abroad. Ideal for overseas company seeking perfect English setting to house senior executive. Minimum three months let. Apply sole agents: Squire, Squire, Hackham and Dudley.

The accommodation comprises: an open-plan living area, with a staircase leading to a gallery. A notable feature is the extensive range of entrances and exists provided. On the ground floor the front door gives access to the mature garden and delightful village beyond. Another door leads to the elegant panelled study, and a third to the light and airy modern service quarters. A fourth door opens into a luxurious bathroom/WC suite, and a full-length south-facing window affords extensive views. On the gallery level is the door to the master bedroom, and another to a small but well-proportioned linen cupboard. A corridor gives access to all the other rooms in the upper parts of the house. Another beautifully equipped bathroom/WC suite opens off the landing halfway up the stairs.

All in all, a superb example of the traditional English set-builder's craft – a place where the discerning theatre-goer will feel instantly at home.

As the curtain rises, the award-winning modern telephone is ringing.

Enter from the service quarters Mrs Clackett, a housekeeper of character. She is carrying an imposing plate of sardines.

(Michael Frayn, *Noises Off*)

Questions

(a)   How do you think you would react to a designer's interpretation of this set, as the curtain rose?

(b)   How do you think the author intends you to react?

(c)   Are there any clues in the text to tell you something of the nature of the play which is to follow?

(d)   Imagine you are designing this set. Write a short list of **Notes** to yourself. What have you singled out, and why?

────── The unknown ingredient ──────

A play cannot exist without an audience. To say that something special happens when a play is first seen and experienced by real people in a real theatre is a commonplace, but it is true, and it is something we may need to remind ourselves of as we sit straining to imagine a live performance, with the printed text of a play open in our laps. A play which is performed is not like a play which is read and seen in our heads. A first performance is not like a rehearsal, however ready and polished the rehearsal may be. A play needs us, in an even more obvious and immediate way than a novel or a poem needs a reader, in order to exist.

A play is an interaction of two sets of people, two kinds of reality, across a theoretical barrier which may be more or less visible. Whether we like it or not, whether we are relaxed in our seats, or on our feet shouting encouragement, or thoroughly uncomfortable, fidgeting and looking at our watches, our reaction is important. The feedback we give is a necessary part of the process. The atmosphere which emanates from us as audience can be sensed by the actors on stage and can modify their performance in subtle ways.

The ways in which we can be called upon to participate are almost infinitely variable. We may feel a very strong *divide* at the edge of a conventional stage, with a proscenium arch, and our share in the production may be largely a matter of atmosphere: actors and watchers alike may sense the fluctuations of an audience's attention through the quality of its silence; the occasional gasps or laughter of the people around us can be a potent force in the shaping of the dramatic experience. But often our involvement is more direct than this. Present-day audiences have become quite familiar with the device of using parts of the auditorium – balcony, boxes, gangways, or even ordinary seats – as performance space. In recent years it has become common for a dramatist to cross the invisible dividing line, or even wear it away almost completely. Possibly we are becoming more blasé about this phenomenon than is good for us or for the plays which use it extensively: but we are surely still sensitive to the reversal of roles when a 'member of the audience' suddenly begins to heckle the actors on stage in a loud and intrusive way and *interrupt the performance*. We may still feel momentary irritation or embarrassment, and that irritation or embarrassment may open the door to other, more complex emotional questions.

Much depends on the conventions of the kind of theatre we are watching and the way in which they shape our expectations. Children's theatre often offers considerable scope for interaction between actors and audience, and no one regards it as *gimmicky*. If, at a pantomime, we are asked to punch a giant inflatable sausage through the air, we probably have little trouble accepting our role as a traditional and necessary element in this kind of theatre. In the serious context of a Shakespearian tragedy we would probably find it at worst outrageously inappropriate and at best distracting. Yet Elizabethan audiences had no qualms about making their presence heard and felt! Perhaps we should do well to remind ourselves of how comparatively recently in the history of theatre our fixed theatres with their comfortable seats and electric lighting and sophisticated scene-changes developed, how comparatively recently audiences have been allowed to be comfortable and anonymous in their own space of darkness. We have only to think of a primary-school production, acted at floor-level and with no gradations of lighting, to be able to understand the real and vital part an audience can play.

Exercise 4

The extract which follows is taken from a speech at the beginning of a play which uses the resources of true theatre to pose serious moral questions very indirectly – so indirectly, in fact, that until the play has ended the audience is caught up inextricably in the games played by the two main characters. It is only afterwards that all the questions can surface.

Read the speech which follows, and try to imagine you are in a real theatre audience.

BRI *comes on without warning. Shouts at audience.*

BRI: That's enough! (*Pause. Almost at once, louder.*) I said enough! (*Pause. Stares at audience. He is thirty-three but looks younger. Hardly ever at rest, acts being maladroit but the act is skilful. Clowning may give way to ineffectual hectoring and then self-piteous gloom.*)

Another word and you'll all be here till five o'clock. Nothing to me, is it? I've got all the time in the world. (*Moves across without taking his eyes off them.*) I didn't even get to the end of the corridor before there was such a din all the other teachers started opening their doors as much as to say what the hell's going on there's SOME-BODY'S TALKING NOW! (*Pause, stares again, like someone facing a mad dog.*) Who was it? You? You, Mister Man? . . . I did not *accuse* you, I *asked* you. Someone in the back row? (*Stares dumbly for some seconds. Relaxes, moves a few steps. Shrugs.*) You're the losers, not me. Who's that? (*Turns on them again.*) Right – hands on heads! Come on, that includes you, put the comb away. Eyes front and sit up. All of you, sit up! (*Puts his own hands on his head for a while, watching for a move, waiting for a sound, then takes them down. Suddenly roars.*) Hands on head and eyes front! YOU I'm talking to! You'll be *tired* by the time I've finished. Stand on your seat. And keep your hands on your heads. Never mind what's going on outside, that joker at the back. Keep looking out here. Eyes front, hands on heads.

(Peter Nichols, *A Day in the Death of Joe Egg*)

Questions

(a)   How do you think an audience would react to this speech?

(b)   Can you give reasons?

(c)   How do you think the relationship between actors and audience would be changed by the time Bri reached the end of this speech?

(d)   What implications will that change have for the play which is to follow?

(e)   How appropriate is this school-teacher as a 'warm-up man'? Are 'warm-up men' desirable when we are raising serious questions?

—— What is going to happen? ——

At the beginning of a play, something signals to the audience that a theatrical presentation is beginning. In the terms of a traditional naturalistic (see the Glossary on page 256) theatre, this is usually the opening of a curtain. In other kinds of theatre – theatre in the round, street theatre – there may be nothing so tangible, but still there is a moment when the audience goes silent with expectation of what is to follow. This is the moment which corresponds to the moment when we, as students of drama, open the printed play and read the words printed on its first page of text. We ask ourselves at once, as we do on the first page of a novel, what is going to happen.

But what is going to happen in a play is subtly different from what is going to happen in a novel. There is little place for scene-setting: only what refers directly to what an audience can be shown in the physical realities of a stage set, and what can be conveyed acceptably through the dialogue itself. A dramatist cannot use tenses to superimpose different times with the same freedom a novelist can: he or she is restricted to what can actually be shown and what an audience can grasp. And, again, a theatre audience is not able to go back and read parts of the text again, juxtaposing different parts of it and comparing and asking questions: the important features of a drama must be memorable, or they are nothing.

If the play involves realistic characters in a realistic framework, we do of course also ask some of the questions we might ask if the same material were re-cast in an undramatic form and available to us as fiction. In practice, we often do find ourselves asking: 'But why are they doing that? Who is she? What will happen if he . . . ?' But if we are experiencing the play fully as theatre, those questions are a part of larger, more immediate questions: when we are on a rollercoaster we are first and foremost aware of the *terrain* itself. The first and most important question is – and should be – 'When we get to the top of this slope, what then?' If we feel none of that tension and excitement, a potentially very interesting play is in fact little more than an alternative way of reading fiction. Our involvement is the most real part of 'what is going to happen'. When we attempt to analyse parts of the printed text, we should be careful never to lose sight of all those elements which keep us on the edge of our seats, which make us uncomfortable and then allow us to relax. We should be aware of what pulls us closer into the development of the action, and aware of what distances us from it. This, rather than any *plot* which could be summarised in story form, is the real dramatic development of a piece of theatre. When we ask ourselves what is happening, we should be careful not to overlook our own central role in the proceedings.

Exercise 5

Study the following two openings, trying to reproduce in your imagination something of the atmosphere of a real performance. Then answer the questions.

[*A room which used to be the children's bedroom and is still referred to as the 'nursery'. There are several doors: one of them leads into ANIA's room. It is early morning: the sun is just coming up. The windows of the room are shut, but through them the cherry trees can be seen in blossom. It is May, but in the orchard there is morning frost.*

Enter DOONIASHA, carrying a candle, and LOPAKHIN with a book in his hand.]

LOPAKHIN. The train's arrived, thank God. What time is it?

DOONIASHA. It's nearly two. [*Blows out the candle.*] It's light already.

LOPAKHIN. How late was the train then? Two hours at least. [*Yawns and stretches.*] How stupid I am! What a fool I've made of myself! Came here on purpose to go to the station and meet them – and then overslept! . . . Dropped off to sleep in the chair. Annoying . . . I wish you'd woken me up.

DOONIASHA. I thought you'd gone. [*Listens.*] Sounds as if they're coming.

LOPAKHIN. [*also listens*]. No. . . . They'll have to get their luggage out, and all that. . . . [*Pause.*] Liubov Andryeevna has been abroad for five years, I don't know what she's like now. . . . She used to be a good soul. An easy-going, simple kind of person. I remember when I was a boy about fifteen, my father – he had a small shop in the village then – hit me in the face and made my nose bleed. . . . We had come to the manor for something or other, and he'd been drinking. I remember it as if it happened yesterday: Liubov Andryeevna – she was still young and slender then – brought me in and took me to the washstand in this very room, the nursery it was then. 'Don't cry, little peasant,' she said, 'it'll be better before you're old enough to get married' . . . [*Pause.*] 'Little peasant'. . . . She was right enough, my father was a peasant. Yet here I am – all dressed up in a white waistcoat and brown shoes . . . But you can't make a silk purse out of a sow's ear. I am rich. I've got a lot of money, but anyone can see I'm just a peasant, under my skin. [*Turning over pages in the book.*] I've been reading this book, and I haven't understood a word of it. I fell asleep reading it. [*Pause.*]

DOONIASHA. The dogs didn't sleep all night: they know their masters are coming.

LOPAKHIN. What's the matter, Dooniasha?

DOONIASHA. My hands are trembling. I feel as if I'm going to faint.

(Chekhov, *The Cherry Orchard*)

Set in darkness. Crash against front door. MARTHA'S laughter heard. Front door opens, lights are switched on. MARTHA enters, followed by GEORGE.

MARTHA: Je*sus* . . .

GEORGE: . . . Shhhhhhh. . . .

MARTHA: . . . H. Christ . . .

GEORGE: For God's sake, Martha, its' two o'clock in the . . .

MARTHA: Oh, George!

GEORGE: Well, I'm *sorry,* but . . .

MARTHA: What a cluck! What a cluck you are.

GEORGE: It's late, you know? Late.

MARTHA [*looks about the room. Imitates Bette Davis*]: What a dump. Hey, what's that from? 'What a dump!'

GEORGE: How would I know what . . .

MARTHA: Aw, come on! What's it from? *You* know . . .

GEORGE: . . . Martha . . .

MARTHA: WHAT'S IT FROM, FOR CHRIST'S SAKE?

GEORGE [*wearily*]: What's what from?

MARTHA: I just told you; I just did it. 'What a dump!' Hunh? What's that from?

GEORGE: I haven't the faintest idea what . . .

MARTHA: Dumbbell! It's from some goddam Bette Davis picture . . . some goddamn Warner Brothers epic. . . .

GEORGE: *I* can't remember all the pictures that . . .

MARTHA: Nobody's asking you to remember every single goddamn Warner brothers epic . . . just one! One single little epic! Bette Davis gets peritonitis in the end . . . she's got this big black fright wig she wears all through the picture and she gets peritonitis, and she's married to Joseph Cotten or something. . .

GEORGE: . . . Some*body* . . .

MARTHA: . . . some*body* . . . and she wants to go to Chicago all the time, 'cause she's in love with that actor with the scar. . . . But she gets sick, and she sits down in front of her dressing-table . . .

GEORGE: What actor? What scar?

MARTHA: *I* can't remember his name, for God's sake. What's the name of the *picture*? I want to know what the name of the *picture* is. She sits down in front of her dressing-table . . . and she's got this peritonitis . . . and she tries to put her lipstick on, but she can't . . . and she gets it all over her face . . . but she decides to go to Chicago anyway, and . . .

GEORGE: *Chicago*! It's called *Chicago*.

MARTHA: Hunh? What . . . what is?

GEORGE: The picture . . . It's called *Chicago*. . . .

MARTHA: Good grief! Don't you know *anything*? *Chicago* was a thirties musical, starring little Miss Alice *Faye*. Don't you know *anything*?

GEORGE: Well, that was probably before my *time*, but . . .

MARTHA: Can it! Just cut that out! This picture . . . Bette Davis comes home from a hard day at the grocery store. . . .

GEORGE: She works in a grocery store?

MARTHA: She's a housewife; she buys things . . . and she comes home with the groceries, and she walks into the modest living-room of the modest cottage modest Joseph Cotten has set her up in. . . .

GEORGE: Are they married?

MARTHA [*impatiently*]: Yes. They're married. To each other, Cluck! And she comes in, and she looks around, and she puts her groceries down, and she says, 'What a dump!'

GEORGE [*pause*]: Oh.

MARTHA [*pause*]: She's discontent.

GEORGE [*pause*]: Oh.

MARTHA [*pause*]: Well, what's the name of the picture?

GEORGE: I really don't know, Martha. . . .

MARTHA: Well, think!

GEORGE: I'm tired, dear . . . it's late . . . and besides . . .

MARTHA: I don't know what you're so tired about . . . you haven't *done* anything all day; you didn't have any classes, or anything. . .

GEORGE: Well, I'm tired. . . . If your father didn't set up these goddamn Saturday night orgies all the time. . .

MARTHA: Well, that's too bad about you, George. . .

GEORGE [*grumbling*]: Well, that's how it is, anyway.

MARTHA: You didn't *do* anything; you never *do* anything; you never *mix*. You just sit around and *talk*.

GEORGE: What do you want me to do? Do you want me to act like you? Do you want me to go around all night *braying* at everybody, the way you do?

MARTHA [*braying*]: I DON'T BRAY!

GEORGE [*softly*]: All right . . . you don't bray.

MARTHA [*hurt*]: I do not bray.

GEORGE: All right. I said you didn't bray.

MARTHA [*pouting*]: Make me a drink.

GEORGE: What?

MARTHA [*still softly*]: I said, make me a drink.

GEORGE [*moving to the portable bar*]: Well, I don't suppose a nightcap'd kill either one of us. . .

MARTHA: A nightcap! Are you kidding? We've got guests.

GEORGE [*disbelieving*]: We've got what?

MARTHA: Guests. GUESTS.

GEORGE: GUESTS!

MARTHA: Yes . . . guests . . . people. . . . We've got guests coming over.

GEORGE: When?

MARTHA: Now!

(Edward Albee, *Who's Afraid of Virginia Woolf?*)

Questions

(a) If we extract the information about *plot* from the first extract, what picture can we build up of characters and events?

(b) Do these characters or events already raise any questions in your mind? What questions?

(c) What other, more dramatic information is there?

(d) What picture of characters and events do we gain from the second extract?

(e) Are there already suggestions of areas of conflict?

(f) What is dramatic about this beginning?

(g) In which of these two extracts would you, as a potential member of the audience, feel more involved? Which would you feel the more intrigued by?

(h) Are the last two questions the same? Are your answers to them the same?

───── Back to basics ─────

We have already mentioned pantomine as a salutary reminder of what theatre can do. The tendency in most dramatic writing of the late 19th and early 20th centuries was to see these resources as having very little to offer serious theatre. The rollercoaster effect was perhaps less important than a steadily building dramatic concentration which had to do with the 'real', believable characters and the audience's identification with them. The ramatist was more of a chemist than a mechanic: we were asked to be present at the mixing of dramatic elements and observe the volatile mixture which resulted. Much modern theatre may seem more manipulative than this. There may be no real place that we are asked to believe in, no real characters. The movement of the play is not so much in the conjunction of events and characters as in the ebb and flow of the dialogue and action itself.

As character is less believable, stage business comes into its own. What happens on stage may not allow us to interpret it in the comfortable, ordinary terms we use to interpret people and events in our everyday lives. Tones of voice, gestures, actions, even slapstick, are no longer a convenient way of building up an audience's sense of a *well-rounded* character. They become important in themselves. They may be hilariously funny, and at the same time obscurely threatening. Our relationship with them is in a sense the play. And when we leave the theatre at the end of the performance, the meaning of the play cannot possibly be discussed without taking them into account.

In this context, language itself becomes both more and less important. It is less important as a reliable source of information. In many modern plays we may find it hard to build up a coherent picture of a recognisable human situation. But words may become more important in themselves, conveying double meanings, or ambiguous meanings, or even drawing our attention to the inadequacy or silliness of language itself.

Exercise 6

Read the following extract from the beginning of a one-act play first published and performed in the 1960s, and answer the questions.

A late evening in the future.

KRAPP's *den.*

Front centre a small table, the two drawers of which open towards the audience.

Sitting at the table, facing front, i.e. across from the drawers, a wearish old man: KRAPP.

Rusty black narrow trousers too short for him. Rusty black sleeveless waistcoat, four capacious pockets. Heavy silver watch and chain. Grimy white shirt open at neck, no collar. Surprising pair of dirty white boots, size ten at least, very narrow and pointed.

White face. Purple nose. Disordered grey hair. Unshaven. Very near-sighted (but unspectacled). Hard of hearing. Laborious walk.

On the table a tape-recorder with a microphone and a number of cardboard boxes containing reels of recorded tapes.

Table and immediately adjacent area in strong white light. Rest of stage in darkness.

KRAPP *remains a moment motionless, heaves a great sigh, looks at his watch, fumbles in his pockets, takes out an envelope, puts it back, fumbles, takes out a small bunch of keys, raises it to his eyes, chooses a key, gets up and moves to front of table. He stoops, unlocks first drawer, peers into it, feels about inside it, takes out a reel of tape, peers at it, puts it back, locks drawer, unlocks second drawer, peers into it, feels about inside it, takes out a large banana, peers at it, locks drawer, puts keys back in his pocket. He turns, advances to edge of stage, halts, strokes banana, peels it, drops skin at his feet, puts end of banana in his mouth and remains motionless, staring vacuously before him. Finally he bites off the end, turns aside and begins pacing to and fro at edge of stage, in the light, i.e. not more than four or five paces either way, meditatively eating banana. He treads on skin, slips, nearly falls, recovers himself, stoops and peers at skin and finally pushes it, still stooping, with his foot over edge of stage into pit. He resumes his pacing, finishes banana, returns to table, sits down, remains a moment motionless, heaves a great sigh, takes keys from his pockets, raises them to his eyes, chooses key, gets up and moves to front of table, unlocks second drawer, takes out a second large banana, peers at it, locks drawer, puts back keys in his pocket, turns, advances to edge of stage, halts, strokes banana, peels it, tosses skin into pit, puts end of banana in his mouth and remains motionless, staring vacuously before him. Finally he has an idea, puts banana in his waistcoat pocket, the end emerging, and goes with all the speed he can muster backstage into darkness. Ten seconds. Loud pop of cork. Fifteen seconds. He comes back into light carrying an old ledger and sits down at table. He lays ledger on table, wipes his mouth, wipes his hands on the front of his waistcoat, brings them smartly together and rubs them.*

KRAPP: (*briskly*). Ah! (*He bends over ledger, turns the pages, finds the entry he wants, reads.*) Box . . . three . . . spool . . . five. (*He raises his head and stares front. With relish.*) Spool! (*Pause.*) Spooool! (*Happy smile. Pause. He bends over table, starts peering and poking at the boxes.*) Box . . . thrree . . . thrree . . . four . . . two . . . (*with surprise.*) nine! good God! . . . seven . . . ah! the little rascal! (*He takes up box, peers at it.*) Box thrree. (*He lays it on table, opens it and peers at spools inside.*) Spool . . . (*he peers at ledger*) . . . five . . . (*he peers at spools*) . . . five . . . five . . . ah! the little scoundrel! (*He takes out a spool, peers at it.*) Spool five. (*He lays it on table, closes box three, puts it back with the others, takes up the spool.*) Box thrree, spool five. (*He bends over the machine, looks up. With relish.*) Spooool! (*Happy smile. He bends, loads spool on machine, rubs his hands.*) Ah!

(Samuel Beckett, *Krapp's Last Tape*)

Questions

(a) What does 'A late evening in the future' suggest to you? If you were the director of the play, or its single actor, how might you interpret this phrase? How far would we be aware of it as members of an audience?

(b) What effect would Krapp's appearance have?

(c) Describe the effect that would be produced by the stage lighting. How do you think a real audience would react to it?

(d) What would be the effect of the stage business with the banana?

(e) How is the playwright using language in Krapp's first speech?

(f) Which is the more important, what Krapp says, or what he does?

(g) How will these opening moments of the play have coloured our expectations of what is to follow?

Commentary

Exercise 1

If you are anything like me, the chances are that the plays or films you walked out of actually disgusted you in some way. Since strong reactions are by definition dramatic reactions, it is perhaps not surprising if playwrights and film-directors are perpetually pushing out the boundaries of what an audience finds palatable and acceptable. The line between what revolts an audience and what moves an audience can be a thin one. We may also have walked out in boredom, or at least felt tempted to. If we have never walked out of a play because it bored us and yet can admit that we have on occasion been bored by a performance, it may be that our expectations of the theatre are in fact rather too literary. Often when we are reading a novel, we are content to tell ourselves, 'Well, I'm not quite *into* it yet. I can't judge it yet.' With a play we *can* judge, even at the beginning. We may not be able to judge from an isolated moment whether or not it is, ultimately, a good play, a satisfying experience. But we can almost invariably tell from our own reactions whether a play is at a given moment *dramatic*. If we lose sight of that reaction in favour of something less immediate, we are already beginning to lose sight of what a play really is.

Exercise 2

(a) This is a complex question and one which deserves more detailed study. All we can do for the purposes of this exercise is to try to focus our attention on what is easy to do on stage but difficult or impossible to do on radio, and vice versa.

Obviously on radio we have only dialogue and sound-effects to set the scene. We have no visual resources to convey a character's appearance, his or her age, or facial expression, or gestures. If they are important, we have only voices to convey them. On radio there is no obvious visual way of suggesting intimacy or distance between characters: though voices can do a lot, they can't do everything. But sometimes visuals can be cumbersome: scene-changes conventionally depend on stage-hands and ropes and pulleys; ageing usually calls for sophisticated make-up. Modern production techniques may have done much to simplify the mechanics of time and place on stage with their less representational approach. But radio drama can intercut different times and settings with the same ease a novel can.

A comparison of the two dramatic texts could not fail to underline functional differences in the dialogue itself, as well as obvious differences in any instructions for staging. The text written for radio would probably be noticeably freer in its handling of time and place.

(b) It seems to me that the unwritten potential of a stage play is necessarily wider. A radio play is so completely dependent on its dialogue and on the creative ordering of that dialogue that the author's responsibility here is surely almost complete. A good stage dramatist is likely to leave a wider margin of interpretation for director and cast: because of the very nature of the medium, there are more variables. Dialogue no longer has such complete responsibility; it is part of a much larger whole.

(c) The radio play is surely more literary, in the sense that it is closer to a kind of art that is *written*. More of it is written and less is open to the participation of the other artistic disciplines (such as stage and lighting and costume design, mime, dance) that go to make up a stage performance.

Exercise 3

(a) The answer to this question is of course subjective. When I saw the play, the impression made initially by the set was hard to define. The scene at stage level was conventional and even boring. But the gallery, with its almost absurdly numerous doors, introduced an element of something slightly humorous and unexpected.

(b) The answer to this is less subjective. We have all sorts of clues in the funny and original way in which the author has chosen to frame his stage-directions in the flattering and untrustworthy language of a rather slick estate-agent. As we read it, we cannot fail to be aware of the joke, to laugh with the author in an atmosphere of complicity (perhaps at the actors' expense?), and to feel self-consciously aware of ourselves as *discerning theatregoers*. When I saw the play, not much of this was in fact translated into what was initially happening on stage. Inevitably one asks oneself how much of it *could* have been discernible in the actual set. Not much, perhaps, no matter how scrupulous and keen an eye for detail the director had. But perhaps the way in which these stage-directions are written is the *literary* (or reader's) equivalent of other elements in the performed play which will come later. George Bernard Shaw made his play, *Pygmalion*, more readable by adding *literary* elements to it in a comparable way. These two playwrights, by giving us as readers the flavour of the drama which is to follow, are making double sure that we treat the text that is to come with the dramatic imagination it deserves.

(c) There are clues in the double location of the set at the very beginning, echoed in the self-conscious and ironic 'a superb example of the traditional English set-builder's craft – a place where the discerning theatregoer will feel instantly at home.' From this and from the 'imposing plate of sardines' we know at once that what is to follow will include a substantial dose of comedy. Again, from simply witnessing the stage set and Mrs Clackett's entrance, we should probably not have such insight: we should be in a state of suspended reaction until Mrs Clackett first made us laugh with her garbled and unlikely telephone conversation and antics with the sardines. Even then, we should not realise that this is a *play within a play*, as the stage-directions immediately hint to us.
Perhaps the only clue that would be perceptible to a real theatre audience is the exaggerated number of doors.

(d) I think that even from these initial directions it is possible to tell that the doors are crucial, and that however one chooses to deal with them, it will affect the nature of the whole play. If I were designing this set, I would give considerable thought to the level of illusion that was desirable: how far the audience *believes in* this set will be crucial in the balance of values in the play itself.

Exercise 5

(a) We know Liubov Andryeevna is returning after five years and that she is not alone. Lopakhin, a rich business-man who began life as a peasant and by his own admission has never fully escaped his peasant origins, has come to her house intending to go and meet her from the train. We learn that Liubov Andryeevna used to be 'a good soul. An easygoing, simple kind of person' who bathed his face once after an episode of violence. Yet there is already a strong suggestion of social and personal tension here. We learn that Dooniasha is nervous at her mistress's return.

(b)   The central question they raise has to do with the phenomenon of change. We infer that Liubov Andryeevna has changed, at least outwardly, since the time of Lopakhin's youth, as he himself has. Both in the words the characters say and in the uneasy, expectant way they behave, we are being made to wonder about the meaning of change.

(c)   The most dramatic information is perhaps in the suggestion of the morning with its frosted cherry-blossom (which surely would be hardly visible to a real audience) and in Dooniasha's 'My hands are trembling. I feel as if I'm going to faint.' The expectation that is built up is ambiguous: is it an expectation of blossoming, or of frost?

(d)   We have a picture of a couple returning late (and probably somewhat drunk) from a party. We already have the picture of a kind of intimacy built on friction between them. We already have a strong impression that American culture plays a large part in their relationship.

(e)   From Martha's first word and George's reaction to it, we know her language is louder and more obviously histrionic than his is. He seems to hate her loudness; she is perpetually accusing him of being stupid. We suspect too that some of the tension is connected with her father, and that some of it revolves around the questions of ages and ageing.

(f)   Their entrance is itself dramatic. The lights go on suddenly and immediately this couple bursts in on us and starts fighting in our presence. The way Martha harasses George with questions and insults makes us wonder already if and how this tension can escalate and how it can be resolved. We may also laugh, but the initial shock and anxiety surely linger to colour our laughter.

(g) and (h)   The answers to these two questions are subjective. But however you reply to them it is worth asking yourself why you feel as you do, and how the two reactions are related.

Exercise 6

(a)   It may well suggest something of a contradiction: it seems to me that devices used to evoke lateness are rarely if ever connected with the kind of conventions used to suggest the future. A director could convey lateness partly by his or her choice of lighting, and an actor could convey it in his voice in all sorts of ways (fatigue, dislocation, use of silence, etc.)

but to suggest the future without recourse to conventions of set or costume would seem to be an impossibility.

(b) Krapp's appearance is an odd combination of depressing and clown-like elements. In context it could make us laugh, or, just as easily, appear as a kind of threat.

(c) It is surely alienating, combining as it does the connotations of outer darkness and the interrogation chamber.

(d) It would surely make us laugh. It might also embarrass us, breaking the invisible wall between actor and audience, and leaving us very insecure of how we are to react or what kind of spectacle we are watching. The fact that it is 'one of the oldest gags in the business' also traps us: it's corny, but is it funny, or embarrassing?

(e) He is using the words in an almost *un-verbal* way – as if words themselves were a kind of gesture. The way Krapp plays with the sound of 'spool' has the effect of emptying it of meaning and making it sound absurd. It would surely give us a feeling of dislocation, the kind of feeling we all get occasionally when a correctly spelled word looks suddenly wrong. Language is no longer to be trusted – it is precisely as funny and slippery and suggestive as the banana.

(f) In a sense they are the same. At this point in the play, words and gestures are in fact very similar in the function they perform. They *throw* us, they make us laugh, they make us uneasy. After a while they might begin to exasperate us.

(g) This will vary from individual to individual, but most of us will surely be expecting a very strange world where stark solitude goes with buffoonery. We probably expect to laugh, but we probably already expect that laughter to be ambiguous and uncomfortable.

8

LAUGHING AND CRYING

Catharsis

If we can begin to appreciate how important we ourselves are as the audience in what happens in a theatre, it makes sense to ask ourselves why we go to a play. What do we expect to get out of it? Do we expect first and foremost to be entertained? Do we expect to be improved in some way, intellectually or morally, hoping that when we step out into the night air afterwards we shall somehow be wiser or more sophisticated people? Do we hope to be transported into an imaginary world, or to be made to think objectively about our own? Do we feel that the job of *real* theatre is to move us profoundly, or do we feel that we are moved and disturbed enough by our everyday lives?

These questions are never resolved. We ask them again at each new theatrical experiment, perhaps even at each performance we witness. Twentieth-century dramatists have produced tremendous upheavals in the history of dramatic writing by answering them differently. Whether we are studying a contemporary farce, a Shakespearian history, a medieval morality play or a Greek tragedy, we cannot afford to ignore them. Are we to be changed by our experience? And if we are, how is that change to be effected?

Possibly the most seminal theoretician of the theatre of all time was Aristotle in the fourth century BC. Apart from analysing and classifying aspects of Greek theatre as it appeared to him, and developing a vocabulary of drama which is still largely in use today, Aristotle gave considerable thought to the ways in which a dramatic performance, and tragedy in particular, worked on its audience. At the centre of his descriptions of what constitutes plot and character and what conditions contribute to dramatic intensity, is the idea of *catharsis*. Critics have argued about whether the term itself is a medical one (purging) or whether it is a metaphor drawn from a more abstract, spiritual area of experience. But it is clear that Aristotle saw theatre as an intimate relationship between the ups-and-downs of characters on stage and the degree to which we as audience would feel for or with them. And it is clear too that how an audience felt was seen to be related to an audience's general moral and spiritual well-being: if we could feel pity and fear as we witnessed the inevitable and largely undeserved sufferings of characters on the stage, we would emerge from the dramatic experience somehow purified, better able to cope with the traumas and moral ambiguities of our own lives.

The most complete description Aristotle gives us of *catharsis* is not to be found with most of his other dramatic theory in the *Poetics*, but in the *Politics*, in the context not of drama but of music:

> 'Take pity and fear, for example, or again enthusiasm. Some people are liable to become possessed by the latter emotion, but we see that, when they have made use of the melodies which fill the soul with orgiastic feeling, they are brought back by these sacred melodies to a normal condition as if they had been medically treated and undergone a catharsis. Those who are subject to the emotions of pity and fear and the feelings generally will necessarily be affected in the same way; and so will other men in exact proportion to their susceptibility to such emotions. All experience a certain catharsis and pleasant relief. In the same manner cathartic melodies give innocent joy to men.'

> (Aristotle, *Politics*, quoted by Humphrey House in *Aristotle's Poetics* (Rupert Hart-Davis, 1961), p. 107)

The business of drama is not only to bring us pleasure. It is also to make us *feel*, and, just as importantly, as we feel, to bring us back to a kind of balance. A good play with a sensitive audience is, as we would say today, genuinely *therapeutic*. It is a *therapy* which ideally goes deep enough to modify our whole relationship with our ordinary existence.

This, in turn, has all sorts of implications for the ingredients of good dramatic writing. If feeling and, ultimately, moral growth, are the criteria, then the emphasis is on a certain kind of drama with a certain kind of plot and a certain kind of characters. It must be 'real' – but not too real. The characters must be close – but not too 'close'. The structure must be 'tight' – but not so tight that the poetry itself is lost.

Aristotle may have been the first to formalise the phenomenon of theatre as a relationship, a tension between more and less realism, more and less distance, but it is a tension which has stayed with us ever since. Every century has come up with a different answer, a different version of what constitutes the ideal balance. Some of the greatest of our European dramatists have changed the nature of theatre by defying that optimum balance in a new and revolutionary way. But we have not yet so far superseded Aristotle and his theories as to claim that *catharsis* (though we may call it by another name) can be left out of the equation. We surely still find strong emotion – pity, terror, or joy – a memorable part of what drama can do, and to some extent we still define other kinds of theatre against that memory.

Exercise 1

Think about any dramatic performances you have been present at in the past few years (or less, if you are lucky or rich enough to go to the theatre frequently!) Include amateur performances, children's performances, and so on. (If you never get the chance to go to a live performance, you can change the emphasis of this exercise slightly to make use of trips to the cinema, or your experience of TV or radio drama.) Ask yourself:

(a)   How close did I feel to what was happening on stage?

(b)   How close did I feel to the characters?

(c)   Which factors in the production/acting were most responsible for how far I identified with what was happening?

(d)   What emotion did I feel?

(e)   How comfortable was it at the time?

(f)   How did it affect me afterwards?

——————— What moves us? ———————

If we accept that emotion in the theatre can act as a kind of catalyst to change us and perhaps, in changing us, to change the world, we need to think about how theatre can bring about this emotional involvement.

One of the ways a play can achieve this undoubtedly has something to do with a playwright's conception of character. Perhaps Aristotle's vision of a character who would be distanced from us by belonging to the world of myth and yet fallible enough to be recognisably human still has its place. But there are other ways of achieving this balance. All sorts of dramatic devices can be used to make a character's delight or suffering somehow slightly larger than life, while he or she retains his or her essential humanity. If we watch closely, we shall almost invariably perceive some element of stylisation which amplifies conflict and reactions, and in many cases allows us as audience to feel safe enough to *let go*. One could certainly argue that too much realism can be simply depressing, that the way to make *reality* work on stage is to temper it with some degree of stylisation. In fact our Anglo-Saxon heritage prepares us to expect this. If we have seen or read plays by Shakespeare, we are already used to handling different levels of realism, and we probably recognise very readily that different levels of identification are no bar to our overall response.

Exercise 2

Try to think back over all the plays you have ever seen. (If you are a keen theatre-goer, you will need to be more selective.) Of all the performances you remember, which moved you most? What was it about the performance that moved you? Can you try to analyse it in more detail? How far was the emotion a function of the particular performance or production? How far was it *written into* the play itself? Can you remember what led up to the most moving moment? Were other moments or elements of the play or performance in a recognisably different register?

Exercise 3

Read the following three extracts carefully and try to visualise what is happening. Several readings should be enough to give you some (inadequate!) sense of the emotional charge in these scenes:

CORDELIA

How does my royal lord? how fares your majesty?

KING LEAR

You do me wrong to take me out o' the grave:-
Thou art a soul in bliss; but I am bound
Upon a wheel of fire, that mine own tears
Do scald like molten lead.

CORDELIA

Sir, do you know me?

KING LEAR

You are a spirit, I know: when did you die?

CORDELIA

Still, still, far wide!

DOCTOR

He's scarce awake: let him alone awhile.

KING LEAR

Where have I been? Where am I? – Fair daylight? –
I am mightily abus'd. – I should e'en die with pity.
To see another thus. – I know not what to say. –
I will not swear these are my hands:- let's see.
I feel this pin prick. Would I were assured
Of my condition.

CORDELIA

O, look upon me, sir,
And hold your hands in benediction o'er me:-
No, sir, you must not kneel.

KING LEAR

Pray, do not mock me:
I am a very foolish fond old man,
Fourscore and upward, not an hour more nor less;
And, to deal plainly,
I fear I am not in my perfect mind.
Methinks I should know you, and know this man:
Yet I am doubtful: for I am mainly ignorant

What place this is; and all the skill I have
Remembers not these garments; nor I know not
Where I did lodge last night. Do not laugh at me;
For, as I am a man, I think this lady
To be my child Cordelia.

CORDELIA
And so I am, I am.

KING LEAR
Be your tears wet? yes, faith. I pray, weep not:
If you have poison for me, I will drink it.
I know you do not love me; for your sisters
Have, as I do remember, done me wrong:
You have some cause, they have not.

CORDELIA
No cause, no cause.

KING LEAR
Am I in France?

KENT
In your own kingdom, sir.

KING LEAR
Do not abuse me.

DOCTOR
Be comforted, good madam: the great rage,
You see, is kill'd in him; and yet it is danger
To make him even o'er the time he has lost.
Desire him to go in; trouble him no more
Till further settling.

CORDELIA
Will't please your highness walk?

(Shakespeare, *King Lear*)

[Dysart is the psychiatrist treating Alan, who is deeply distressed after an incident in which he blinded the horses in a local stable. In the course of their dialogue, the events in Alan's spiritual life which have led up to the moment of violence are dramatised. Lighting, humming, stylised godlike horse-costumes, all contribute to an atmosphere of emotions bigger and older than we can understand.]

ALAN: I bet this room's heard some funny things.
DYSART: It certainly has.
ALAN: I like it.
DYSART: This room?
ALAN: Don't you?
DYSART: Well, there's not much to like, is there?
ALAN: How long am I going to be in here?
DYSART: It's hard to say. I quite see you want to leave.
ALAN: No.
DYSART: You don't?
ALAN: Where would I go?
DYSART: Home . . .

[*The boy looks at him.* DYSART *crosses and sits on the rail upstage, his feet on the bench. A pause.*]

Actually, I'd like to leave this room and never see it again in my life.
ALAN: [*surprise*]: Why?
DYSART: I've been in it too long.
ALAN: Where would you go?
DYSART: Somewhere.
ALAN: Secret?
DYSART: Yes. There's a sea – a great sea – I love . . . It's where the Gods used to go to bathe.
ALAN: What Gods?
DYSART: The old ones. Before they died.
ALAN: God's don't die.
DYSART: Yes, they do.

[*Pause.*]

There's a village I spent one night in, where I'd like to live. It's all white.
ALAN: How would you Nosey Parker, though? You wouldn't have a room for it any more.
DYSART: I wouldn't mind. I don't actually enjoy being a Nosey Parker, you know.
ALAN: Then why do you do it?
DYSART: Because you're unhappy.
ALAN: So are you.

(Peter Shaffer, *Equus*)

THOMAS. Now to Almighty God, to the Blessed Mary ever Virgin, to the blessed John the Baptist, the Holy apostles Peter and Paul, to the blessed martyr Denys, and to all the Saints, I commend my cause and that of the Church.

          While the KNIGHTS *kill him, we hear the*

CHORUS. Clear the air! clean the sky! wash the wind!
    take stone from stone and wash them.

The land is foul, the water is foul, our beasts and ourselves defiled with blood.

A rain of blood has blinded my eyes. Where is England? where is Kent? where is Canterbury?

O far far far in the past; and I wander in a land of barren boughs: if I break them, they bleed; I wander in a land of dry stones: if I touch them they bleed.

How can I ever return, to the soft quiet seasons?

Night stay with us, stop sun, hold season, let the day not come, let the spring not come.

Can I look again at the day and its common things, and see them all smeared with blood, through a curtain of falling blood?

We did not wish anything to happen.

We understood the private catastrophe,

The personal loss, the general misery,

Living and partly living;

The terror by night that ends in daily action,

The terror by day that ends in sleep;

But the talk in the market-place, the hand on the broom,

The night-time heaping of the ashes,

The fuel laid on the fire at daybreak,

These acts marked a limit to our suffering.

Every horror had its definition,

Every sorrow had a kind of end:

In life there is not time to grieve long.

But this, this is out of life, this is out of time,

An instant eternity of evil and wrong.

We are soiled by a filth that we cannot clean, united to supernatural vermin,

It is not we alone, it is not the house, it is not the city that is defiled,

But the world that is wholly foul.

Clear the air! clean the sky! wash the wind! take the stone from
the stone, take the skin from the arm, take the muscle from the
bone, and wash them. Wash the stone, wash the bone, wash
the brain, wash the soul, wash them wash them!

(T S Eliot, *Murder in the Cathedral*)

Questions

(a) How far could the emotion generated by each of these scenes be
said to rest on contrast?

(b) If there are contrasts, what are the contrasting elements in each?

(c) Is there an element of stylisation in each scene?

(d) Choose the extract which moves you most. Get hold of a copy of the
play it was taken from, and read (or re-read) it in one sitting. Is your
reaction to the original extract the same when you read it now in context?
What has gone before to prepare or enhance this moment? How does the
emotion of this moment colour what comes after?

Real feeling

I think few watchers or readers of plays would dispute that the way in
which we respond emotionally to the ups and downs of the play is related,
directly or indirectly, to a playwright's conception of realism and the
stance he or she chooses to adopt with respect to it. In some ways
theatre is akin to the novel. Both commonly *relate* a series of fictional
happenings, involving fictional characters with whom we can identify to a
greater or lesser extent. We are used to the *willing suspension of
disbelief* in both contexts. But the differences are nevertheless enormous. In a novel we may need a pinch of drama to help us accept
something our imaginations find hard to swallow. But theatre *is* drama.
We can experience it, whether we *believe in* it or not. We do not have to
be convinced that actors are really animals to be saddened or delighted
by a performance of *Cats*. Watching *Don Giovanni* or *The Winter's Tale*,
we can actually *see* a 'statue' come alive on stage in a way which makes
our belief or disbelief irrelevant.

Some of the most powerfully emotive theatre is also some of the most profoundly 'artificial'. (We can, of course, argue about whether artifice in theatrical terms means the same as stylisation, or whether in fact there is more artifice in the *realistic* stages and characterisation we associate with Ibsen and late 19th-century drama.) If we can visualise the starkness of a Greek amphitheatre under the open sky, with its masked actors, its chorus and its poetry, we begin to understand how as audience we can experience drama without being *taken in* by its details.

Exercise 4

Study the following extract from the tragic climax of Sophocles' *King Œdipus*:

> ATTENDANT: The King saw too, and with heart-rending groans
> Untied the rope, and laid her on the ground.
> But worse was yet to see. Her dress was pinned
> With golden brooches, which the King snatched out
> And thrust, from full arm's length, into his eyes –
> Eyes that should see no longer his shame, his guilt,
> No longer see those they should never have seen,
> Nor see, unseeing, those he had longed to see,
> Henceforth seeing nothing but night . . . To this wild tune
> He pierced his eyeballs time and time again,
> Till bloody tears ran down his beard – not drops
> But in full spate a whole cascade descending
> In drenching cataracts and scarlet rain.
>   Thus two have sinned; and on two heads, not one –
> On man and wife – falls mingled punishment.
> Their old long happiness of former times
> Was happiness earned with justice; but to-day
> Calamity, death, ruin, tears, and shame,
> All ills that there are names for – all are here.
> CHORUS: And he – how is he now? Does he still suffer?

> (translated by E F Watling)

What elements of stylisation or 'artificiality' can you find in this extract? Which parts of it seem to speak to us the most immediately and directly? Is the final impression, for you, of something close to the real world, or of something remote? How emotive is the Attendant's speech?

Exercise 5

With the advent of Ibsen and a movement called Naturalism towards the end of the 19th century, the relationship between performers and audience began to undergo subtle changes. As what happened on stage began to look less obviously theatrical and more *real*, it became ever easier for spectators to identify with characters' dilemmas and to share their often violent emotions. Yet this identification was, in a sense, passive. Audiences were situated firmly in one space, and actors in another, and the actors' space was apparently its own complete world. This kind of realism (which may actually be very far from a 'photographic' or documentary imitation of ordinary existence) is the principle behind what is often called the *fourth wall* view of theatre: the idea is that an invisible fourth wall separates the stage from the watchers, preventing any direct interaction between the two. The effect of the *fourth wall* is often, paradoxically, to free our imaginations to become part of the fictional space we see in front of us, in the same way we might expect to enter imaginatively into the world of a 19th-century novel. Something has changed. We are feeling with the characters on the stage in a way which spectators of Classical, Medieval or even Elizabethan drama surely could not. And yet we are probably less aware of the emotions we are feeling, less *in touch* with their implications. Is it the force of our involvement which has changed, or its quality?

Read the following two dramatic extracts carefully and take time to compare them (in your own terms) before you try to answer the questions:

EKDAL. Hm. It's poor fun, going for one's morning walk alone.

HEDVIG. Didn't you feel like shooting, Grandpapa?

EKDAL. It's not shooting weather today. So dark in there you can hardly see in front of you.

HEDVIG. Don't you ever feel like shooting anything besides the rabbits?

EKDAL. Surely the rabbits are good enough, aren't they?

HEDVIG. Yes, but what about the wild duck?

EKDAL. Ha, ha! Are you afraid I shall shoot your wild duck for you? Not for the world, bless you! Never!

HEDVIG. No, I expect you couldn't. Because it must be difficult to shoot wild ducks.

EKDAL. Couldn't? I should jolly well think I could!

HEDVIG. How could you manage it, Grandpapa? I don't mean with *my* wild duck, but with others.

EKDAL. I should make sure of shooting it in the breast, you know; that's the surest place. And then, you must shoot *against* the lie of the feathers, you see, not *with* the feathers.

HEDVIG. Do they die, then, Grandpapa?

EKDAL. Oh yes, they die all right, so long as you shoot properly. Well, I must go in and tidy myself. Hm – you see – hm. [*Goes into his room.*]

[*Hedvig waits a moment, glances towards the door, goes across to the bookcase, streches up on tip-toes, takes the double-barrelled pistol from the shelf and looks at it. Gina, with her brush and duster, comes in from the living-room. Hedvig puts down the pistol quickly and unnoticed.*]

GINA. Don't go meddling with your father's things, Hedvig.

HEDVIG. [*moving away from the shelves.*] I only wanted to tidy up a little.

GINA. You'd better go into the kitchen and see if the coffee's keeping hot; I'll take the tray with me when I go down to him.

(Ibsen, *The Wild Duck*)

[[. . .] *the ceiling opens. A pink cloud comes down. On it the Three Gods rise, very slowly.*]

SHEN TE. Oh, don't, illustrious ones! Don't go away! Don't leave me! How can I face the good old couple who've lost their store and the water seller with his stiff hand? And how can I defend myself from the barber whom I do not love and from Sun whom I do love? And I am with child. Soon there'll be a little son who'll want to eat. I can't stay here! [*She turns with a hunted look toward the door which will let her tormentors in.*]

THE FIRST GOD. You can do it. Just be good and everything will turn out well!

[*Enter the witnesses. They look with surprise at the judges floating on their pink cloud.*]

WANG. Show respect! The gods have appeared among us! Three of the highest gods have come to Setzuan to find a good human being. They had found one already, but . . .

THE FIRST GOD. No 'but'! Here she is!

ALL. Shen Te!

THE FIRST GOD. She has not perished. She was only hidden. She will stay with you. A good human being!

SHEN TE. But I need my cousin!

THE FIRST GOD. Not too often!

SHEN TE. At least once a week!

THE FIRST GOD. Once a month. That's enough!

SHEN TE. Oh, don't go away, illustrious ones! I haven't told you everything! I need you desperately!

[*The Gods sing.*]

THE TRIO OF THE VANISHING GODS ON THE CLOUD

> We, alas, may never stay
>> More than a fleeting year
> If you watch your treasure long
>> 'Twill always disappear.

> Down here the golden light of truth
>> With shadow is alloyed
> That is why we take our leave
>> And go back to the void.

SHEN TE. Help! [*Her cries continue through the song.*]

> Our anxious search is over now
>> Let us to heaven ascend
> The good, good woman of Setzuan
>> Praising, praising to the end!

[*As Shen Te stretches out her arms to them in desperation, they disappear above, smiling and waving.*]

(Brecht, *The Good Woman of Setzuan*)

Questions

(a) In which of these two contexts are we as audience likely to feel more?

(b) Why do you think this is?

(c) Is there a character you identify with readily in the first extract?

(d)   What do you feel for the characters in the second extract?

(e)   How do you think you might react to the second extract if you saw it on stage?

(f)   How far does the setting itself condition our response?

(g)   Which of the two extracts do you find the more exciting?

—————— **The witches' brew** ——————

For the ancients, comedy and tragedy were separate genres, each with its own rules and conventions. What was an appropriate inspiration in terror and pity could hardly be suitable material for laughter.

But we in the 20th century seem to like our poisons mixed. Frequently, in our reactions to all kinds of drama – popular drama on TV or radio, as well as in live stage productions – we may find ourselves laughing and at the same time wondering whether what we are laughing at is not in fact more tragic than ludicrous. We may find that increasingly the *terror and pity* with which a tragic piece of theatre inspires us are heightened and deepened by a dose of painful laughter.

Possibly as English audiences we have been predisposed to this mixture by our exposure to Shakespeare. We may remember from our school days learning to look at scenes full of fools and drunkards and grave-diggers, not just as funny in themselves, but as a key to something more serious. But it is in our own century, with the advent of the absurdist playwright Samuel Beckett and his highly unorthodox and at the time controversial play, *Waiting for Godot* (1953), that audiences have experienced how completely inextricable these apparently contradictory emotions can become.

Sometimes the line between comedy and tragedy is extremely thin. In our everyday lives we may not ever manage to distinguish satisfactorily between what is potentially funny and what is potentially tragic. What we call *black* humour bridges the two almost completely. On the stage, this narrow distinction can be put to good use. Whether it is a matter of laughing and crying by turns, or laughing and crying simultaneously, a dramatic writer who mobilises both these impulses is inviting us to experience a more complete representation of our own lives, with all their contradictions. But with the tension of these opposing demands on us, we also face insecurity. The anxiety that a 20th-century absurdist drama can generate in us is itself a fertile theatrical experience. The play which *throws* us is often the play which will linger uncomfortably in our memories, as we continue to puzzle out what comment it is making on our values in our own lives.

Exercise 6

Read the following two extracts through several times, imagining you are a member of a real audience, and make a note of your reactions. Then work through the questions which follow.

OLD WOMAN: Oh! you *are*, my dear, oh you *are* really, you are *so* . . . so . . . you could have been something in life, much more than a Quartermaster-General.

OLD MAN: Don't let us be boastful . . . we should be satisfied with the little we have . . .

OLD WOMAN: Perhaps you've wrecked your career?

OLD MAN [*suddenly starts crying*]: Wrecked it? Dashed it to pieces? Broken it? Oh! Where are you, mummy? Mummy, where are you? . . . hee, hee, hee, I'm an orphan. [*Groaning*] . . . an orphan, a norphan . . .

OLD WOMAN: Mummy's with you, what are you afraid of?

OLD MAN: No, Semiramis, my pet. You're not my mummy . . . an orphan, a norphan, who will look after me?

OLD WOMAN: But I'm still here, my love!

OLD MAN: That's not the same . . . I want my mummy, so there! You're not my mummy.

OLD WOMAN [*stroking him*]: You're breaking my heart. Don't cry, little one.

OLD MAN: Hee, hee! Leave me alone; hee, hee! I feel all cracked and smashed, I've a pain, my career is hurting me, it's all in pieces.

OLD WOMAN: There, there!

OLD MAN [*sobbing, with his mouth wide open, like a baby*]: I'm an orphan . . . a norphan.

OLD WOMAN [*trying to coax him into being quiet*]: My little orphan boy, you're breaking mummy's heart, my pet. [*She has already started rocking the disillusioned old man backwards and forwards on her knees.*]

OLD MAN [*sobbing*]: Hee, hee, hee! Mummy! Where's my mummy? I've lost my mummy.

OLD WOMAN: I'm your wife, so now I'm your mummy, too.

OLD MAN [*giving in a little*]: It's not true, I'm an orphan, hee, hee.

OLD WOMAN [*still rocking him*]: My little sweetheart, my little orphan, norphan, porphan, borphan, morphan.

OLD MAN [*still sulky, but coming round slowly*]: No . . . I don't want to, I wo-o-on't!

OLD WOMAN [*singing softly*]: Anorphan-lee, anorphan-lo, anorphan-lah, anorphan-lu, anorphan-lay.

OLD MAN: NO-o-o-o . . . No-o-o-o.

(Eugène Ionesco, *The Chairs*)

OLD MAN: Alas! . . . Alack! . . .

OLD WOMAN: Alas! . . . Alack! . . .

OLD MAN: . . . Our bodies will fall far from one another, we shall rot in watery solitude . . . Let us not complain too much.

OLD WOMAN: We must do what must be done! . . .

OLD MAN: We shall not be forgotten. The eternal Emperor will remember us, always.

OLD WOMAN [*echo*]: Always.

OLD MAN: We shall leave some trace behind, for we are not towns, but people.

BOTH [*together*]: A street will bear our names!

OLD MAN: Let us be united in time and eternity, if not in space, as we were in trial and tribulation; let us die at the same moment . . . [*To the impassive, motionless Orator*] Once more, then . . . I am depending on you . . . You must tell everything . . . Bequeath the messsage to everyone . . . [*To the Emperor*] With Your Majesty's permission . . . Farewell, to all of you. Farewell, Semiramis.

OLD WOMAN: Farewell, to all of you! . . . Farewell, my love!

OLD MAN: Long live the Emperor! [*He throws confetti and paper streamers over the invisible Emperor; a fanfare of trumpets is heard; a brilliant light, as from a firework.*]

OLD WOMAN: Long live the Emperor! [*Confetti and paper*

streamers over the Emperor, then over the impassive, motionless Orator, and over the empty chairs]
OLD MAN [*more confetti, etc.*]: Long live the Emperor!
OLD WOMAN [*more confetti, etc.*]: Long live the Emperor!
[THE OLD COUPLE *at one and the same time both jump through their windows, crying 'Long live the Emperor!' A sudden silence; the firework's glare has gone, an 'Ah!' is heard from both sides of the stage, and the glaucous sound of bodies striking water. The light is no longer coming through the great door and the windows: there is only the dim light there was at the beginning; the wide-open windows gape black, the curtains flapping in the wind.*]

(Eugène Ionesco, *The Chairs*)

Questions

(a)   One of these passages occurs very near the beginning of the play, and one almost at the end. Can you tell from the text whether anything has happened between them?

(b)   How do you think an audience would react to the first of these two extracts, seeing it performed on stage?

(c)   What in the first extract is comic?

(d)   Is the comedy tempered with something else?

(e)   Can you point to something in the text which might be partly responsible for the complex emotion it arouses?

(f)   How might the effect of the second extract differ from the effect of the first?

When we have tried to answer all these questions, there is one more question which we shall inevitably find ourselves asking. As students of theatre we can and should try to chart the dramatic movements within a play, to see where the emotional peaks and troughs are and what are the mechanics behind them. But to follow our own reactions is also to watch ourselves being manipulated. Perhaps successful theatre is always, in a sense, manipulation, yet it is only intermittently that we feel it as such. We may be more or less moved, and more or less aware of ourselves as moved. It is surely the distance a playwright chooses to create between the events which take place on the stage and the audience's own lived reality which, more than any other factor, determines the quality of our response. In some cases, as we shall see in the next chapter, it may not be in a playwright's interest for his or her audience to be *moved* at all.

--------------------- **Commentary** ---------------------

Exercise 1

It is impossible, of course, for me to go through the endless personal variations here. What creates a feeling of closeness between a stage production and any one member of its audience may be totally at odds with another person's experience. Again, distance is not the result of *one* factor, but the interaction of several. Take the example used in the previous chapter of the effect produced when a character on stage addresses the audience directly. Ultimately the effect is not produced by this one device in isolation: the device will work differently in different contexts. In one context it will result in a feeling of alienation; in another, it can be a trigger of powerful emotion.

Any of the resources at the dramatist's or director's or actors' disposal can be similarly double-edged, according to the uses to which they are put, and the company in which they find themselves.

However you may have replied to questions (a) to (d), your answers to questions (e) and (f) will be particularly interesting: the cumulative effects of realism or stylisation in text and production cannot fail to influence audience response in one way or another. Ask yourself now whether ultimately the level of your identification with the characters and happenings on stage meant your memory of the experience was an emotional or a thought-provoking one. Are the two interdependent? Or are they to some extent mutually exclusive?

Exercise 2

Again, answers to these questions will be subjective. They will undoubtedly overlap somewhat with and perhaps enlarge on your answers to **Exercise 1**. The aim here is to make you aware of the *invisible* element in a piece of dramatic writing which remains open to interpretation by director and actors, and of the active role you yourself as a member of the audience inevitably play in the dramatic whole. Nevertheless, if you learn to look at the text attentively, you will find yourself becoming steadily more aware of the clues and *silences* which are the dramatist's gift. If we were to direct a production, our choices might well be very different from those of another director. Nevertheless, if they are good choices, they can be rationalised by a study of what the text actually does give us. They must answer to the play's whole meaning as we perceive it, and they must translate and reinforce that meaning for an audience.

Exercise 3

(a)   The emotional impact of all three of these extracts seems to me to depend largely on our perception of unexpectedly contrasted elements.

(b)   The scene from *King Lear* contains many contrasts. If we know the play, even by hearsay, we shall have a strong picture of Lear's ever older and more 'cracked' presence which contrasts movingly with his youngest daughter Cordelia's youth and soundness of mind and body. His 'ravings' are poetic with imagery and wild repeated rhetorical questions. Her interventions are poetic in their stripped simplicity. Against his mono-logues they shine with the truth of despair. Together they create a tragic duo which is unforgettable, culminating in the last simple, childlike, wise, desperate question:

'Will't please your highness walk?'

In the case of the *Equus* extract, the contrast is not so much inside this scene itself, as between the momentary lull of this moment in which psychiatrist and patient *meet*, in more ways than one, and the violence of the emotion and social constraints which surround it. The scene also depends on a partial role-reversal: we expect the patient to suffer and the doctor to be immune and aloof. Here we see Dysart himself as vulner-able, as abandoned by the gods, in exactly the same way Alan is. There are electric moments in the play when Alan becomes suddenly powerful, and we see that the suffering is also Dysart's, and society's, and our own.

In the third extract, the most striking contrast is between what we see and what we hear: the violence, however ritualised, of the killing we witness, and the formality, however violent the meanings of the words themselves, of the verse chorus. Although Eliot's poetry here is not formal in the traditional ways (it does not use systematic rhyme or a sustained, regular metre), this is nevertheless very formal, rhetorical language. It is full of repetitions. Regular or not, its powerful rhythms impose themselves on our consciousness with the inexorable beat of ritual music or incantation.

(c)   Yes. Surely there is, though, oddly enough, it is (perhaps) least obvious in the extract from *King Lear*, where it penetrates us in the quality of the poetry. In the scene from *Equus*, the dialogue itself is not obviously poetic or stylised, though the simple language does contain reminders that we are in a surreal world of men-gods-horses, all the more striking against this background of present-day psychological concerns. In the *Murder in the Cathedral* extract, there is obvious stylisation not only in the dramatist's choice of verse and the kind of verse he has chosen as his medium, but also in the decision to use a Chorus, complete with all its associative baggage of stylisation and dramatic function in the very different context of Greek tragedy.

(d)   The answer to this part of the exercise is too long and complex to cover adequately here. If you have read your chosen play attentively you will, in any case, not need a 'teacher' to read it again on your behalf. Have confidence in your own ability to talk about the mechanics of what is happening in a play. You can be sure that a moment of great drama has been *set up* by many factors in a play's development. Have faith in your own ability to react to them, to think about them, and ultimately to analyse them. You will find that your discussion of a play does not have to be particularly *technical*, as long as you are ready to use your imagination to visualise the play in performance and to talk about the 'ups and downs' of that imagined performance in a thoughtful and coherent way.

This last part of the exercise should have been a particularly useful one, in that it highlights the relationship between an attentive reading of a small part of the text of a play and a more representative reading of the same play as a dramatic whole. A fragment of text may suddenly reveal to us the dynamics which have been only latent in a play's development; a whole play may be *feeding* a few intensely dramatic moments.

Exercise 4

The attendant's speech contains elements of formal stylisation in its sound: presumably the translator's rhythms are to some extent an echo of the rhythms of the Greek original, though other sound-echoes may well have been lost. But there are many other formal patterns there too: repetitions which echo the theme of repetition, of a destiny which falls back to earth in blood in lines 10–13; the antithetical (balance and contrast) movement of the speech as a whole and certain of its parts (11.16–18) which reinforces the theme of impossible, unthinkable union. There is stylisation there too even in the decision to relate these tragic events indirectly and not to show them on stage.

The effects of these different forms of stylisation are cumulative. The whole speech is an almost unbearable combination of graphic narrative and distance. Then the Chorus' simple questions cut right through all these rhetorical elements, as if to the bone.

For me, this is where the real world finally, painfully, intrudes.

Exercise 5

(a) The answer to this must be to some extent subjective (and culturally relative), but I would guess that most audiences would be likely to feel much more in the context of the scene in the first extract.

(b) I think this is largely because we are so used to naturalistic (or at least unobtrusively non-naturalistic) drama that realism of setting, dialogue, character and events acts as a kind of licence: it is *safe* to feel in this context. If there is symbolism here, it is a symbolism we can welcome. We are anonymous, in the dark; no one is likely suddenly to turn a light on us and make us uncomfortable. We can let ourselves be moved to tears or laughter, and *no one need know*. Even without the physical facts of theatre, lighting, set and acting style, there are distinct signs here to tell us that our role as potential audience of the second extract will have very little to do with this kind of invisible support and reassurance.

(c) I should think that it would be eminently possible to identify with any of these three characters here. Gina says little, but what she says is ordinary and convincing, and allows us the possibility of imagining behind her words as much or as little of a real life as we like. Old Ekdal is not obviously sympathetic, yet his hesitations allow us the same freedom to make him a real and complex character, with potential conflicts and contradictions. Against this background of understated adult lives, Hedvig's clear questions must surely seem to come from the needy child in all of us.

(d) I would guess that most readers would be unlikely to feel anything at all for these characters.

(e)   Your response to this question will of course be an individual one. If we are used to being *carried away* by any drama we watch, we might conceivably find it very tedious. Yet if we look at the elements of this *package*, we can see that it has much to recommend it – music, drama and special effects.

(f)   If we try to imagine in detail a setting for this scene, we shall probably find ourselves in difficulties almost immediately; before we can decide *how* to stage this, we have to work out for ourselves how real it is, and how real it ought to be. If the stage design were for a 'real' naturalistic room (we are in fact told that it is a courtroom), coupled with sophisticated techniques which might soften the 'dream' intrusions and make them more acceptable, we should find ourselves interpreting the whole scene in the light of those decisions. If the set is minimal and the Gods apparently quite as real as Wang or Shen Te, then we shall react to the message of the scene quite differently.

(g)   It is impossible for me to answer this on your behalf. But whichever way you reply to this question, your answer will tell you something important about your own values and responses as a member of an audience, real or imaginary. This in turn should help you to look again at your critical standpoint. Can you visualise ever choosing differently?

Exercise 6

(a)   It seems to me that there is no way of telling from a comparison of these passages whether a lot has happened in the intervening play, or very little. We begin with a dialogue between two old people, and we almost end with one. True, they commit suicide in this second extract, but we might ask ourselves how alive and well they appear to us at the beginning. If anything, they are more 'sane' here: more worldly, more 'positive' in their outlook. There is talk of the Emperor. The Orator has come to give his message. If anything has changed here, it is the language itself, which has grown old – from the meaningless baby-talk in the first extract to the equally meaningless, but at least conventionally understandable clichés of the second extract.

(b)   I don't know about you, but I have a feeling this first scene would always hover somewhere between real comedy and something far more disturbing.

(c)   The sudden transformations are surely funny as well as surprising. The wordplay (*orphan, norphan,* etc.) would be funny initially, as would the incongruity of this babyish old man who sobs that '[his] career is hurting [him].' Whether it would continue to be funny with the verbal escalations of 'my little orphan, norphan, porphan, borphan, morphan' and the grotesque and pathetic lullaby is another matter entirely.

(d)   The comedy here undoubtedly *is* tempered with pathos, but then most comedy surely is. (Think about classic TV comedy like *Steptoe and Son,* or even the 'blacker' *Monty Python* sketches). But there is another element too. The grotesque distortion can go so far and it is funny; if it oversteps the mark it generates unease. We are not *sure* here whether we should still be laughing or not. This use of what ought to be simply farcical to generate discomfort or even fear in the audience (even as we are still laughing!) is one of the most fertile and provocative techniques of absurd drama.

(e)   A number of examples could be chosen here. We have already talked about the old man's incongruous regression to babyhood and the way in which words are used and used again and over-used until they become quite meaningless. We could also mention the 'hee, hee!' of the old man's sobs – is he crying or laughing?

(f)   It is stylised in more obvious ways. The way the old woman echoes her husband, the way the two speak in unison, the conventional, empty gesture of confetti, coupled with fanfares, the empty chairs which witness those speeches and gestures – all combine to produce an effect which is surely sinister, if not slightly sickening, in the disorientation it hints at.

Now try to get hold of a copy of *The Chairs* and read it straight through. The enormous dramatic fact which is central to the play has intentionally been skirted by our discussion. I think you will be surprised to see how the elements we have talked about fit into the play's development, contribute to its power, and reinforce our astonishment at what is actually happening on stage.

9

DISTANCE AND IRONY

────────── **The wheel and the leg** ──────────

'Theatre,' wrote the early 19th-century French poet and dramatist Guillaume Apollinaire, 'is no more the life it interprets than the wheel is a leg.' We have already touched briefly on Naturalism as a crucial movement in the historical development of theatre as we know it. But we have not yet looked more closely at the assumptions on which Naturalism rests. Movements in the theatre, like movements in any other branch of literature, are very rarely close-knit groupings which will fit readily into a moment in time or a particular geographical place. Literary tendencies are much more likely to be awkward, straggly conceptions which have forerunners and latecomers, and cut across expected boundaries of nationality, language and literary genre. If we are not careful we can find ourselves working more as detectives than as critics, trying to disentangle this or that hidden influence, and reducing literary identities to ciphers in their possible relationship to a prestigious 'suspect number one'.

Nevertheless there *are* groupings and tendencies which can be talked about meaningfully, if not definitively labelled and described. Naturalism may still be very much with us. In the drama enjoyed by the average adult in our western society, it is almost certainly the most dominant influence. In our films and television, our radio drama, and a substantial proportion of our stage drama, the late 19th century still shapes our expectations as no other period of our theatrical heritage now can. The assumptions Naturalism rests on seem to have embedded themselves so deeply in our culture that we usually accept the complaints that, 'it didn't seem real,' or 'it just wasn't convincing' without question. How could anything that didn't convince us be worth watching? How could a performance which began by announcing to us, 'What you are about to watch is completely unreal' be anything but rather childish escapism?

Yet, in the late 1920s, one immensely important and innovative dramatist – Bertolt Brecht – was certain that it could. The assumptions on which Naturalism in the theatre is based are very close to the assumptions which underlie the Naturalist novel: that the greatest seriousness and scientific truth lie in an illusion so perfect it is almost photographic. By losing our own identity for the sake of this nearly perfect copy of life as we know it, we can come closer to the principle behind all life. We hope to gain the truest picture of reality by suppressing our part in it. The experiment unfolds in front of us. The dramatist mixes human substances and we watch them fizz, change colour, explode.

But the choice between Realism and *escapism* is a false choice. There is nothing intrinsically more 'real' about the novel which carries us almost bodily into its fictional world, or about the stage-set which looks uncannily like our Aunt Margaret's sitting-room. After all, we are real people in a real theatre watching a real play. What can be more truthful than for us to be aware of that fact at every juncture of the drama? We may no longer enter the play so fully in our imagination, but instead we are entering it more truthfully, not just with our ears and eyes and emotions, but with our heads still very firmly on our shoulders. And, perhaps even more importantly, we have no need to stop in some dark corner of the stairs to put our *real life* identity together again on the way out. Whatever we have experienced in the theatre is ours to take home with us.

The influence of Brecht and his company, the Berliner Ensemble, founded in 1949, has been crucial for the development of modern theatre. Like Shakespeare and Molière before him, he was a practitioner. His theories about the nature of theatre and its significance as a means to moral and political awareness and understanding were not merely theories. His conception of what he called 'epic theatre' grew out of real dramatic presentations and the reactions of real audiences. What

Brecht called the *Verfremdungseffekt* (what we generally hear referred to in English as the *alienation-* (*or A-*) *effect*) was the result of a real conviction: the conviction that if we were allowed to forget ourselves in theatre as in a warm bath, we would step out of it not much cleaner than when we stepped in (the image is mine, and not Brecht's own!). Theatre should be mentally invigorating, reminding us of its function and our own needs with its all too visible plumbing, using unexpected changes of flow and temperature to remind us perpetually that it carries a message.

Exercise 1

Brecht was of course not the only dramatist to reject the underlying beliefs of Naturalist drama. As early as the turn of the century, for example, the French dramatist Alfred Jarry had used techniques similar to some of Brecht's for more purely iconoclastic purposes. He already used a mixture of masks, cardboard cut-outs and placard scene-changes in his farcical and grotesque *Ubu* plays. Brecht's techniques are more sophisticated, and his justification of them more serious and systematic. But we can still recognise an element of Surrealist drama in the clashes of context and expectation which shape the grotesque and sinister figure of Arturo Ui.

(a)   Imagine you are a member of the audience for what you have heard is to be a serious production of a serious dramatic work. The actors make a point of 'mingling' with the audience before the performance and during the interval. Do you feel:

     (i) threatened?
     (ii) flattered?
     (iii) intrigued?

(b)   When the scene first changes during the performance, the lights are not dimmed and the actors themselves shift furniture and props in a matter-of-fact way. Do you:

     (i) assume the company is too poor to pay stagehands?
     (ii) ask yourself if there is anything in the play itself which might justify this treatment?
     (iii) hardly notice it, because it happens so often in contemporary theatre?

(c)   The play you are watching uses a lot of music. It seems to you to be intrusive. Do you:

     (i)   try to ignore it and enjoy the play as best you can in spite of it?
    (ii)   ask yourself what kind of music you yourself would have chosen?
   (iii)   momentarily forget the play, and enjoy the music for its own sake, inappropriate or not?

(d)   You are at a performance of *The Resistible Rise of Arturo Ui*. While the Chicago businessman Ui perfects his voice, gestures and persona in front of a mirror, a movie-screen at one side of the stage shows stills of Hitler. Do you watch:

     (i)   the screen?
    (ii)   Ui?
   (iii)   both as best you can?

Exercise 2

Brecht expressed his theory of the theatre in his poetry, as well as in his copious prose. It seems to me that in deciding to adopt a new stance with respect to the currents of dramatic writing and performance which dominated the theatre of his youth, he was making a decision which is not merely his own, but one which is central to all drama. The most fundamental values of any play rest on the position it adopts with respect to reality. Should it 'hold as 'twere the mirror up to nature' (*Hamlet*), or should it try to go one better? Every time a play is written, rehearsed, or performed, that question has to be answered one way or the other.

Look closely at the following poem, and then answer the questions that follow:

On Judging

You artists who, for pleasure or for pain
Deliver yourselves up to the judgement of the audience
Be moved in future
To deliver up also to the judgement of the audience
The world which you show

You should show what is; but also
In showing what is you should suggest what could be and is not
And might be helpful. For from your portrayal
The audience must learn to deal with what is portrayed.
Let this learning be pleasureable. Learning must be taught
As an art, and you should
Teach dealing with things and with people
As an art too, and the practice of art is pleasurable.
To be sure you live in a dark time. You see man
Tossed back and forth like a ball by evil forces.
Only an idiot lives without worry. The unsuspecting
Are already destined to go under. What were the earthquakes
Of grey prehistory compared to the afflictions
Which we suffer in cities? What were bad harvests
To the need that ravages us in the midst of plenty?

(from *Bertolt Brecht Poems*, ed. Willett and Manheim, p. 308)

Questions

(a)   What does this poem say about the responsibilities of the artist?

(b)   What is implied here about the function of theatre?

(c)   The poem seems to change direction at line 14. How is this last section relevant?

(d)   How do you react to these ideas?

(e)   Could they be applied to *all* theatre? Could they be applied to Shakespeare or Chekhov? Or the play you saw last?

—————— Irony and its uses ——————

Irony can take many forms in the theatre, as it can in fiction. The verbal ironies we explored in the context of first-person narration in the novel can also operate on stage, though the necessary balance of subtlety and comprehension is probably harder for a dramatist to achieve. The classic visual ironies probably work better: the pickpocket having his pocket picked is likely to be a lot funnier on stage than he would be, caught between the pages of a novel.

But some forms of irony seem to lend themselves even more completely to the conditions of theatre. The irony we call *dramatic irony* is a situational irony which comes into existence when an audience knows more of what is going on than do one or more of the characters on stage. At a very simple, obvious level it is the irony we perceive when the pantomime dame comes and stands just where we know the flour-sack is about to drop. At a more serious level, it is the passage Muecke quotes from Sophocles:

> 'And it is my solemn prayer
> That the unknown murderer, and his accomplices,
> If such there be, may wear the brand of shame
> For their shameful act, unfriended, to their life's end.'

The irony is quite complex here, operating as it does on several levels: not only does the audience, primed with knowledge of the myth on which the drama is based, realise that the murderer Œdipus is cursing is in fact himself, but even the detail of his chosen imagery ('brand of shame') seems to prefigure his eventual blinding. 'Unknown' takes on a new meaning; 'unfriended' takes on a new meaning if we already know what is to become of Jocasta and her children.

The question of how irony affects an audience's relationship with the character who is the object of it is a fascinating one. We cannot truly be empathising with a character if we know more than he or she does. We have been put in a position to look down on events and often to foresee their outcome, while the character is still wrestling with conflicts and indecision that we know to be quite futile. In this sense, irony is distance. It separates us irretrievably from a character and the emotional turmoil he or she may feel. Yet in another sense, irony *builds* a relationship between character and us, the members of the audience who are in a position to help and illuminate, and change the dramatic outcome, while at the same time being quite helpless, condemned by our role as theatre audience to sit still and quiet in our seats. We have only to hear very small children shouting to the dame, 'Look out, he's behind you!' to understand that the irony of *being in the know* is imposing a real tension on us. As adult watchers of classical tragedy, we may not jump up and shout, 'Don't do it, Œdipus!' Nevertheless, for the drama to function, a part of us at least must want to. In situations like these, we do sometimes feel intensely for the character who is *at risk*. Yet it is not the ordinary human sympathy aroused by real people in our real lives, but a product of the theatrical experience itself. Probably even as we feel it we are acutely aware that if we *were* to shout, 'Don't do it!' the theatrical conventions and our own necessary collusion in them would immediately be painfully, embarrassingly obvious!

Exercise 3

Read the following short extracts, together with any brief contextual explanations which precede them, and answer the questions:

[We, as audience, know that Juliet is not dead, but has taken a potion which will make her appear to be dead, in order to escape the necessity of marrying Paris.]

ROMEO

[. . .]   Ah, dear Juliet,
Why art thou yet so fair? shall I believe
That unsubstantial Death is amorous,
And that the lean abhorred monster keeps
Thee here in dark to be his paramour?
For fear of that, I still will stay with thee;
And never from this palace of dim night
Depart again: here, here will I remain
With worms that are thy chamber-maids; O, here
Will I set up my everlasting rest;
And shake the yoke of inauspicious stars
From this world-wearied flesh. – Eyes, look your last!
Arms, take your last embrace! and, lips, O you
The doors of breath, seal with a righteous kiss
A dateless bargain to engrossing death! –
Come, bitter conduct, come, unsavoury guide!
Thou desperate pilot, now at once run on
The dashing rocks thy sea-sick weary bark!
Here's to my love! [*drinks*] – O true apothecary!
Thy drugs are quick. – Thus with a kiss I die.

(Shakespeare, *Romeo and Juliet*)

[We know from the previous scene between Willy and his employer that, far from being cherished and well-treated by the company

— 216 —

which he has worked for all his life, Willy is being pushed aside, perhaps even put out to grass, in favour of younger talent.]

BEN: Now look here, William. I've bought timberland in Alaska and I need a man to look after things for me.

WILLY: God, timberland! Me and my boys in those grand outdoors!

BEN: You've got a new continent at your doorstep, William. Get out of these cities, they're full of talk and time payments and courts of law. Screw on your fists and you can fight for a fortune up there.

WILLY: Yes, yes! Linda, Linda!

[LINDA *enters as of old, with the wash.*]

LINDA: Oh, you're back?

BEN: I haven't much time.

WILLY: No, wait! Linda, he's got a proposition for me in Alaska.

LINDA: But you've got – [*To* BEN] He's got a beautiful job here.

WILLY: But in Alaska, kid, I could –

LINDA: You're doing well enough, Willy!

BEN [*to* Linda]: Enough for what, my dear?

LINDA [*frightened of* BEN *and angry at him*]: Don't say those things to him! Enough to be happy right here, right now. [*To* WILLY, *while* BEN *laughs*] Why must everybody conquer the world? You're well liked, and the boys love you, and someday – [*to* BEN] – why, old man Wagner told him just the other day that if he keeps it up he'll be a member of the firm, didn't he, Willy?

WILLY: Sure, sure. I am building something with this firm, Ben, and if a man is building something he must be on the right track, mustn't he?

BEN: What are you building? Lay your hand on it. Where is it?

(Arthur Miller, *Death of a Salesman*)

[Nina, chasing her dream of becoming an actress, and fascinated by the more worldly Trigorin, has cut herself off from her home, her past, her reputation, the ideal 'artist's' life of dreams which Trepliov is still ineffectually pursuing.]

NINA. [. . .] I became petty and common, when I acted I did it stupidly. . . . I didn't know what to do with my hands or how to stand on the stage, I couldn't control my voice. . . . But you can't imagine what it feels like – when you know that you are acting abominably. I'm a seagull. No, that's not it again. . . . Do you remember you shot a seagull? A man came along by chance, saw it and destroyed it, just to pass the time. . . . A subject for a short story. . . . That's not it. [*Rubs her forehead.*] What was I talking about? . . . Yes, about the stage. I'm not like that now. . . . Now I am a real actress, I act with intense enjoyment, with enthusiasm; on the stage I am intoxicated and I feel that I am beautiful. But now, while I'm living here, I go for walks a lot. . . . I keep walking and thinking . . . [. . .]

TREPLIOV [*sadly*]. You have found your right path, you know which way you're going – but I'm still floating about in a chaotic world of dreams and images, without knowing what use it all is. . . . I have no faith, and I don't know what my vocation is.

(Chekhov, *The Seagull*)

Questions

(a) Say as much as you can about the central irony of the Shakespeare extract and the way it affects our reactions to Romeo's words.

(b) Would it distance us as members of a real audience, or would it bring us closer?

(c) Describe the functioning of dramatic irony in the Arthur Miller extract.

(d) Which character is the object of the irony in the Chekhov passage.

(e) In any of these extracts, are there characters who *half-know* what we know (i.e. who in theory *ought* to know the truth but are unable for some reason to grasp its significance?)

(f) How close would an audience feel, do you think, to a character who is blinded, not by events outside his or her control, but by insensitivity or pig-headedness?

Plays within plays

When we see ourselves and our surroundings reflected in a mirror, we may react to the experience in various different ways. Most of the time we probably hardly think about the phenomenon, but only, 'Goodness, look at that spot!' or 'Have I forgotten to comb my hair today?' Sometimes we may sit in front of the glass in a dream, feeling as if something of ourselves or our world is actually caught deep inside it. Only very occasionally will we become aware of the mechanics of the reflecting process, the light, the angle, the dust on the surface.

In the theatre, when a playwright suddenly makes us aware of different levels of reality and our own relationship to them, he or she is exploiting what is potentially a vital dimension of every dramatic experience: in making us self-conscious about what we are seeing, he or she is also making us *think*.

The distancing techniques that Brecht used so systematically are one way of making an audience aware of the artifice of theatre and its real requirements in our own space and time. But there are other ways of questioning our relationship with what is happening on stage. Like a telescope which may be held at either end, the *play within a play* is just as likely to magnify what is happening as to distance it, but whatever we see, we are somehow aware of our hands on the barrel, the distorting lens next to our eye.

The *play within a play* may not immediately *alienate* us in the way the Brechtian screen does. After all, the fact that characters within the play we are watching are themselves putting on a dramatic performance does not *logically* invalidate those characters' reality. Real people do sometimes put on plays. But if we are at all impressionable, the secondary play will surely remind us that this is a play we are watching, that our relationship to it parallels the relationship of the play within a play to characters on stage, and that our life will go on outside the theatre, just as theirs does inside. When we draw inferences about the characters we are almost certainly half-aware that we ourselves are also subject to influence. We are not being shown what characters and events are, so much as *what theatre is*. And what is more *real* for us as audience than that vital relationship?

Exercise 4

Read the following two extracts, relating them as well as you can to the whole plays from which they are taken. (For the second extract it may help you to look back at exercise 3.)

QUINCE

Francis Flute the bellows-mender.

FLUTE

Here, Peter Quince.

QUINCE

You must take Thisby on you.

FLUTE

What is Thisby? a wandering knight?

QUINCE

It is the lady that Pyramus must love.

FLUTE

Nay, faith, let not me play a woman; I have a beard coming.

QUINCE

That's all one: you shall play it in a mask, and you may speak as small as you will.

BOTTOM

An I may hide my face, let me play Thisby too: I'll speak in a monstrous little voice; – 'Thisne, Thisne,' – 'Ah, Pyramus, my lover dear! Thisby dear, and lady dear!'

QUINCE

No, no; you must play Pyramus:– and, Flute, you Thisby.

BOTTOM

Well, proceed.

QUINCE

Robin Starveling the tailor.

STARVELING

Here, Peter Quince.

QUINCE

Robin Starveling, you must play Thisby's mother. – Tom Snout the tinker.

SNOUT

Here, Peter Quince.

QUINCE

You, Pyramus' father; myself, Thisby's father; -Snug the joiner, you, the lion's part:– and, I hope, here is a play fitted.

SNUG

Have you the lion's part written? pray you, if it be, give it me, for I am slow of study.

QUINCE

You may do it extempore, for it is nothing but roaring.

BOTTOM

Let me play the lion too: I will roar, that I will do any man's heart good to hear me; I will roar, that I will make the duke say, 'Let him roar again, let him roar again.'

(Shakespeare, *A Midsummer Night's Dream*)

NINA. The men, the lions, the eagles, the partridges, the antlered deer, the geese, the spiders, the silent fishes of the deep, starfishes and creatures unseen to the eye – in short, all living things, all living things, having completed their mournful cycle, have been snuffed out. For thousands of years the earth has borne no living thing, and this poor moon now lights its lamp in vain. The cranes no longer wake in the meadows with a cry, no longer are May beetles heard humming in the groves of lime trees. It is cold, cold, cold. . . . It is deserted, deserted, deserted. . . . It is terrifying, terrifying, terrifying. . .

[*Pause*]

All living bodies have turned to dust and the Eternal Master has transformed them into stones, into water, into clouds, while their souls have all been merged into one. The common soul of the world is I – I. . . . The souls of Alexander the Great, of Caesar, of Shakespeare, of Napoleon, and of the basest leech are contained in me! In me the consciousness of men is merged with the instinct of the animals; I remember all, all, all, and live every single life anew in my own being!

[*Will-o'-the-wisps appear.*]

ARKADINA [*in a low voice*]. This sounds like the Decadent School.

TREPLIOV [*imploringly and reproachfully*]. Mamma!

(Chekhov, *The Seagull*)

How do you think each of these *plays within a play* is likely to comment on the whole play that we are seeing? How much of the commentary is explicit? What is implied more obliquely in each case?

Exercise 5

Read the two extracts which follow and compare them. They are in fact taken from the same play, Pirandello's *Six Characters in Search of an Author*, which was first produced in 1921. The whole structure of Pirandello's drama is based on the play of reflections between two different classes of characters. Pirandello's exploration of the nature of dramatic truth is itself highly dramatic: an audience could hardly have a better illustration of the fundamental questioning of values which informs the best modern theatre.

PRODUCER (*to the* PROMPTER): Now if you'll get into position while they're setting the stage. . . . Look, here's an outline of the thing. . . . Act I . . . Act II . . . (*he holds out some sheets of paper to him*). But you'll really have to excel yourself this time.

PROMPTER: You mean, take it down in shorthand?

PRODUCER (*pleasantly surprised*): Oh, good man! Can you do shorthand?

PROMPTER: I mayn't know much about prompting, but shorthand. . . .

PRODUCER: Better and better. (*Turning to a* STAGE-HAND.) Go and get some paper out of my room. . . . A large wadge. . . . As much as you can find!

(*The* STAGE-HAND *hurries off and returns shortly with a thick wadge of paper which he gives to the* PROMPTER.)

PRODUCER (*to the* PROMPTER): Follow the scenes closely as we play them and try and fix the lines . . . or at least the most important ones. (*Then, turning to the* ACTORS). Right, ladies and gentlemen, clear the stage, please! No, come over this side (*he waves them over to his left*) . . . and pay careful attention to what goes on.

LEADING LADY: Excuse me, but we . . .

PRODUCER (*forestalling what she is going to say*): There won't be any improvising to do, don't you worry!

LEADING MAN: What *do* we have to do, then?

FATHER (*wounded, speaking with sharp resentment*): Don't laugh! Don't laugh like that, for pity's sake! It is in this fact that her drama lies. She had another man. Another man who ought to be here.

MOTHER (*with a cry*): No! No!

STEPDAUGHTER: He's got the good luck to be dead. . . . He died two months ago, as I just told you. We're still wearing mourning for him, as you can see.

FATHER: But it's not because he's dead that he's not here. No, he's not here because . . . Look at her! Look at her, please, and you'll understand immediately! Her drama does not lie in the love of two men for whom she, being incapable of love, could feel nothing. . . . Unless, perhaps, it be a little gratitude . . . to him, not to me. She is not a woman. . . . She is a mother. And her drama. . . . And how powerful it is! How powerful it is! . . . Her drama lies entirely, in fact, in these four children. . . . The children of the two men that she had.

MOTHER: Did you say that I had them? Do you dare to say that I *had* those two men . . . to suggest that I wanted them? (*To the* PRODUCER.) It was his doing. He gave him to me! He forced him on me! He forced me. . . . He forced me to go away with that other man!

STEPDAUGHTER (*at once, indignantly*): It's not true!

MOTHER (*startled*): Not true?

STEPDAUGHTER: It's not true! It's not true, I say.

MOTHER: And what can you possibly know about it?

Questions

(a) In which of these two extracts do the characters seem the more *real*?

(b) Can you pin this impression of reality down to something one or more of the characters actually does or says?

(c) Is there anything else in these two scenes which would condition the way we as audience would respond to what is happening?

(d) Can you draw any more general conclusions from your answer to question (a) about the play as a whole?

(e) Turn back to **Chapter 7, exercise 3** (page 169) and compare the dramatic device that is being used here to the ironic implications which

flavour Michael Frayn's stage directions at the beginning of *Noises Off*.
Are there any parallels here? Is this kind of dramatic device more likely to
make us laugh or cry? Or will it in the end do neither?

——— Framing the characters ———

The *play within a play* may be a small episode in a predominantly realistic
central action. It may, as in Pirandello's *Six Characters in Search of an
Author* or in Michael Frayn's *Noises Off*, provide the whole structure of a
play in which the 'actors' and the 'characters' vie with one another to
carry conviction. The *inner* play may be almost the whole play, with the
outer play relegated to the status of a rather ornate frame. For all
practical purposes we can ignore it, and yet it is still present, as gold-
painted scrollwork might remain to remind us that even the most
photographic of paintings is still an artefact, something set apart from our
ordinary lives, something we judge differently from how we judge our
own lives, to which we apply a different set of standards.

Shakespeare used this distancing effect in *The Taming of the Shrew*.
The entire play is framed in a practical joke played on Christopher Sly, a
character who takes no part in the central action. In the text as it stands,
the drunken Sly is in bed with his 'wife' throughout the enactment of the
real drama. His presence, awake or asleep, drunk and uncomprehend-
ing, is a constant dumb commentary on the events and characters we see
centre-stage. The play may end on a 'higher' note, with the focus on
Kate's new submissive persona, but Sly and his bed manners are a
reminder that we may be well advised not to believe all we hear and see.

Exercise 6

Read the following openings, and think about their implications for the
drama which follows. Then answer the questions.

[*Enter* CHORUS]
[CHORUS]

O for a Muse of fire, that would ascend
The brightest heaven of invention, –
A kingdom for a stage, princes to act,

And monarchs to behold the swelling scene!
Then should the warlike Harry, like himself,
Assume the port of Mars; and at his heels,
Leash'd-in like hounds, should famine, sword, and fire,
Crouch for employment. But pardon, gentles all,
The flat unraised spirits that have dared
On this unworthy scaffold to bring forth
So great an object: can this cockpit hold
The vasty fields of France? or may we cram
within this wooden O the very casques
That did affright the air at Agincourt?
O, pardon! since a crooked figure may
Attest in little place a million;
And let us, ciphers to this great accompt,
On your imaginary forces work.
Suppose within the girdle of these walls
Are now confin'd two mighty monarchies,
Whose high-upreared and abutting fronts
The perilous narrow ocean parts asunder:
Piece-out our imperfections with your thoughts;
Into a thousand parts divide one man,
And make imaginary puissance;
Think, when we talk of horses, that you see them
Printing their proud hoofs i' th' receiving earth; —
For 'tis your thoughts that now must deck our kings,
Carry them here and there; jumping o'er times,
Turning th'accomplishment of many years
Into an hour-glass: for the which supply,
Admit me Chorus to this history;
Who, prologue-like, your humble patience pray,
Gently to hear, kindly to judge, our play.   [*Exit.*

(Shakespeare, *King Henry the Fifth*)

[[. . .] TOM *enters dressed as a merchant sailor from alley, stage left, and strolls across the front of the stage to the fire-escape. There he stops and lights a cigarette. He addresses the audience.*]

TOM: Yes, I have tricks in my pocket, I have things up my sleeve.
  But I am the opposite of a stage magician. He gives you illusion

— 225 —

that has the appearance of truth. I give you truth in the pleasant disguise of illusion. To begin with, I turn back time. I reverse it to that quaint period, the thirties, when the huge middle class of America was matriculating in a school for the blind. Their eyes had failed them, or they had failed their eyes, and so they were having their fingers pressed forcibly down on the fiery Braille alphabet of a dissolving economy.

In Spain there was revolution. Here there was only shouting and confusion.

In Spain there was Guernica. Here there were disturbances of labour, sometimes pretty violent, in otherwise peaceful cities such as Chicago, Cleveland, Saint Louis . . .

This is the social background of the play.

[MUSIC]

The play is memory.

Being a memory play, it is dimly lighted, it is sentimental, it is not realistic.

In memory everything seems to happen to music. That explains the fiddle in the wings.

I am the narrator of the play, and also a character in it. The other characters are my mother Amanda, my sister Laura, and a gentleman caller who appears in the final scene.

He is the most realistic character in the play, being an emissary from a world of reality that we were somehow set apart from. But since I have a poet's weakness for symbols, I am using this character also as a symbol; he is the long-delayed but always expected something that we live for. There is a fifth character in the play who doesn't appear except in this larger-than-life-size photograph over the mantel.

This is our father who left us a long time ago.

(Tennessee Williams, *The Glass Menagerie*)

Questions

(a) Superficially, these extracts seem to have a little in common. How alike are they in fact?

(b) With which of them do we as audience feel the more involved?

(c)   Is either of these opening speeches in any way destructive?

(d)   Choose one of the extracts and try to talk about this opening speech in terms of the function it is performing.

Exercise 7

The plays we have looked at so far in this context have used irony on the whole as a means to greater seriousness. Each of the three speakers in exercise 6 addresses us with a gravity and directness which may undercut the comfortable values we have inherited from Naturalist theatre, but which do nothing to undercut theatre itself. Rather, we are led to question more closely the whole phenomenon of theatre and our relationship with what is happening on stage; we are more likely to carry the questions posed by the play out with us into our real lives, and to let them continue to nourish us intellectually and morally. Even Shakespeare's Sly episode at the beginning of *The Taming of the Shrew* poses serious questions about the 'real' play which follows, at the same time as it makes us laugh.

But the deflation may be more systematic than this. The ironies of the *play within a play* structure may be used more intrusively to deflate and devalue the *inner* play, or even to invalidate themselves. Any seriousness there is is in the satirical implications of our laughter. There is often not very much difference between the technique which makes us agonise and the technique which makes us scoff. Both involve manipulations of distance. Language, tone, context are everything here. In a play as in a poem, it is the *total pattern* we need in the end to come back to; it is the *total pattern* which helps us to interpret the meanings of all its parts.

Look at the following extract. How is the *framing* device used here? What is it that triggers our laughter? Does that laughter contain more serious questions? How do Moon and Birdboot differ from the introductory speakers in the previous exercise?

MOON: What? Oh yes – what do you make of it, so far?
BIRDBOOT (*clears throat*): It is at this point that the play for me comes alive. The groundwork has been well and truly laid, and the author has taken the trouble to learn from the masters of the genre. He has created a real situation, and few will doubt his ability to resolve it with a startling denouement. Certainly that is

what it so far lacks, but it has a beginning, a middle and I have no doubt it will prove to have an end. For this let us give thanks, and double thanks for a good clean show without a trace of smut. But perhaps even all this would be for nothing were it not for a performance which I consider to be one of the summits in the range of contemporary theatre. In what is possibly the finest Cynthia since the war –

MOON: If we examine this more closely, and I think close examination is the least tribute that this play deserves, I think we will find that within the austere framework of what is seen to be on one level a country-house weekend, and what a useful symbol that is, the author has given us – yes, I will go so far – he has given us the human condition –

BIRDBOOT: More talent in her little finger –

MOON: An uncanny ear that might have belonged to a Van Gogh –

BIRDBOOT: – a public scandal that the Birthday Honours to date have neglected –

MOON: Faced as we are with such ubiquitous obliquity, it is hard, it is hard indeed, and therefore I will not attempt, to refrain from invoking the names of Kafka, Sartre, Shakespeare, St. Paul, Beckett, Birkett, Pinero, Pirandello, Dante and Dorothy L. Sayers.

BIRDBOOT: A rattling good evening out. I was held.

(Tom Stoppard, *The Real Inspector Hound*)

Choose one of the last four plays quoted in this chapter to read in its entirety. How far does the complete reading conflict with the impressions you formed from doing the exercises?

—————————— Commentary ——————————

Exercise 1

The format of this exercise may look frivolous, but the implications of the questions it asks are quite serious. These dramatic choices have consequences for real audiences at real productions, and different solutions imply different positions with respect to the purpose of theatre.

(a) Probably none of these responses is the Brechtian ideal. Better to feel intrigued than flattered or threatened, certainly, but better still to treat the visibility of the actors as one element in the total presentation and go on to wonder about the meaning of the play as a whole.

(b) (ii) has to be the most Brechtian of the answers here. (iii) implies that present-day directors would have to resort to an escalation of alienation techniques in order to produce the same effect as Brecht's own theatre company had in the 1950s. But as in question (a), we can go beyond the mere consciousness of the mechanics of the production and *use* the state of mind it produces in us to look at the play itself with new eyes.

(c) A combination of responses (ii) and (iii) might be useful here. Everything in a play is there to be experienced; obviously if we try to ignore one element in a production we are voluntarily making ourselves insensitive to a part of its message. Wondering what music we ourselves might have chosen could be a way of focusing on exactly *how and why* the given music is not appropriate and so on what precise effect the clash of values we perceive is producing.

(d) (iii) Watch both. The two images are fertile in suggested parallels, but also in incongruities. When you leave the theatre, your head will still be buzzing with the many questions the comparison raises.

Exercise 2

(a) According to the poem, it is the artist's responsibility not only to show the world as it is but also to suggest a possible better future. It is his or her responsibility to present this alternative vision in such a way that the audience is able to digest and use it, while taking pleasure in the process. The responsibility is not just to entertain, but to teach people how to live.

(b) This implies that the function of theatre is not merely a representational one. It is not enough for theatre simply to be truthful and reproduce what *is*. By choosing to make its own bones visible, art can teach us about anatomy in general (my image, not Brecht's).

(c) This last section of the poem refers obliquely to the Depression of the pre-War years and the rise of Nazism. It gives the 'what is' in 1.6 substance and the 'what could be' of 1.7 a meaning. Brecht's theatrical world is not just a concept: it carries a definite political and ideological message, linked to real events and a specific moment in history.

(d)   Your own reaction is of course personal, but it has implications for your whole view of theatre and what constitutes the dramatic. Think about it in relation to your values as 'critic' of the play you saw most recently.

(e)   Does Shakespeare give us the world 'as it is' or a vision of something better? Does Chekhov? Does a play which immerses us in a 'reality' we recognise without question imprison us in that reality, or can claustrophobia teach us indirectly 'what could be and is not/ and might be helpful'?

Exercise 3

(a)   The central irony of the first extract is that while Romeo is devastated by Juliet's death and prepares to follow her, we, the audience, know she is not in fact dead but only appears to be dead. The irony has as much to do with our status as audience as it does with what is happening on stage: in real life, we should jump up and tell Romeo he is mistaken, but in a theatre we are powerless to intervene. The irony gives tragedy an 'edge', at the same time making us obscurely aware that what we are watching is, after all, only a play. Perhaps the release of tragic emotion has something to do with the safety we feel: perhaps (and here we are quite at odds with Brecht!) it is *because* we perceive theatre as artificial that we can afford to experience it fully? Knowing more about Romeo's tragic circumstances than he does himself, we feel all the force of his words. Look at the double meanings of 'Why art thou yet so fair?' and the questions that follow it. The last seven lines of Romeo's speech are even fuller of ambiguities: desperation, sea-sickness, love, all have a different meaning in the context of what we know, from the meaning they have for Romeo as he says them.

(b)   It would surely do both. It creates distance between us in order to make us experience Romeo's pain dramatically in terms of our own impotence.

(c)   Here the relationship is complicated by Miller's handling of time in the play. This scene follows the scene in which Willy learns the truth about his career, yet there is an indication in the words 'as of old' that we may be flashing back in time, to a period in which Willy could not have known about the failures of his future self. Yet the placing of these two scenes leaves us with the suspicion that he *ought* to know it. His younger self has just witnessed his older self: surely the writing is already on the wall? What all three characters say here is not just ironic, but also painfully suggestive of a whole fabric of self-delusion.

(d)   This is a difficult question, as it would be for the Arthur Miller extract we have just been considering. To some extent (and overtly) it is Nina, pathetically half aware of her own mental and spiritual disintegration. But it is also, and more tellingly, Trepliov, who seems totally unaware of her suffering, appealing to us as he does for a pity we have already given Nina at his expense.

(e)   Yes. Willy, Trepliov and Nina are all in varying degrees examples of this.

(f)   This kind of irony does tend to distance us emotionally from a character. Yet even here there may be circumstances which exonerate the character from full possession of the truth and make his or her inability to accept it all the more poignant. Sometimes, of course, ironies of this sort can be a powerful source of comedy. In Molière's *Tartuffe*, the central character in the drama obstinately refuses the evidence of his own ears: treated to a catalogue of illness among members of his family, all he can think of is his 'poor' protégé, Tartuffe, himself suffering only from a large appetite and very thick skin!

Exercise 4

Of course these two *plays within a play* are very different. The extract from *A Midsummer Night's Dream* is overtly funny. The play within the *Seagull* is not funny, though it is in many ways strange and incongruous, and retrospectively it is full of ironies.

But what these two *plays within a play* have in common is that they both lead us as audience into a kind of reality which is not the reality of the play as a whole. *Pyramus and Thisbe* may be a caricature, but its cast is all the more real for being stupid and big-headed and generally clueless as actors. They are both more and less real than the figures of the *Dream* itself, and make us think about and question the values of the whole drama which frames them. Trepliov's play is unreal and stylised. There is a kind of poetry in the – at times faintly comic – ideal vision of this fictional playwright, and in Nina's young voice as it conjures up this other-worldly apocalypse. When we remember this dramatic performance in the light of Nina's far more real destruction towards the end of the play (see Ex. 3 page 217) the unreality of Trepliov's vision becomes a comment on a whole set of artistic attitudes, and their responsibility for pain in the real world.

The first extract seems to me to comment on the whole of *A Midsummer Night's Dream* only indirectly. But the indirect commentary is far-reaching, under its mask of humour. The whole basis of sexual identities and sexual relationships is thrown into question (and this would have carried an extra humorous charge for an Elizabethan audience, used to the female roles' being taken by male actors). The nature and function of drama itself do not escape the implications of the clowning: we are reminded that drama is something artificial, where casting is arbitrary and disguises only a convention; above all we are reminded that one purpose of drama is entertainment – that however serious the play, there must still be space in it for us to relish the roar of a 'lion'.

The actual text of the second extract echoes retrospectively in our minds as a comment on the emptiness and sterility of a whole social order and the aesthetics it has fostered: indirectly, it comments ironically on that order. Arkadina's interruption is truer and more sinister than she knows.

Exercise 5

(a) There is no logical reason why the characters of the first extract should seem unreal. As actors in rehearsal, they in fact dramatise what we *know* to be happening: a real *performance* subject to the unifying conception of a real director. Nothing about their language or behaviour does anything to undermine this relationship with us. Yet surely the characters of the second extract seem far more vivid and alive?

(b) The text of the first extract (which actually occurs somewhat later in the play than the second extract) is if anything more idiomatic than that of the second extract. Both are broken up and fragmentary, resembling *real* dialogue. If anything, the language of the second extract is more literary and formal. There are enormous differences of tone and content. But perhaps the most important factor in the vitality of the characters of the second extract is in the drama itself. They hardly speak a word without contesting something. They butt in and argue and shout each other down irrepressibly.

(c)   The very fact that the reality we are offered in the first extract is a theatrical reality conditions our response, in the same way as Brecht's intrusive stage techniques do, by reminding us that we are after all in a theatre and that this is *only* a play we are watching. The miracle of Pirandello's six characters is that they survive *despite* these visible reminders.

(d)   Even though Pirandello's entire play is based on this conflict between what we 'know' to be real and what *seems* real to us, in the end it is what we believe that triumphs over what we 'know'. The play is even more a play about truth than it is a play about dramatic representation.

(e)   There are many parallels here and yet the emphasis and the ultimate effect are quite different. Whether we are more likely to laugh or cry is an individual matter. When the two different sets of characters interact, the incongruities are likely to make us laugh at first. But in Pirandello's play we may also find ourselves involved in something more serious.

Exercise 6

(a)   In some ways they are in fact similar. They both make a very explicit appeal to us to enter some *other* world of the mind which is not the physical world of the stage we see in front of us. Perhaps in both cases the very fact of *asking* us to use our imaginations makes it harder at first for us actually to 'let go'. But there are also obvious differences.

(b)   One of the most important of these is our degree of involvement with the speaker. Shakespeare's Chorus is a purely functional, impersonal figure. Tennessee Williams' Tom may begin as a magician, a manipulator, but something in our relationship with him changes in the last sentence.

(c)   The second extract is to some extent destructive: it is doing something which is almost the dramatic equivalent of some of the novel-openings we met in Chapter 1 – we already know the gentleman caller will come in the final scene. Part of our interest in 'plot' has been destroyed. Our sense of time is also being tampered with overtly in a way which may make us self-conscious and uncomfortable.

The first extract seems to me to be pre-empting less of what is to follow, though it does set the scene for us in more ways than one. But is the convention itself destructive? If you were directing either play, how would you handle the prologue?

(d)   There is no space here to answer this in detail. The best answer is in an attentive reading of the play you have chosen. You might like to look too at the beginnings of Jean Anouilh's *Antigone* and Thornton Wilder's *Our Town*, which will provoke related but subtly different questions.

Exercise 7

Here the use of the *framing* device has an effect which is subtly different from that of the previous extracts. It is used to undercut the inner play, not merely indirectly by its greater vitality and the implication that it is more real, but by a very direct commentary on the conventions of a certain kind of conventional drama and the unthinking expectations of the audiences and critics it deserves. In the end, the ironies are more complicated than this: the humour of silly exchanges between Moon and Birdboot are a prelude to a more general devaluation, which includes the events of their own lives as surely as the events we see on stage. Our laughter is triggered here primarily by these critics' use of language – pompous and inane, full of cliché and ironies at both the play's and their own expense. Under that language lies the question of what language *is* appropriate for the discussion of drama, serious or otherwise. Is *any* language ultimately appropriate? Can we do any better? Moon and Birdboot are set up to destroy the play they are watching, for themselves and for us, but also, ultimately, to destroy themselves. It is impossible to take any of the characters in this play seriously, yet the play itself remains in a sense serious, despite the general massacre.

LITERATURE
AND MESSAGE

— Does literature have a message? —

However deeply we study literary texts and compare them with one another, there are always questions which refuse to be resolved. Perhaps one of the most central, and one of the most difficult, is the whole problem of whether literature conveys a message – or, if it conveys many messages, whether one particular message surfaces as more important and influential than all the others. Should literature aim to persuade us, to convince us of something, or should it only suggest possibilities, leave us free to find our own answers to the troubling areas it can present to us more powerfully than we might have presented them to ourselves? Is it concerned with conveying truth, or with conveying a kind of dream-reality which the onus is on us to analyse for meaning? Can literature teach us to live better? Should it change our values and have repercussions for our decisions in the *real* world?

Didactic literature has plenty of respectable precedents. We have inherited from the Ancients a deep-seated belief that a work of art may and should make us better men and women. The first-century (BC) poet, Horace, formulated the same conviction in his famous '*dulce et utile*' – the work of art is not simply *sweet* but also intrinsically useful. A play can teach us about our own society and potentially about the dynamics of any social set-up. A novel can teach us about the workings of the human mind. A poem can teach us about ourselves and through ourselves and our limitations, about what still escapes us.

Yet different ages have reacted in their different ways against *committed* literature. If, with one generation, literature swings towards the expression of a particular moral, political or religious ideology, the next generation may swing it back with a vengeance. *Art for art's sake* is not just a late 19th-century phenomenon. It has probably always had its adherents. But the idea of a literature which is *empty* of ideas is perhaps as sterile and problematic as an *art for Marxism's sake* – or feminism's sake, or conservation's sake, or Christianity's. Again, the sensitive issue when it comes to literature is the issue of language: language cannot *not* express something. It is inevitable that individual words and sentences and fragments of dialogue will carry a meaning, and legitimate or even necessary that that meaning should reflect the serious concerns of the writer. What is crucial is that these primary meanings should still be part of a pattern. A paragraph of propaganda is a paragraph of propaganda. Four paragraphs of warring propaganda arranged to reflect on and contrast with one another would already be a kind of literature.

Exercise 1

For some reason, we seem more able to accept an 'involved' authorial stance in the theatre than we do in a poem or even a work of fiction. Perhaps our image of the theatre as a genre is of something less *essential* and more ephemeral. We are very aware that our presence is actually physically necessary to what is happening on stage, and the two-way process which acts on us as our reaction in turn acts on the quality of acting and production. It seems natural that a play should reflect the concerns of its time in a direct and immediate way. It is easy sometimes to overlook the necessary organisation which transforms ideology into drama and makes it watchable.

In the novel the debate is not usually nowadays about commitment, so much as about what is seen as *largeness* and *smallness*. Contemporary taste and much contemporary fiction seem to lean towards the idea that for novels social subjects are still the most appropriate. It is easier to admire Joyce's *Ulysses* for its portrayal of 1904 Dublin than for the other things it does.

Poetry is the most extreme example, perhaps because poetry is traditionally 'singing about' something rather than 'talking about' something, and it is harder to sing about Thatcherism than it is to sing about the moon. But we have only to think of the popularity of a contemporary poet like Tony Harrison to realise there is no intrinsic contradiction between poetry and political awareness. His Gulf War poems are no less *poetic* for dealing explicitly with painful political issues – far from it. Yet the organisation which has shaped them is as important here as it is in less overtly committed writing: a reporter's view of the same anecdotal material would not move us in the same way.

Look at the following prose poem. Read it carefully several times. If possible, read and re-read it over a few days, thinking about the questions which follow.

THE COLONEL

WHAT YOU HAVE HEARD is true. I was in his house. His wife carried a tray of coffee and sugar. His daughter filed her nails, his son went out for the night. There were daily papers, pet dogs, a pistol on the cushion beside him. The moon swung bare on its black cord over the house. On the television was a cop show. It was in English. Broken bottles were embedded in the walls around the house to scoop the kneecaps from a man's legs or cut his hands to lace. On the windows there were gratings like those in liquor stores. We had dinner, rack of lamb, good wine, a gold bell was on the table for calling the maid. The maid brought green mangoes, salt, a type of bread. I was asked how I enjoyed the country. There was a brief commercial in Spanish. His wife took everything away. There was some talk then of how difficult it had become to govern. The parrot said hello on the terrace. The colonel told it to shut up, and pushed himself from the table. My friend said to me with his eyes: say nothing. The colonel returned with a sack used to bring groceries home. He spilled many human ears on the table. They were like dried peach halves. There is no other way to say this. He took one of them in his hands, shook it in our faces, dropped it into a water glass. It came alive there. I am tired of fooling around he said. As for the rights of anyone, tell your people they can go fuck themselves. He swept the ears to the floor with his arm and held the last of his wine in the air. Something for your poetry, no? he said. Some of the ears on the floor caught this scrap of his voice. Some of the ears on the floor were pressed to the ground.

May 1978 Carolyn Forché

Questions

(a)   How much of the impact of this prose poem is in fact due to the apparently factual information conveyed in it?

(b)   Do we need to trust this information implicitly for the poem to move us as it surely does?

(c)   What is the poet doing with juxtaposition here?

(d)   As far as possible, try to rearrange the poem into separate lists of statements, each dealing with a single kind of information (e.g. innocuous statements about daily life, statements about food, statements more obviously loaded with political implications, statements about suffering). Read your separate lists one after the other. Do they still move you in the same way?

——— Literature and morals ———

From the way we discussed narrative tone and viewpoint in **Chapter 3**, it must have been obvious that morality in literature is a complex question. We are not likely at this point to fall into the trap of calling *Lady Chatterley's Lover* an 'immoral' book because of the explicit sexual references it contains, nor even to conclude that an evil story-teller makes for an evil story. We are not likely to dismiss *Paradise Lost* on the grounds that Satan is a more attractive character than Adam and Eve, or *Mansfield Park* on the grounds that the worldly-wise and witty Crawfords are considerably more interesting than the 'real' hero and heroine of the novel.

Nevertheless, there *is* a genuine question here. If, even after we have thoroughly digested all the underlying patterns of a book, a play, or a poem, the world-view which informs that work of literature still seems to us to be fundamentally evil, or oppressive, or ungenerous, how can that work of literature still be 'good'? Is literature really divorced from honesty, and generosity and compassion? Aren't the human values which emanate from it themselves potentially ugly or beautiful? Can we truthfully say of a book, 'Yes, this is lovely' without endorsing its values? Can a nihilistic book move us as much as one which affirms what we hold precious?

It seems to me that if we aspire to a kind of criticism which is purely formalist, which tries to be objective and even scientific, at times we are forced to say that it can. But if we see the phenonemon of literature as a relationship between writing and reading, between what is offered and what we bring to it, we shall be dissatisfied with any approach which leaves no space for morals. One of the glories of literature is that it can enlarge our conception of humanity and answer our very deepest needs.

This is the point at which literature and myth meet. Myth uses story-telling to explain the inexplicable, to help us live through what at first we feel too frightened to face. The best works of literature are mythical in this sense: instead of literal truth they give us answers which we recognise as *true* and appropriate at a very deep level of our shared cultural consiousness. They help us to live by answering our deepest unstated questions. We *recognise* rightness in literature as we recognise the figure who holds the key to an important secret in one of our own dreams.

Exercise 2

Think back over all the works of literature you have read and the plays you have seen, and try to remember if any of them felt perfectly *right* to you in this sense. Ask yourself if this *rightness* could be analysed in terms of formal coherence. Was there an implied morality which coloured the writing in some way? Is it possible to separate it out from the book's structure?

Can you think of any books you have found morally suspect or unpleasant? What were your reasons for this? Are they legitimate reasons?

—— Language about language ——

What protects literature from becoming propaganda is its layers of meaning. When we walk into a room we may feel at once from the decor, 'Well, I know what the people who live in *this* house are like!' But we move into the house ourselves and decide to strip off the old paper. Under the heavy gilt flock is a discreet floral, under that a nursery design, and under that a discoloured remnant from the 1930s. We are not dealing with one family, but with many, each of them making an implied statement about the people who lived here before.

Literature is language about language. Words already mean something, sentences already mean something. But if I put them together in inventive combinations, the way I have combined them will itself mean something. If I invent a character with explicit ideas about politics or religion, art or morality, I am making a statement through that character. But the relationship between that character and my whole book qualifies that statement and may even completely negate it. I can write dramatic dialogue to make my audience feel uncomfortable or even humiliated, yet the play itself may show my public that the ups and downs of dramatic interaction are a part of something much larger, based on seriousness and respect.

This is the phenomenon the structuralists call *metalanguage*. Metalanguage demands of us something we could call *meta-awareness*. We *hear* the language of literature and listen to ourselves hearing it. We are reacting to words and phrases and sentences on several levels at once.

This could sound intimidating, or even well-nigh impossible, but in fact if you have reached this chapter you have probably already been doing it for some time. Your own answers to my questions and your further thoughts about them will have made you more at ease with the multiple meanings of a work of literature than you yourself probably realise. My guess is that if you were *put off* by ambiguity when you started, you are by now more intrigued than threatened.

The fact is that by *saying something about saying something*, literature is not in the end *saying* anything. It is *doing* something. It is doing something as surely as a painting or a musical composition *does* something. The verbal artist plays in the no-man's land between one kind of *saying something* and another. The best writers do not *have something to say*. They make something which says itself, in a way which is tailor-made to fit readers of quite different shapes and sizes.

— What the poet really meant to say —

Twenty or thirty years ago it was still a commonplace to find a work of literature judged by comparison with a writer's intention. So much the better if a novelist or poet had stated his or her intention clearly in a letter or a theoretical document of some kind. Failing that, critics could try to reconstruct an unstated intention from biographical and historical material, or by studying other works by the same author. Often the evidence of 'intention' in the work itself was treated only as a last resort, seen as a rather inadequate or unreliable source of evidence because it seemed to take us back to where we started.

But critical opinion about the usefulness of this kind of artistic intention has changed. A creative writer's intentions for his or her work are notoriously unreliable: the poem that was intended to be long and came out short may not necessarily be a failure. A 'little' novel intended to help the novelist *get his or her eye in* may be more important than he or she knew. The poem may turn into prose, the prose into poetry; the story intended primarily for children may move thousands of adults, and the story intended for adults may have a different – but equally valuable – appeal for children.

The example usually cited to underline the shortcomings of intention as a yardstick is Blake's poem 'Jerusalem'. Here is a poem most of us know, have sung, probably from childhood. We got to know it intimately, met it with our own cultural expectations, invested it with spiritual and emotional meanings of our own, meanings which enhance its aesthetic effect for us and perhaps for future generations. Yet if we know anything about Blake and his view of the organised religion of his time, we are forced to concede that the 'real meaning' of the poem is quite different from the one we regard as vital: the 'dark Satanic mills' in question have very little to do with the evils of industrialisation; they are a concealed metaphor for the Church itself. However beautiful the poem, what it says about religion is probably the opposite of our earliest understanding. If we judge this poem with reference to the poet's intentions, we must say goodbye to much of what originally moved us. In a sense, we amputate something from the poem. If we are being faithful to the facts of its genesis, we have to admit we are wrong to find it beautiful in the way we do.

A writer's intention is less dangerous if we can find it inside the text of the work of literature itself. But this is not saying very much, because this will involve us in an appreciation, not only of individual statements and images in the work, but of its whole organisation, the implied scale of values that comes from the relative emphasis the writer's pattern gives them. In other words, *implicit* intention is not very different from any aesthetic criterion.

Surely if we take *any* static, universal criterion, we are doing violence to what literature is? I should be surprised if I read any of the extracts in this book in precisely the same way as any of you have. I should be even more surprised if any of our readings were to be identical to those of our children or grandchildren. To propose *any* single criterion of beauty in a work of literature, even if it is the author's own, is reductive. The author has no special authority. He or she has created a combination of words in a language which belongs to us all, which itself goes on growing and changing, shedding old meanings and usages and taking on new ones. The writer makes a bet with the future – not that 'what he or she really means to say' will survive, but that *something* will survive, that the pattern itself will be suggestive enough for new readers to have new meaningful relationships with it.

Exercise 3

Take time to look back through this book again, stopping to re-read any of the extracts which have appealed to you particularly. Note down the page references for those which have touched or moved you. Then try to whittle down your list to a single extract or poem.

(a)   Now, in a couple of sentences, try to write down to your own satisfaction 'what the writer really meant to say'.

(b)   What kind of poem or book or play is this *meant* to be? Is it passing or failing the test?

(c)   Look again at what you have written in answer to question (a). Why do you think the writer didn't actually say what you have written?

The unwrapped gift

Twenty or thirty years ago, most self-respecting literary critics also eventually found themselves talking about something called 'form' and something called 'content'. It was quite common to think of the work of literature as if it were something made of moulded plastic: there was the shape of the mould and the chemical composition of the material, and woe betide the artist if the plastic was inferior or the shape of the mould unsuitable!

Nowadays, at least among academic critics, this conception is a rare one. Critics of quite diverse persuasions have come to question the relationship between literature and its *material*, to understand that when the medium of art is language, it can make no sense to try to separate form and content in this way. Forms are as various as the nuances of language itself, in all its possible combinations. Content *is* in one sense just words, and words already have meaning and a kind of shape to them.

How can it be possible to peel off the form from a work of literature and see what is left? In literature *everything means*. The most external of formal devices triggers changes in the substance of what it shapes. Think of a story and tell it to yourself backwards. Is it the same? Can its 'content' really be the same?

Perhaps it *is* just possible to talk about form and content at the level of individual words. There is the sound-sequence our mouth and larynx make, or the sequence of symbols on the printed page. In themselves they mean nothing. There is no obvious reason why the word 'rabbit' should *contain* the meaning we attach to it. But at the level of literary choices, these distinctions disappear: a writer's organisation of his or her work cannot be arbitrary in this way. A writer chooses to say things in certain ways because their meaning will be changed by them. In a poem there *is* a necessary relationship between rhyme, rhythm or line-length and 'what the poet is saying'. 'What the poet is saying' is what he or she chooses to do.

If literature is a gift, it is an unwrapped gift, or a gift which has somehow absorbed and been changed by its own wrapping, like a bar of chocolate that has melted in our pockets. If we try to prize off those elusive shreds of aluminium foil with our fingers, we shall never have the experience of that mess of sweet metal in our mouths.

The way we can avoid doing this is by being constantly aware of relationships. Every time we feel ourselves touched or moved or disconcerted we should ask ourselves *what* is producing the effect. Every time we discover a fragment of pattern, we should replace it in the *whole* pattern and ask ourselves what its importance is. Each time a piece of foil sticks in our teeth, we should ask ourselves how it makes us feel about the lump of chocolate that is left.

For, gift or not, a work of literature is a kind of relationship, something that happens between us and the writer, between our eyes or ears and the text on the page. When we open a book, we are inviting something, allowing a potential relationship to come into existence. On his or her first page a writer makes us a kind of promise. How that promise will be kept is as much our business as it is the writer's own.

Like any relationship, literature has two sides to it. The whole of this book has been aimed at making you more aware of the reader's side, and, incidentally, of the attractions of what is being offered. We owe it to literature and to ourselves to read well. If we can read well, literature will reward us.

Exercise 4

Now it is time to go off and read in their entirety the books and plays I have quoted or others you yourself have chosen, without a set of formal questions to answer on the last page. By this time you can make up your own questions. From now on the onus will be on the writer to answer them!

—————— Commentary ——————

Exercise 1

(a)   At first glance, much of the impact of this prose-poem is due to the 'facts' it contains, from the gratings on the windows and the broken glass embedded in the walls to the final horrifying picture of the grocery-bag of human ears emptied on the table. If we look at it more closely, though, we can see how even this appalling *information* is not so much shocking in itself as shocking in context. The context is built up as carefully as the escalation of the *facts* themselves, so that by the end of the poem the tension between the two orders of experience is almost unbearable. Perhaps in the end it doesn't matter very much whether this final scene is an actual occurrence or a hallucinatory possibility.

(b)   On one level, we do need to believe it. But is this belief the same as the belief we give to a trustworthy news source?

(c)   She is showing us very forcibly the sheer human outrage of a violence which is apparently *ordinary*, integrated in the little concerns and self-gratifications of a comfortable daily existence. The whole movement of the poem's many juxtapositions is *dramatic*: the reader is made to live through the poet's own unfolding awareness of what the abuse of power really means.

(d)   At the beginning of the poem, this exercise should not pose too many problems, but towards the end it becomes impossible. When we meet the grocery-bag in one sentence and the ears in the next, we are already in difficulties. When we get to the image of the dried peach halves, it is no longer possible to separate the different orders of experience. The poet herself acknowledges the unthinkable fusion in her intercalated statement, 'There is no other way to say this.' The Colonel toasts his outrages with the question, 'Something for your poetry, no?' How do we answer? How does the poet answer?

Exercise 2

I can think of my own answers to these questions, but your answers will be your answers and you will be able to justify them if you try.

Exercise 3

This exercise is in a sense destructive, and is intended to make you aware of how reductive this kind of approach can sometimes be. The essential here is not what you have written, but the thoughts you have had about writing it, and the unbridgeable gap between any *statement* of the meaning of a work of literature and the richness of the work of literature itself.

WHERE TO GO
FROM HERE

The simple answer to this is *read*. The more you read, the more deeply and critically you will read and the more rewarding literature will become. But reading alone is not enough. Literature is a living thing which depends on your active participation – in your imagination and also in the flesh. Studying theatre means attending performances, listening to the radio, watching TV drama critically, and not just sitting in an armchair with a printed play open in your lap. Studying poetry means opening your eyes and ears to poetry in all its forms – from poetry on the underground and the buses to the sudden unexpectedly poetic piece of advertising. Ideally it means listening to poetry on the radio (and you would be surprised how often a poem is broadcast on Radios 4 and 3!) and taking advantage of live poetry readings in your area. Studying fiction also means thinking about what *fiction* is, in all its forms. Novels and short stories are not something sacred just because they are printed. Thinking about fiction on film and the television – or even about the daily lies we tell others and ourselves – will help you to come closer to what story-telling actually means and how it can adapt itself to different media.

Reading can also be quite lonely, and following your nose in the choice of books can sometimes be limiting. Often an Adult Education or WEA course can broaden horizons by pushing you to study a text you would never have chosen, asking questions you might not have thought to ask yourself. Courses of this kind can be a wonderful forum for the exchange of ideas, and incidentally a good way to make new friends who share your growing interest. If there are no courses in your area, you could start a reading group: members usually meet regularly in one another's houses and take turns to suggest a book for all to read and discuss. The discussion could be more structured if the proposer of a book were to come armed with a list of his or her own questions, problems, and likes/dislikes.

Even if you are housebound or live in a remote part of the country, you can make critical reading a more *shared* activity by beginning a kind of circular letter which is added to by each group member and which eventually becomes a rich exchange of enthusiasm and critical ideas.

Reading the text itself is the most important thing. You have your own valuable critical response to each text. If you have a copy with an introduction, read the text first and think about it before you read what the writer of the introduction has to say. By then what he or she says will make sense, and you will know whether or not you are agreeing with it. Why start your relationship with a book second-hand? You wouldn't choose a mate by looking at him or her through a friend's glasses.

Read the text itself before you read any critical material. Take time to think about it, on its own, with other texts by the same author, and others it reminds you of. Then give yourself the stimulating experience of finding out what other people have thought about the book. A critic may delight you by seeming to have read the same book you yourself have, or perplex you by seeming to have read a different book entirely. He or she may surprise you by seeing things you haven't noticed or disappoint you by not being sensitive to what you know is there.

It doesn't matter. It is all stimulating. It is all debate. It doesn't mean that you are wrong, or your own response invalid, only that there may be more to this book than you thought!

— Suggestions for further reading —

On fiction

ed. Miriam Allott, *Novelists on the Novel* (Routledge, 1959)
Erich Auerbach, *Mimesis: The Representation of Reality in Western Literature* (Doubleday Anchor, 1953)

Wayne C Booth, *The Rhetoric of Fiction* (University of Chicago Press, Chicago and London, 1961)

E M Forster, *Aspects of the Novel* (Edward Arnold, 1927; now Penguin)

Percy Lubbock, *The Craft of Fiction* (Cape, 1921)

On theatre

John Allen, *A History of the Theatre in Europe* (Heinemann, 1983)

Peter Brook, *The Empty Space* (Granada, 1977)

Philip Cook, *How to Enjoy Theatre* (Piatkus, 1983)

Raymond Williams, *Drama and Performance* (Muller, 1954; now Penguin)

Raymond Williams, *Drama from Ibsen to Brecht* (Chatto & Windus, 1952; now Penguin)

On poetry

Tony Curtis, *How to Study Modern Poetry* (Macmillan, 1990)

C Day Lewis, *The Poetic Image* (Cape, 1965, first published 1947)

Ruth Miller and Robert A Greenberg, *Poetry, An Introduction* (Macmillan, 1981)

Winifred Nowottny, *The Language Poets Use* (The Athlone Press, 1962)

Anthony Thwaite, *Poetry Today, A Critical Guide to British Poetry 1960–1984* (Longman, 1985)

On literature and writing

Nathalie Goldberg, *Writing Down the Bones* (Shambhala, Boston and London, 1986)

Ted Hughes, *Poetry in the Making* (Faber, 1967)

D C Muecke, *Irony* (Methuen, 1970)

Linda Nochlin, *Realism* (Penguin)

René Wellek and Austin Warren, *Theory of Literature* (first publ. in the USA 1949; Cape, 1949; now Penguin)

——— GLOSSARY ———

What I have tried to do here is to give simple working commentary/ definitions for the words which have become or remained a part of my own critical vocabulary, and of those that I myself have used in the body of this book. If you are in need of a dictionary definition of a given literary term and you cannot find it in these pages, there are many dictionaries of literary and critical terms available. Your local library will probably have some of them (my own town library boasts four), or at least a good general dictionary which will have entries for the most current words.

For a good, accessible commentary which deals with many of the terms I have used, and makes useful connections between them, I can refer you to John Peck and Martin Coyle's *Literary Terms and Criticism: A Student's Guide* (Macmillan, 1984), which also contains a very helpful chapter on modern developments in literary criticism. For the knottier and more elusive critical concepts, the Methuen Critical Idiom series is a very valuable aid in focusing on the problems, if not in solving them!

Note: The words marked with an asterisk are used sometimes with and sometimes without capital letters. When they begin with a capital, their meaning is more precise, generally referring to a particular historical phenomenon or literary movement, or to the characteristics of that movement as they have influenced other more recent writers and texts.

Without a capital, the words mean something looser and vaguer. Nevertheless the two meanings are connected, so that it is always useful to think about both words and compare them – the more precise literary term and the wider meanings it has acquired in the public imagination.

Absurd, theatre of the   A term often used to describe the work of modern dramatists like Beckett, Ionesco, Pinter and Albee; not only do strange things happen in these plays, but the conventions of 'normal' social exchange in general, and language in particular, are undermined.

Affective fallacy   A term defined by the critics Wimsatt and Beardsley in their *Verbal Icon* as *a confusion between the poem and its results (what it is and what it does)*: what Wimsatt and Beardsley saw as the error of projecting our own subjective reactions on to the aesthetic value of what we read.

Alliteration   (especially in poetry) a sound (usually a consonant) repeated at the beginning of words which are near to one another.

Antithesis   A balance of two opposing ideas, or words, or groups of words.

Assonance   A pattern of repeated sounds (usually vowels) in poetry.

Autonomy   The seeming independence of the fictional character who seems to take on a life of his or her own, beyond what his or her fictional or dramatic function demands.

Ballad   A song-like poem which tells a story.

Bildungsroman (German for *formation novel*)   A novel which describes the formative experiences and development of its hero or heroine.

Blank verse   A verse form dating from the 16th century and consisting of unrhymed lines with a regular 5-stress iambic rhythm (iambic pentameters).

Caesura   A brief pause or breath-break in the middle of a line of poetry.

Catharsis   (Greek *purgation*)   Emotional release in drama or art (O.E.D.); Aristotle's term for the therapeutic resolution of the pity and fear aroused by tragedy.

Classical*   Often opposed to **Romantic** in the continental literary traditions, and meaning an ideal of harmony and appropriateness modelled on the values of ancient Greek and Roman writers and thinkers.

Classicism* See **classical**. Classicism was a historical literary and dramatic phenomenon across 17th- and 18th-century Europe. The term may also be used to describe the influence of classical themes, myths and aesthetic values in the work of modern art.

Concrete poetry Poetry which is printed in such a way as to make a recognisable design or picture on the page.

Diction The vocabulary used by a writer, a poet's choice of particular words.

Dramatic irony On the stage this kind of irony depends on the gap between a character's grasp of his or her situation and an audience's understanding of it. In fiction, where the character in question is the narrator of the story, we might call the resulting irony *narrative irony*.

Ellipsis (from the Greek leaving out) A kind of compression or concentration of language, especially associated with poetry; it involves the *leaving out* of something we would normally expect to be present.

End-stopped lines In poetry, lines which are self-contained in terms of meaning, breaking 'naturally' where the natural pauses and/or punctuation marks occur.

Enjambement (from the French *stepping over*) The opposite of end-stopping: the meaning and grammatical structure of a line of poetry run from one line to the next, 'stepping over' the visual break as if it were an invisible fence.

Epic One of the oldest of literary genres and traditionally the greatest: the epic is a long poem which tells a story of heroic deeds, usually in a 'large' and comprehensive manner.

Epic theatre Brecht's term for a kind of theatre which would use alienation techniques to appeal more to the audience's reason than to their feelings in its presentation of social and political problems.

Epistolary novel A novel in which events are narrated in letters exchanged by the various characters.

Farce A very old form of comedy based on the simplest and most fundamental kind of laughter, a genre which still survives today.

Eye-rhyme Occurs when two words look as if they ought to rhyme but are actually pronounced differently, e.g. *mouth* and *uncouth*.

Feminine rhyme A rhyme which consists of two syllables, the first stressed and the second unstressed, as in *pity* and *city*.

Foot A group of syllables which forms a unit of rhythm. In English a metrical foot conventionally consists of one stressed and one or more unstressed syllables.

Fourth wall In drama of a Naturalist tendency, the invisible 'fourth wall' of the stage which separates the 'reality' of the play from the other reality of its audience.

Free verse Poetry which is not written in lines of regular length or metre. Ideally this does not imply formlessness.

Genre A literary type or class. The main Classical genres were epic, tragedy, lyric, comedy and satire. The list of existing literary genres nowadays would look quite different.

Haiku A very short Japanese verse form. A haiku has three lines, of five, seven and five syllables respectively. Conventionally it is a poetic miniature which uses nature and the seasons to suggest an idea or emotion.

Half-rhyme A form of rhyme which depends on words with one or more *rhyming* consonants but *unrhyming* vowels, e.g. *life* and *loaf*, or *rain* and *sign*. This kind of rhyme is particularly associated with the First World War poet, Wilfred Owen.

Iambic A metre which is made up of feet consisting of an unstressed syllable followed by a stressed syllable. Iambic pentameter (a five-foot iambic line) is probably the most common metre in English verse, the *background expectation* against which our other verse-forms and experiments present themselves to us.

Ideology The system of ideas at the basis of an economic or political theory (OED); the implicit system of values and beliefs which is embedded in any work of literature.

Image In a more general sense, an image may be anything a poem makes us *see*; more specifically, we use the word to describe figurative (or non-literal) uses of language, and especially metaphor and simile.

Indirect free style (also sometimes called 'free indirect speech') A technique used by many contemporary novelists, but particularly associated with the nineteenth-century French novelist, Flaubert: we are presented with a character's perception of a situation, but there are no quotation marks or tense-changes or explicit introductory words (*she thought* . . .) to warn us that the viewpoint has shifted to become more personal. The technique has had major repercussions for the development of the modern novel.

Intentional fallacy The most important of the 'fallacies' explored by Wimsatt and Beardsley in *The Verbal Icon*: the misleading critical practice of interpreting a writer's work in the light of its author's apparent intentions.

Interior monologue A narrative technique associated with 20th-century novelists like James Joyce, Virginia Woolf and William Faulkner: a character's fragmentary thoughts and feelings are presented in an apparently haphazard way which can suggest the spontaneity and fragmentation of real thought in our lives.

Internal rhyme Rhyme between a word at the end of a line and a word inside the line, or between two or more words inside the line.

Intrusive narrator A narrator who *intrudes* into his or her narrative, making us aware of the existence of a story-teller and of the artifice of the story (as when a narrator addresses us as 'dear reader' and proceeds to comment on the characters or their morals).

Irony Irony depends on a reader's or spectator's awareness of a gap between what is *said* and what is *meant*. Verbal irony may be a gentler version of sarcasm. Other, situational ironies may depend on what is implicit rather than explicit: in a play or a novel we may have a clearer veiw of events and situations than the characters themselves do, and this knowledge may colour our response to the story in a way which is painful or piquant.

Italian sonnet The Italian or Petrarchan sonnet is made up of an eight-line section which rhymes ABBA ABBA, and a six-line section (CDE CDE). The second section usually resolves the conflict implicit in the first.

Lyric One of the ancient Classical genres, originating in song. Nowadays it usually means a short poem which expresses personal feelings.

Masculine rhyme A rhyme in which the final, rhymed syllable is stressed, e.g. *leaf* and *grief*, or *appeal* and *reveal*.

Metaphor A figure of speech in which one thing is described in terms of another (or in terms which apply more naturally to and therefore suggest another). Metaphor is not a single, simple device, but a continuum – with effects which can range from almost imperceptible coloration to outrage. In one form or another, most modern conceptions of poetry seem to depend on it.

Metonymy Traditonally, a figure of speech in which a part or an attribute of something stands for the thing itself. Recent Russian and French critics have enlarged the definition and seen metonymy as an alternative linking device (one thing standing for what it occurs next to or with), in some cases as important as metaphor.

Metre The rhythmic pattern of stressed and unstressed syllables in poetry.

Mimesis Imitation of reality in art. The term is generally used to describe the more 'photographic' kinds of realism, and is closely associated with Erich Auerbach's critical classic, *Mimesis* (1957).

Mimetic Imitating reality in a Naturalistic, 'photographic' way (see **mimesis**).

Myth Usually a story of collective origin which uses the fictional behaviour of super-human characters to explain problems and mysteries in real life.

Narration Story-telling. It implies a teller.

Narrative A story which is told.

Narrative distance For practical purposes, this is usually considered to be the implied distance between the narrator's voice and interpretation of events and those of the author as they are perceptible within the text. There is usually a correlation between this distance and the distance we feel as we read between the narrator and ourselves.

Narrative intervention The intrusion of the narrator into the story to explain or comment, often humorously. When a narrator is already dramatised, his or her intervention is less intrusive. When the intervention is more unexpected, the effect is to pull us up short and make us suddenly aware of the mechanics of what we are reading.

Narrative poetry Poetry which tells a story.

Narrative viewpoint The point of view from which the story is told. This is closely related to decisions about how far the narrator is to have insight into his or her characters' thoughts and motivation. It also has implications for the grammatical person in which the novel is written.

Narrator In a novel or short story (or poem), the voice that tells the story. Not to be confused with the author, even in an autobiographical novel which uses 'I'.

Naturalism* Naturalism is generally thought of as a late 19th-century development of Realism, associated with the French novelist, Emile Zola. It claims to be scientific, reflecting a deterministic view of humanity very much influenced by Darwin and his successors. In the theatre, naturalistic drama is particularly associated with Ibsen. Naturalism has continued into the 20th century as a powerful force in fiction and drama, particularly in Russia and the US.

Novel A long fiction in prose. It is hard to define the novel more closely than this, and even the debate about what 'long' might mean is not easy to resolve. The word itself comes from the Italian *novella, piece of news, tale.*

Novella A prose fiction which is somewhere between a novel and a short story in length. A genre which has flourished particularly in Germany.

Omniscience A novelist's decision to see into the minds of all his or her characters.

Onomatopoeia Words which sound like what they mean (e.g. *quack* or *pitter-patter*) In poetry, onomatopoeia may sometimes be a matter not so much of a single word but of the way in which several words are combined.

Petrarchan sonnet See **Italian sonnet.**

Proscenium arch In a conventional present-day theatre, this is the space filled by the curtain. A proscenium arch theatre lends itself particularly to naturalistic values and styles of production.

Prose poem A poem in prose. The prose poem is problematic because it raises nearly insoluble questions about the nature of poetry itself. There are usually few or no effects of patterned sound or typography to tell us this is a poem. Usually it is the density of language and the economical, associative nature of the images which earn it the title of poetry.

Protagonist The principal character in a drama or work of fiction.

Realism* A set of aims and values normally associated with the 19th-century novel and 19th-century painting and particularly with French novelists like Stendhal and Balzac who were concerned with 'holding up a mirror' to reality, with painting society in all its breadth and banality. In England we might connect this kind of ambition with Dickens or George Eliot, in Russia with Tolstoy. Realism is a powerful but elusive set of literary values, well explored by Linda Nochlin in her *Realism* (Penguin). It is probably still the greatest single influence in contemporary fiction.

Rhetoric   The art of using language persuasively. One of the ancient Classical disciplines. Now we often use the word in a derogatory sense.

Rhetorical   We speak of a rhetorical device when language is used in a particular way for a particular purpose. A rhetorical question is a question which does not expect an answer. We often use *rhetorical* loosely to describe language which is inflated and empty.

Rhyme   Matching sounds or combinations of sounds. The minimum unit is a vowel (*stay* and *play*), but rhymes may be much richer (*sinister* and *minister*). The matching sounds may occur at the ends of lines or within them.

Romantic*, Romanticism*   Romanticism was a literary and aesthetic movement which spread across Europe in the first half of the 19th-century, probably originating in Germany. Romanticism is a term which is almost impossible to define. Tendencies which loom large are a concern with the self and with subjective emotion, a new preoccupation and identification with the natural world and a new interest in history, coupled with a paradoxical delight in tumultuous renewal in all its forms. Romanticism was a major influence on all literary genres, but particularly on poetry, where it opened up a new creative domain with the central importance it gave to the faculty of the imagination.

Round, theatre in the   The term given to a dramatic performance which takes place in a (usually lower) space surrounded, or almost surrounded, by the audience. Not only are the mechanics of 'curtain-raising' and scene-changes affected, but the style of acting, the status of the reality presented and the whole dynamic relationship between actors and audience.

Self-consciousness   In fiction, this is the usual term used to describe parts of the text which seem to make us aware of the artifice of the text we have in our laps, and of ourselves as readers. They may be passages which have an 'extra' abstract meaning about the actual practice of writing, or they may be the novelist's equivalent of the *play within a play* technique.

Semantic gap   (*Semantics* is the branch of linguistics which deals with meaning). When we are discussing a poem, the semantic gap is the distance in meaning between the two sides of an explicit or implicit comparison. If the poet compares a dictionary to a telephone directory, we say the semantic gap is narrow. If he or she compares a dictionary to a coral necklace, we would say it was much wider.

Shakespearian sonnet   Unlike those of the Italian or Petrarchan sonnet, the lines of the Shakespearian sonnet are grouped in three quatrains (four-line stanzas) and a couplet, rhymed ABBA CDDC EFFE GG.

Simile   An explicit comparison which uses the word *like* or *as*.

Sonnet   A 14-line verse-form, in English usually in iambic pentameters, which also follows a conventional pattern of rhyme and stanza-breaks. See **Italian sonnet** and **Shakespearian sonnet.**

Stanza   A group of lines in a poem. *Stanza* is a more precise way of referring to what we often call a verse. (*Verse* has several possible meanings.)

Stream of consciousness   See **interior monologue**. The words are particularly associated with James Joyce's *Ulysses*.

Structuralism, structuralist*   Structuralism is an interdisciplinary movement which has grown up since about the 1950s. It began in the field of linguistics and spread via anthropology to literary criticism. It has adherents in disciplines as far apart as mathematics and psychology, in countries as far apart as Russia and the U.S. In literary criticism, the emphasis is on the patterns of relationship and opposition which form the underlying structure of a work of literature, and on how these patterns relate to others in different social or aesthetic 'languages'.

Style   A characteristic way of writing. As a critical term, *style* is probably less useful than it seemed to be 50 years ago. A discussion of *style* or *stylistics* tends to blur the distinction between author and narrative persona and introduce misleading separations of form and content.

Surrealism, surrealist*   An aesthetic movement which grew up in Europe in the 1920s, and which has had enormous repercussions on world painting, literature, cinema, sculpture, etc. The Surrealists believed in dreams, the images of the subconscious, spontaneity and childhood as so many tools in the search for a deeper truth.

Symbol   Something which stands for something else. The distinction between symbol and implicit metaphor, if it exists at all, is a very fine one.

Synaesthesia   The mixing of sense-impressions, the describing of one sense-impression in terms of another (e.g. *a thin note, a warm colour*).

Syntax   *Syntax* is often used simply as a synonym for *grammar*. It refers to a writer's organisation and ordering of parts within his or her sentences and the way in which that organisation affects their meaning.

Tale A short narrative in prose or verse. It may be the product of a communal oral culture, rather than a short literary story written by an individual. If it *is* written by an individual, it will probably reflect a folk tradition.

Tautology The unnecessary repetition of ideas as in *at this moment in time*.

Tenor and vehicle Are terms coined by IA Richards in his *Philosophy of Rhetoric* (1936) to denote the two parts of a comparison. The *vehicle* is the metaphor-word and the *tenor* is what it means.

Transferred epithet A figure of speech in which the epithet (qualifying adjective) is transferred from the noun it would logically describe to another, e.g. 'a wicked pack of cards' (T S Eliot).

Trochaic Trochaic metre is in a sense the reverse of iambic – a *falling* as opposed to a *rising* rhythm. Each foot is made up of a stressed syllable followed by an unstressed syllable. The most famous example in English is Longfellow's *Hiawatha*.

Unreliable narrator In fiction, a narrator who is not to be trusted, i.e. whose assessment of a situation or whose moral interpretation of it may differ from the author's and our own. Such narrators can appear sympathetically naïve, or dishonest, or downright repellent. Their narratives can generate anything from laughter to horrified fascination, from pity to disgust.

ACKNOWLEDGEMENTS

The author and publishers would like to thank the following for permission to reproduce material in this volume:

Anvil Press Poetry for 'Love in a New Language' from *Human Rites* (published 1984) by E A Markham on page 148. Bloodaxe Books Ltd for 'Buzzard' on pages 97 and 112 and an extract from 'West Kennet Long Barrow' on pages 110 and 93 both from *Frances Horovitz: Collected Poems* (Bloodaxe Books/Enitharmon Press, 1985) by Frances Horovitz, and 'New Car' by C K Williams on page 98. Calder Publications Ltd for extracts from *The Chairs* by Eugène Ionesco, from Collected Plays Volume 1, translated by Donald Watson. Copyright © this translation by John Calder (Publishers) Ltd, 1958. On pages 201–3. Jonathan Cape for extracts from *Who's Afraid of Virginia Woolf?* by Edward Albee on pages 175–178, *Latecomers* by Anita Brookner on page 68, 'The Colonel' from *The Country Between Us* by Carolyn Forché on pages 237–8, *The French Lieutenant's Woman* by John Fowles © John Fowles, 1969, on pages 37–8, *The Cement Garden* by Ian McEwan on page 28. Carcanet Press Limited for 'Vico's Song' from *Collected Poems (1985)* by Edwin Morgan on page 124. Century Hutchinson Ltd for an extract from 'Learning Chinese' by Libby Houston from *The Poetry Book Society Anthology (1988–1989* David Constantine) on page 130. Chatto & Windus for two extracts from *A Word Child* by Iris Murdoch on pages 35–6. Kelly Cherry for an extract from 'Letter to a Censor' from *Natural Theology* by Kelly Cherry, © Kelly Cherry, published by Louisiana State University Press, 1988, on pages 126–7. Curtis Brown, London, on behalf of Random House Inc. for two extracts from *The Sound and the Fury* by William Faulkner on page 31 (copyright 1929 by William Faulkner, renewed 1956 by William Faulkner), and an extract from 'The Bluffalo' from *How Beastly* (1980) by Jane Yolen, published by Collins World (republished 1992 by Boyds Mills Press, copyright © 1980 Jane Yolen, on page 99. André Deutsch Ltd for extracts from *Voyage in the Dark* (edition 1967) by Jean Rhys on pages 74–5 and *Equus* by Peter Shaffer, from *Three Plays* by Peter Shaffer (first published by Penguin), on pages 192–3. The Ecco Press for 'The Drowned Children' © 1976, 1977, 1978, 1979, 1980 by Louise Glück. From *Descending Figure* by Louise Glück, first published by The Ecco Press in 1980. Reprinted by permission on pages 148–9. Faber and Faber Limited for extracts from *Krapp's Last Tape* by Samuel Beckett on pages 180–1, *The Pyramid* by William Golding on page 78, *A Day in the Death of Joe Egg* by Peter Nichols on pages 172–3, 'Miss Drake Proceeds to Supper' from *Sylvia Plath: Collected Poems edited by Ted Hughes* by Sylvia Plath on pages 9–10, *The Bell Jar* by Sylvia Plath on page 9, 'Wuthering Heights' from *Crossing the water* by Sylvia Plath on page 144, *The Real Inspector Hound* by Tom Stoppard on pages 227–8, for 'Murder in the Cathedral' from *The Complete Poems and Plays of T S Eliot* by T S Eliot on pages 194–5, for 'Mushrooms' from *The Colossus* by Sylvia Plath on pages 153–4, for 'An Otter' from *Lupercal* by Ted Hughes on page 107. Victor Gollancz Ltd for an extract from *Lucky Jim* by Kingsley Amis on page 52. Grove Press Inc. for an extract from *The Erasers* by Alain Robbe-Grillet, translated by Richard Howard, on page 69. Hamish Hamilton and A Norah Hartley for an extract from *The Go-Between* by L P Hartley on